GW00370810

Risk, Complexity and ICT

Edited by

Ole Hanseth

Professor of Information Systems, University of Oslo, Norway

and

the late Claudio Ciborra

Professor of Information Systems, London School of Economics and Political Science, UK

Edward Elgar
Cheltenham, UK • Northampton, MA, USA

© Ole Hanseth and Claudio Ciborra, 2007

All rights reserved. No part of this publication may be reproduced, stored in a retrieval system or transmitted in any form or by any means, electronic, mechanical or photocopying, recording, or otherwise without the prior permission of the publisher.

Published by
Edward Elgar Publishing Limited
Glensanda House
Montpellier Parade
Cheltenham
Glos GL50 1UA
UK

Edward Elgar Publishing, Inc.
William Pratt House
9 Dewey Court
Northampton
Massachusetts 01060
USA

A catalogue record for this book
is available from the British Library

Library of Congress Cataloguing in Publication Data

Risk, complexity, and ICT/edited by Ole Hanseth and Claudio
    Ciborra.
        p.   cm
    Includes bibliographical references and index.
    1. Management information systems. 2. Risk management.
    3. Computer networks—Security measures. I. Hanseth, Ole,
    1954–   . II. Ciborra, Claudio.
    T58.64.R57   2007
    658.4'038—dc22
                                                    2007000151

ISBN 978 1 84542 661 3

Printed and bound in Great Britain by MPG Books Ltd, Bodmin, Cornwall

Contents

Contributors

Margunn Aanestad, PhD, holds a post-Doctoral position in the Department of Informatics at the University of Oslo. She worked within health care and telecommunications before her doctoral study of surgical telemedicine. Her research interests are broadly related to IT in health care.

Jennifer Blechar holds an MSc in Analysis, Design and Management of Information Systems from the London School of Economics and Political Science, UK and a BA in Mathematics from Bryn Mawr College, USA. She is a PhD candidate and research fellow with the Department of Informatics at the University of Oslo, Norway and has several years' experience as a consultant within the telecommunications field. Her research interests involve the design, implementation and use of rich media content services in the mobile industry.

Claudio Ciborra graduated in Electronic Engineering from the Politecnico di Milano, Italy, before pursuing studies in management, economics and organization theory at the University of California, Los Angeles and Harvard University. He held teaching positions at a number of Italian universities and was a Visiting Professor in many European and American universities. He was Chair Professor at the Department of Information Systems and Research Professor at the Centre for the Analysis of Risk and Regulation at the London School of Economics and Political Science. He carried out extensive research in the fields of new technologies, organizational design, learning, knowledge and change.

Miria Grisot, MA, is a PhD candidate at the University of Oslo, in the Department of Informatics at the Information Systems Group, Oslo, Norway. Her research interest is on issues of coordination related to the implementation of IT in hospitals. She holds an MA in Political Science from the University of Bologna, Italy.

Ole Hanseth, PhD, is Professor in the Department of Informatics at the University of Oslo, Norway. His research focuses mainly on the interplay between social and technical issues in the development and use of large-scale networking applications. He is also Visiting Professor at the London School of Economics, Department of Information Systems.

Edoardo Jacucci works in the Strategy Department at Accenture in Oslo. He holds a PhD in Information Systems from the University of Oslo and an MSc degree in Information Systems Engineering at the Politecnico di Milano, Italy. His research focuses on socio-technical conceptualizations of standards and on processes of standard-making in the health care sector in Norway and in South Africa.

Jannis Kallinikos (PhD Uppsala University, Sweden) is a Reader in the Department of Information Systems at the London School of Economics. His major research interests involve the institutional construction of pre-dictable worlds (that is, the practices, technologies and formal languages by which organizations are rendered predictable and manageable) and the investigation of the modes by which current institutional and technological developments challenge the organizational forms that dominated modern-ity. Some of these themes are analysed in detail in his recent book *The Consequences of Information: Institutional Implications of Technological Change* (Edward Elgar, 2006).

Eric Monteiro is Professor in Information Systems at the Norwegian University of Science and Technology (NTNU) and holds an adjunct position at the University of Oslo. Monteiro is broadly interested in organizational implementation and use of integrated information systems. Empirically, his studies cover both public organizations (in particular the health care sector) as well as larger business organizations. He has published his work in outlets including *Computer-supported Cooperative Work*, *MIS Quarterly*, *Science, Technology & Human Values*, *The Information Society*, *Information and Organization*, *Systems Practice and Action Research*, *Information Technology for Development* and *Methods of Information in Medicine*.

Daniel Osei-Joehene is a PhD candidate at the London School of Economics. His research interests focus on risks related to large scale infor-mation systems and organizations.

Knut H. Rolland is Associate Professor at the Department of Computer and Information Science at the Norwegian University of Science and Technology (NTNU), Norway. His main research interest is the manage-ment of information systems across global organizations. In particular, his research explores various intended and unintended consequences of the socio-technical processes of integration and standardization of information systems. His research has been published in a wide range of international IS conferences as well as in *The Information Society* journal.

1. Introduction: integration–complexity–risk – the making of information systems out-of-control

Ole Hanseth

1 INTEGRATION, COMPLEXITY AND RISK

ICT has been closely related to risk throughout its history. On the one hand, ICT is essentially a control technology (Beniger, 1986). It is a technology that helps us better predict and control complex processes in nature (develop new drugs, control nuclear power plants, produce weather forecasts, and so on), society (production control systems, project management tools, and so on), and other technologies (intercontinental ballistic missiles, chemical plants, and so on). This also includes various risk prediction, calculation and management tools. But we have also experienced that ICT solutions have their own risks – risks related to ICT projects as well as systems failures. And a whole series of techniques and tools have been developed to help project managers control risks related to the development of ICT solutions as well as making them reliable by minimizing risks for systems failures.

In spite of all the research on ICT risks and the increased sophistication of the tools and techniques developed, ICT risks still prevail. In fact, there are indications that they are increasing rather than diminishing. This apparent paradox is what has motivated this book. Our interest in inquiring into it stems from two sources. The first is an observed growth in ICT complexity which increases and creates new challenges regarding management and control of the development and use of ICT solutions. The second is theoretical developments in other areas regarding risk. The most important source here is Ulrich Beck's (1986) theory of Risk Society which, together with Anthony Giddens, he has later elaborated further into a more general theory of globalization and modernity called Reflexive Modernization (Beck et al., 1994). Through the formulation of this theory Beck and Giddens argue that risk has become a more dominant and characteristic feature of our society at the same time as the nature of risk has changed. While nature was the dominant source of 'old' risks (like natural catastrophes), 'new' risks have their origin more in our 'created environment', that is our technological and organizational systems. This theoretical development has inspired research on risk-related issues in many disciplines. Within science and technology studies, for instance, it has inspired a great deal of research on science, technology and expertise in relation to various environmental problems like risks related to new bio technologies (see for instance Lash et al., 1996). It has also more recently been adopted by scholars within organization studies (Hutter and Power, 2005) and information systems (Ciborra et al., 2000).

We see these two perspectives as closely related. At the centre of Beck's argument is the assumption that our society is becoming more complex through the development and use of more complex technologies and organizational forms that are both essential to ongoing globalization processes. This increasingly complex world is, still according to Beck (and Giddens), becoming more unpredictable and accordingly increasingly out of control and unmanageable. ICT is increasingly becoming a central part of virtually all technologies. At the same time, ICT in general, and the Internet and applications built on top of it in particular, are central to the ongoing globalization. Consequently, ICT should be central to the creation of the Risk Society. So by adopting Beck's perspective, we might say that ICT has (possibly) changed from a control to a risk technology, that is a technology that generates risks more than it helps us control and manage them.

1.1 Growing ICT Complexity

The British Computer Society (BCS) and Royal Academy of Engineering (RAE) published in April 2004 a report about the state of the art in Software Engineering (SE) and Information Systems Design (ISD) research and practice in the UK, which was called 'The challenge of complex IT projects' (BSC/RAE, 2004). The report, which was the result of a project involving 70 leading UK SE and ISD professors and IT managers, concluded that there was an alarming failure rate in UK IT projects. This failure rate could have been significantly lower, the report concluded, if best practices were adopted. In particular the use of risk management methodologies was lacking. But beyond this, the report also concluded that the high failure rate was a result of the fact that the complexity of ICT solutions has grown rapidly and that existing SE/ISD methodologies do not tackle this adequately. The report further concludes that existing methodologies were developed at a time when IT complexity was at a much lower level, that these methodologies have not scaled regarding complexity (see, for example, Fitzgerald, 2000), and, finally, that new methodologies addressing the growth in complexity have not been developed. From this they draw the conclusion that IT complexity is *the* issue on which basic research is needed. We need then, according to the report, first, to understand this complexity; then new risk management methodologies that can enable us to control this complexity need to be developed.

It is exactly this risk and complexity issue that is addressed by this book. We share the report's views regarding complexity and risk – except, perhaps, for the optimism regarding the possibilities of controlling the risks that are consequences of this complexity. Our primary aim is to get a better understanding of this new complexity: how it emerges, how it evolves, and, finally, what kind of risks it generates. So far our understanding of this complexity makes us rather pessimistic about possibilities for controlling it.

1.2 Complexity and Integration

The BCS/RAE report sees the growth in complexity as a consequence of the growth in computing power and the development of communication technologies. The growth in computing power has enabled our computers to run more complex software; accordingly we have developed such software. The development of communication technologies has enabled us to integrate the complex pieces of software across computers.

We also consider these two factors as being important causes of the growing complexity. But our view on the sources of growing ICT complexity is slightly different. We see integration as the key source. And we do not look at ICT as purified technology. ICT complexity has grown as the number of components and their integration has increased. But just as important, complexity has also increased because of increased integration between ICT components and the organizations and practices using the technology. We will spell out this argument in a bit more detail.

As the computing power has increased, the number of applications in use in any organization has been growing. These applications, or information systems (ISs), support an increasing number of application areas. This implies that the number of types of ISs and use areas has grown as well. In parallel the platforms or infrastructures these applications are running on have become more sophisticated; the number of components as well as types of components included has grown. All these components are linked in various ways. Applications have become increasingly more integrated with each other. The same has happened within the platforms. And the evolution of computer communication technologies has enabled the development of various kinds of new applications, but first of all they have led to an integration of platforms and applications across organizational and geographical borders. This, again, has led to integration (that is, an increasing number of connections) between organizations and their routines, and between their ISs. Over time the use of individual ISs grows (partly directly as its number of users grows, partly indirectly through integration with other ISs). This means that the number of links, and types of links, between the technical systems and the social/organizational also grow. And when ISs are integrated across organizational borders, links are established between the routines and practices in one organization and the ISs and platforms in another. And finally, according to assumptions apparently shared by everyone, everything – in particular IT and business organizations – is changing at an increasingly high speed. In sum, this means that it should be quite obvious that the complexity of IS development and use has grown substantially.

1.3   Complexity

Complexity could be defined in a simple and intuitive way as the 'sum' of the number of components and connections between them. Schneberger and McLean (2003) have proposed a slightly more sophisticated – but still very simple – definition. They see complexity as dependent on a system's number of different *types of components*, its number of *types of links*, and its *speed of change*. While the first definition seems to be close to that adopted by the authors of the BCS/RAE report, we have adopted the latter, which accounts well for the complexity created by increased integration as outlined above. The complexity referred to by the BCS report is not really complex according to this definition because the report only talks about systems of technological components – that is systems where the components and the links between them are all technological. We might say that such systems are just complicated (Latour, 1999, p. 304). One might say, though, that the ICT systems as pure technology contain components of many technological kinds such as data base management systems components, security components and communication components. However, the second definition says that 'real' complexity emerges when components of different kinds are integrated. This is the kind of complexity that emerges when platforms, applications and organizational routines, practices and structures are integrated. This is also illustrated by John Law and Annemarie Mol's (2002, p. 1) (somewhat obscure, perhaps) definition of complexity: 'There is complexity if things relate but don't add up, if events occur but not within the process of linear time, and if phenomena share a space but cannot be mapped in terms of a single set of three-dimensional coordinates.' We interpret this definition as underscoring the same point. A system is not complex if it consists of (or can be reduced to) components of one kind – for instance technological. A system is really complex only when it contains components of different kinds – for instance technical and organizational – and when the problems or issues related to one cannot be reduced to the other, that is we cannot understand the problem by addressing only technological or organizational (or social) issues, we need to understand both and their interactions and interdependencies.

1.4 Complexity and Risk

While the first part of our argument is that increased integration leads to increased complexity, the second is that increased complexity leads to increased risks. The fact that increased complexity leads to increased risks may be intuitive. But from the perspective of integration efforts it is paradoxical, since the motivation behind integration efforts is primarily to increase control (Ciborra et al., 2000). In spite of this, the result of the integration efforts is increased risks, that is less control. The basic argument for this goes as follows: when we are confronted with a complex system, our knowledge and understanding of how different components work and interact, and accordingly how the system as a whole works, will always be incomplete. The components may act and interact in ways we cannot fully predict. When one component acts, or interacts with another component, in an unpredicted way, this may produce outcomes that make other components act or interact in unpredicted ways, and so on. Such unpredictable behaviour may cause the complex system as a whole to sometimes behave in totally unpredictable ways.

The fact that we have only partial knowledge about complex systems has, of course, implications for the consequences of human interventions into complex systems. When we have only partial knowledge about a system, the outcome of our interventions will be partly unpredictable. This brings the concept of *side-effects* to the centre stage. When we change a component about which we have only partial knowledge, after our intervention the component will behave in ways we did not predict or intend. A side-effect of our intervention will be some unpredicted behaviour that will interfere with other components in unpredictable ways, which again will produce new unintended effects, and so on.

The more complex a system is, the more incomplete our knowledge will be, and the more unintended effects our interventions will produce. We can say that the more complex a system is, the more its overall behaviours will be caused by propagation of side-effects rather than intended effects. All this means that the more complex a system is, the more unpredictable the outcome of our interventions – that is the higher risks for negative outcomes of interventions. So: through integration we increase complexity which again leads to increased risks.

Integration is the 'holy grail of MIS' (Kumar and van Hillegersberg, 2000). That means that the way in which integration produces risks is a very fundamental aspect of information technologies. Axelrod and Cohen (1999) make a very similar point:

> If complexity is often rooted in patterns of interaction among agents, then we might expect systems to exhibit increasingly complex dynamics when changes occur that *intensify* interaction among their elements. This, of course, is exactly what the Information Revolution is doing: reducing the barriers to interaction among processes that were previously isolated from each other in time and space . . . Information Revolution is therefore likely to beget a complexity revolution. . . . It is ironic that exploiting the promise of short-run possibilities for better prediction and control can create longer-run difficulties (ibid., p. 26).

2   OUTLINE OF THE BOOK

The argument, or rather, the hypothesis, presented above will be explored in the nine chapters following this. Chapters 1 to 3 form a theoretical section which is followed by an empirical section that includes five chapters – one case study presented in each.

2.1   Theory Section

In the first chapter of the theory section, and the second in the book, Claudio Ciborra reviews the research literature on risks related to ICT and locates this research within the broader field of risk management.

With time and experience, managerial attention to ICT applications such as the study of organizational impacts, management of ICT strategy and redesign of business processes has crossed the boundaries of quantitative risk management and widened its scope. As a result, an organizational/managerial literature about information systems risks and their management in a business-wide perspective has emerged. This ranges from the more micro concerns about how to get the user requirements right (an issue that still overlaps with SE risk management) up to the strategic choice in selecting an application portfolio or an ICT infrastructure, where questions need to be asked about the risks of large ICT investments for a business as a whole.

Ciborra argues that the cultural and professional milieu in which these approaches (or methods and techniques) had been originally tried out led to their emergence as strictly quantitative approaches based on a positivist, probabilistic definition of risk: probability of occurrence of a problem multiplied by the value of its impact. He further argues that this naïve view of risk has dominated the SE discipline and practice since the 1980s. It is supported by a myriad of sub-techniques for identifying risks, measuring impacts and assessing probabilities. To be sure, the methods and techniques are accompanied by words of caution from senior software professionals who suggest that they should be applied with a grain of salt and situational common sense. Here, as often happens in the professional field, formal models seem to get gradually substituted by rules of thumb, prescriptions and war stories disguised as articulated experience.

Ciborra also points to the limitations of existing risk management approaches regarding complexity as it is presented in the theories the research reported in this book draws upon – and as it emerges in the cases analysed. Central to these complex systems is the fact that we have only partial knowledge about how they work, accordingly which risks we may encounter is largely unknown, so we cannot calculate their probability nor imagine their impact. These issues are discussed more extensively in the next chapter where Jannis Kallinikos explores theoretically the relationships between risk and ICT. His focus is on recent developments in the study of risk in relation to the 'essence' of technology in general and large-scale ICT solutions in particular. Traditionally risk has been the concern of specific risk and risk management theories or methodologies (which Ciborra presented and discussed). Kallinikos says that the concept of risk has experienced a remarkable renaissance in the last two decades; now the theories are not primarily about risk per se, but as a central concept in the wider field of social theory. Relevant work includes the works of Beck and Giddens already mentioned, but also Mary Douglas's cultural theory of risk (Douglas and Wildavsky, 1980) and Nicolas Luhmann's (1993) monumental theory. The latter is central to the perspective on risk and complexity as well as technology. On this basis Kallinikos points to three key issues. The first is our relation to our world and the paradoxical fact that the more (scientific) knowledge we have about the world we inhabit and the more advanced technology we develop to help us control our world, the more it seems to move beyond our control, that is the more risks. The best illustrations of this are global warming and the possible implications of climate change, or even worse – the risks for nuclear war that may destroy the whole planet. Kallinikos attributes this paradox to the fact that however much knowledge we produce, our knowledge about our world will be incomplete. In addition, our world and the knowledge about it are not independent. When we are producing more knowledge about our world, we are at the same time constructing a more complex world.

The second issue that Kallinikos discusses relates to time and what he calls our 'future orientation'. At the core of this argument is the fact that our world is inherently contingent and unpredictable. We cannot escape this fact in spite of all advance calculative devices that are supposed to help us predict our future – or at least calculate probabilities of various scenarios. In addition, the contingent nature of our future is a precondition for many activities. The world is constituted as open and plural, amenable to initiatives and interventions that could possibly render it different from the present. Without risk there would be no opportunities and therefore no profit, and without profit, no economic initiatives either.

The third issue that Kallinikos discusses is the relation between technology and risk. Technology is traditionally seen as a tool for control and accordingly risk management or reduction. But there are important limitations to how technology can address the issues mentioned here. Drawing on Luhmann, Kallinikos portrays technology as a structural form whose main characteristics are functional closure and simplification. That means that we can deal with reality by simplifying this into a closed domain and specify how the technology can deal with each element in this domain and its states. Technology, then, has important limitations when it comes to uncertainty – in Kallinikos' words: 'technology deals with the unexpected by excluding it'.

After this general discussion of risk and technology Kallinikos turns towards what is specific for large-scale information systems highlighting three aspects: self-referentiality, interconnectivity and de-sequencing of time. Self-referentiality denotes the fact that information is not just data referring to some reality. The more information we gather and process, the more we will also produce information referring to information. This may bring us towards a sort of autonomous complex system of information and a 'de-anchorage from the immediate reality'. The other two aspects of large-scale information systems relate more directly to the issues regarding integration, complexity and risk discussed above. Through increased interconnection of information systems we create more complex systems which are more challenging to control. And such increased interconnection of systems contributes to what Kallinikos denotes de-sequencing of time, that is processes will increasingly be linked, not only sequentially, but also running in parallel. This kind of link between parallel processes creates what Perrow (1984) defines as interactive complexity (as opposed to linear interactions) and which he sees as a main source of unpredictability and unreliability of technological systems.

The last theory chapter, written by Ole Hanseth (Chapter 4), presents the theories that have inspired the research reported in this book and which form the basis of the hypothesis presented above. This is first of all Ulrich Beck's theory of Risk Society/Reflexive Modernization (Beck, 1986; Beck et al., 1994). Beck's general argument is that the world is increasingly dominated by risks so that it can best be characterized as a Risk Society. Beck does not discuss technology as such – he hardly mentions the term, but implicitly technology is central to his theory. His theory is a social theory, but it is a social theory of our technological society. Central aspects of the theory are risks created by advanced technological systems like pollution and global warming, risks related to nuclear weapons and power plants, bio-technology, and how modern transport, communication and production technologies are rapidly transforming working as well as family life.

Complexity is hardly mentioned in Beck's writings. However, his theory can very well be seen as a complexity theory because what is making risks more central in our world is exactly its growing complexity – a complexity which is created through scientific research and the development of increasingly sophisticated technological solutions. And the core dynamic of this complex world is the propagation of side-effects. Beck highlights one particular pattern of how side-effects often propagate. They are not only creating a chain of side-effects (domino effects), but increasingly often they form boomerang effects – they are reflected back to where the original act triggering the whole changing was taking place and causing the result to be more or less the opposite of what the actor intended. This is what Beck calls reflexivity. And it is exactly the extent to which such reflexive, that is self-destructive, processes are created through the integration of ICT solutions that is at the very centre of this book.

In Chapter 4 Beck's theory is supplemented with and compared to a few others. This includes theories from the Complexity Sciences. Side-effects are also at the centre of these theories. However, their originators and proponents have focused on phenomena different from those of Beck – in particular within the natural sciences and economics (standardization), and they have highlighted other patterns created through the propagation of side-effects. Rather than self-destructive processes, they have focused on self-reinforcing ones. However, the reflexive processes that will be presented in this book are at the same time self-reinforcing. This happens because the processes aiming at controlling complexity achieve the opposite because control is tried to be achieved in ways that increases complexity. Complexity bootstraps and becomes self-reinforcing.

This chapter also presents a third theory of complexity which the research draws upon: Actor-Network Theory (ANT). ANT has traditionally not been labelled a complexity theory, but one might very well say that complexity has been the issue addressed in ANT research. Not complexity in all its varieties, but the complexity created by the dense web of relations between the scientific and the non-scientific (that is social, organizational, political, and so on) within science studies and similarly between the technological and non-technological in technology studies. In line with this we draw upon ANT to disclose and analyse one aspect of the definition of complexity presented above: how elements of different kinds are related.

More recently, complexity has been addressed explicitly within ANT (Law and Mol, 2002). One issue that is highlighted is what is sometimes labelled the 'orders' dis-orders', which means that when we try to make order within a domain or 'world' (by creating a new standard, for instance), unfortunately the domain or 'world' we try to order is connected to other domains or 'worlds' beyond what we are able to see and cope with. Accordingly, when we are trying to make order in one domain, as a *side-effect* we are creating dis-orders in others (Berg and Timmermanns, 2000).

Chapter 4 also presents the most relevant research on complex technologies from the Organization Studies field. This includes first of all Charles Perrow's Normal Accident Theory (1984). He argues that complex technological systems that are tightly coupled and characterized by inter-active complexity (as opposed to sequential interactions) will never be completely safe – accidents are normal. This is because we will never have complete knowledge about how they will operate in all circumstances. Accordingly we cannot make sure they will be free of errors or unpredictable behaviours. Risks are inherent to their existence. In this way Perrow's theory is well aligned with the theories presented above and supports the hypothesis we will explore in our research.

However, some scholars are sceptical to Perrow's theory. This includes in particular Todd La Porte who was the original creator of the theory of High Reliability Organizations (HRO) (La Porte, 1988; 1996; Weick and Sutcliffe, 2001). HRO proponents have also studied complex technological systems finding that there are some that prove to be characterized by very high reliability. The typical example is air traffic control. The main aspects of HROs are their focus on risks and learning from experience. Based on the theory of HROs we could extend the research hypothesis presented above with its complementary opposite by asking if or under what conditions the development and use of the emerging complex ICT solutions could be established as HROs. We have not explored this hypothesis explicitly, but it will be briefly discussed below in light of our empirical material.

2.2 Cases

The five cases will present and discuss a number and variety of complex ICT solutions. They will illustrate

- how complexity is the result of various forms of *integration* efforts,
- what kind of *side-effects* these kinds of integration trigger, and
- what kind of *risks* they create.

The three first cases present project risks (that is risks for project failure), the fourth systems risks (that is risks caused by a system in operation), while the fifth case illustrates a case where loose integration is dominating and where the ICT solutions have been managed rather successfully. Two of the cases illustrate large-scale, ambitious integration efforts where a huge number of tasks within a large organization are supported by one complex application where a huge number of software components are integrated around a shared data base. Some of the software components are providing general and basic functions and are used by most members of the organization while others are supporting highly specialized functions and are used by small user groups. This integration strategy has become very popular during the last decade, and its typical manifestation is the implementation of ERP systems like SAP R/3. The two first cases presented here are not about organizational implementation of a commercial product like an ERP system. The first one, presented by Knut Rolland and Eric Monteiro, is about in-house development of a system by and for a 'global' ship classification company with offices in more than a hundred countries. We follow the system from its conception until it is implemented in most of its offices and even integrated with customers' systems. This is a process where more and more computer (software and hardware) components are integrated with each other, where these components are integrated with organizational routines and practices, and where these routines and practices are integrated with each other. The main elements of the process are

- the implementation of the first version of the system in a few pilot offices and the integration of the new system with the existing data base and legacy system;
- the implementation of the system throughout the organization and the integration with the underlying infrastructures; and, finally,
- the integration of the system with customers' systems and work practices.

Each step in this process triggers major unforeseen side-effects. Many of them are serious and challenging. But, overall, the project has been successful – although its cost and duration were far beyond what was planned and the benefits less significant.

The authors discuss if the side-effects and the risks they represent could be managed by traditional approaches. They conclude that that is not the case. The risks encountered emerge as the scope of the integrated system is expanded, and the risks are unique for each level to which the scope is expanded. So the risks could not be identified and managed by traditional techniques like prototyping. Also, since the risks are different at each level, when encountered at one level, they can neither be predicted based on experience at previous levels, nor be managed based on such experience.

The second case, presented by Ole Hanseth, Edoardo Jacucci, Miria Grisot and Margunn Aanestad, concerns the development and organizational implementation of an Electronic Patient Record (EPR) system. The project started out as collaboration between the five largest and most advanced hospitals in Norway and the Norwegian branch, here called Alpha Norway, of a big international company. The strategy and aim of this project were both very much the same as for the ship classification support system, the difference being application area (hospitals), the role of the software development organization, and the fact that the aim was the development of a system satisfying the need of all Norwegian hospitals.

The overall user requirements for the system were that it should make real the idea of one integrated record for all patients that was shared by all medical personnel in contact with them. This implied that the EPR had to include all information in the paper record and support all work tasks where the paper record was used. This means that the EPR system would be integrated – in one way or another – with all work practices where the patient record is involved, and, implicitly, these work practices would be integrated with each other through the EPR system. In addition, because the system was to be used by five hospitals, the system would also indirectly integrate the work practices of all these hospitals.

Central to the evolution of this project was its relation to other products, activities and strategies inside the software product owner Alpha. A side-effect of choosing a big international company like Alpha as development organization was that the project also became integrated with this organization. This fact first revealed itself when some members of the project team at one of the hospitals were informed at a conference that Alpha was involved in a similar project in the UK. They concluded that sooner or later higher-level management would discover this and that they would decide that Alpha should not develop several systems. Further, they assumed that Alpha would consider Norway the least significant market and close down the Norwegian project. Accordingly, they decided to approach Alpha and propose collaboration between these projects, assuming that if they took the initiative they would be more influential in the development of such a collaboration than if the initiative came from Alpha's headquarters. And so it happened. But that also meant that more user and development organizations became involved and that the system had to support a wider range of work practices. This was, in a way, the starting point of an escalating, self-reinforcing spiral. The increased complexity of the version of the system the hospitals and Alpha now aimed at required more resources, which again implied that they had to look for a larger market to make the investments profitable. A larger market implied involving more hospitals with their own work practices and requirements, which again implied a more complex system and project organization – and more investments, which again required a larger market, and so on. Important steps in this process were Alpha's acquisitions of software companies with competence and products for the health care sector in India and the US.

As the project escalated, so did its strategic status inside Alpha. This meant that it became a more and more central product within its medical division (which included a wide range of instruments like X-ray and other imaging equipment, all with their complex systems to store and manipulate images and other patient-related information), and accordingly it also became more and more important to align and integrate the EPR system with the other products and strategies.

The general pattern of this project was: at each stage, the complexity of the system and the project triggered risk that threatened the whole project. The risks were interpreted as threats caused by lack of alignment with parts of the outside world. Accordingly, the strategy chosen to cope with the risk was to align, that is integrate, the system and project with the un-aligned part of the outside world creating the threat. This again increased the overall complexity, which again created new risks, and so on. After eight years, at Rikshospitalet in Oslo, the EPR included only 20–30 per cent of the information in the patient records, the volume of paper had increased dramatically, the portfolio of information systems with patient record functionality had increased dramatically, and so also had the overall fragmentation of the patient records. The aims and strategies concerning integration had produced a more and more complex socio-technical system where the side-effects were taking over the project. In the end, these side-effects caused the end result to become the exact opposite of what had been intended. The risks identified, largely caused by com-plexity, were managed in a way that created increased complexity and accordingly more serious risks.

The next two cases focus less on the integration process creating a complex system, but rather on aspects of complex systems in operation. The third case, presented by Jennifer Blechar and Ole Hanseth, is a project aiming at replacing the billing system of a telecom operator with a new one. The existing system had been developed in-house. It had been extended and modified for about two decades – since the company started its mobile phone business. The plan was to replace it with a commercial off-the-shelf product as part of the launch of 3G services. This was initially assumed to be a plain and simple process requiring just a couple of months. But as the members of the project that was set up started to work on this task, a more and more complex system was revealed. They discovered that the billing system was very complex in itself. But more important, over the years it had been tightly integrated with an increasing number of components including mobile phone infrastructures (NMT400, NMT 800, GSM, GPRS), a huge number of support or front-end systems (for instance so that subscribers could change their subscription over the Internet), the variety of services and 'call plans' had been growing, and so on. The overall complexity also reflected the rapid speed of change in the mobile phone business in general and within this company in particular. One important implication of this is the fact that new, that is, young and well educated but inexperienced, people were hired all the time while the experienced ones moved upwards into managerial positions or abroad as the company engaged in start-up operations in other countries. All this means that the complexity was determined by the number, and number of types, of components and links between them, but probably first of all by the lack of knowledge about it in the organization due to the rapid growth and change of the systems and the personnel moving around in the organization.

As the complexity revealed itself throughout the project, the actions taken to deal with it in this case also contributed to the increase in the overall complexity, that is the project created new risks and challenges just as much as it helped cope with the ones discovered already. In the beginning more consultants were brought in. This created, first, communication problems, which again triggered the establishment of a more complex project organization. Then, as new complexities revealed themselves, more consultants were brought in. They came from different consultancies to avoid too strong a dependence on just one. This again implied several different methodologies and documentation practices – again: increased communication problems and overall complexities.

Project members became well aware of the presence of risks from an early stage, and risk management methodologies were adopted – but with limited success. There were just too many risks involved. Rather than being resolved, the risks were just shuffled around or transformed into new ones.

The fourth case, presented by Daniel Osei-Joehene and Claudio Ciborra, illustrates risks of integrated systems in relation to the operations they support. The system involved is an integrated email infrastructure in a 'global' bank. This bank had over the years expanded geographically from its home base in Canada to the US and later on to Europe and South-East Asia. Its product portfolio had also expanded from retail banking to virtually any kind of financial services. The overall pattern of this expansion process had been one where new units established in new markets were first experimenting and exploring possibilities, then, as they were growing, their operations were streamlining and more tightly integrating into the rest of the organization. The integration of the email infrastructure took place in a period with focus on streamlining and integration – of both operations and technology. At that time a number of different email systems were in use throughout the organizations. They were delivered by different vendors and operated locally. In addition, they were integrated through a gateway at the bank's headquarters in Toronto. The motivation for the integration was primarily cost containment: replacing the different systems with just one and centralizing its operations would cut licence costs and make the operations of the overall infrastructure much simpler and more efficient. At least, that was assumed to be the case. And it was to some extent true.

The integration of the infrastructure was seen to be a technical issue. But in reality, working practices were in some areas within the bank tightly integrated with the email systems. So the implementation of a shared and integrated, that means also standardized, email infrastructure also implied a sort of integration and standardization of work practices. And these work practices were very different: in some business areas, retail banking for instance, email was used to send simple messages around; after the message was read it was largely irrelevant. In other areas, derivatives trading for instance, email was used extensively, and emails contained important information. The folders with old emails were a kind of business-critical information system. This had significant implications: the first group did not need much storage space to keep old emails, while the latter group really did. And when the integrated infrastructure was established, a space limit was set for how much email each user was allowed to keep. This was done without much knowledge about its possible implications, and the rule was not implemented in a strict sense either. For some users, old email was deleted automatically. But because old emails were so important for some users, this regime was not implemented universally.

Central in this case is one incident – an incident triggered by the interaction of several events, and interaction between side-effects of how the events were responded to. It all started when the London office closed down all equipment during the Easter bank holiday to carry out the regular annual check of the electricity back-up system. After the check, some of the email servers didn't boot. It turned out that the reason was the amount of email stored as the space used for this was far, far beyond the limits set. After some time it was discovered that it would take a considerable time to recover from this failure, and in the meantime most email users in the bank would be affected. Because of the number of users affected, it was decided to go for what was believed to be the fastest, but more risky, recovery procedure. This procedure quickly generated some unforeseen situations, and the way these situations were dealt with triggered new unforeseen side-effects, and so on. The whole email infrastructure was up and running again after one week. The incident did not seem to have any significant long-term negative effects, but during the recovery process, the bank was vulnerable and under unfortunate circumstances, and the crisis could possibly have escalated further to a level that could have been disastrous for the bank. For instance, for a period all users were given full access rights to the whole folder system, which contained a large amount of sensitive information for the bank and its customers. If this fact had become widely known and important sensitive business information about the bank's customers had been spread widely, the reputation of the bank could have been seriously damaged.

The last case, presented by Claudio Ciborra, is a bit different. It includes different technologies, different use areas, and different integration strategies. It is about the evolution of a substantial part of the IS portfolio in a pharmaceutical company over almost two decades. At the centre of this chapter are the various technologies used to support communication within and across the various business areas and national subsidiaries, how these technologies have evolved and been used, and the strategy and managerial practices behind their evolution. The main focus is on the development and use of Intranets over the last few years. Central to the overall picture presented is the very high number and enormous variety of systems, projects, use areas, rapid organization change, and so on – that is, complexity – we find in an organization like this one. From an early stage this complexity has moved beyond what can be managed from a central point and in a coherent manner. This is also true if one looks just at the Intranet. The Intranet – even within one division – is made up of a huge number of more or less independent sub-units and without any central or strict coordination of the sub-units and the activities through which they are developed and enhanced. These sub-units are integrated in various ways and to various degrees. But overall, they are loosely coupled (Perrow, 1984), and not tightly coupled (ibid.) around a shared data base as the systems in the previous chapters are. But what this chapter reports is a case where the Intranet development and use has more or less worked very well.

3   CONCLUDING REMARKS: COMPLEX ICT SOLUTIONS – HIGH RELIABILITY ORGANIZATIONS OR RISK SOCIETY?

The cases presented here should demonstrate quite clearly that ongoing efforts at making large scale integrated ICT solutions indeed create complex socio-technical systems that also embed numerous risks. The cases illustrate a wide range of different kinds of risks that are produced by side-effects of a wide range of different activities and components. Questions to

be discussed related to the cases are: were the risks caused by poor practices? Could more of the risks have been predicted? Would the adoption of
'best practices' within software engineering and risk management have
made a difference? As far as we can judge, 'best practices' were followed in
the cases reported. Or at least, we cannot find that any decisions were made
or actions taken that were against what is considered best practices. And
the risks that were not predicted, like those related to the scaling up of the
IS in the ship classifications case, for instance, could not easily have been
predicted. Similarly, the fact that the establishment of the integrated email
infrastructure in the bank case should involve the kind of risks that actually emerged also seems quite hard to predict to us – at least within the
framework of established software engineering practices. However, among
the cases there is at least one that needs some discussion before the conclusion that 'best practices' would not help may be considered valid. This is
the mobile telecom operator case. In this case, a major challenge was that
the project members could not find people in the organization that knew
how the existing billing system was working and how it was integrated
within its context. One might easily argue that any organization needs to
make sure that they have competent people knowing how its systems work.
And this is what any textbook would say – unless it is considered so obvious
that it is unnecessary to say it. So in this way this organization did *not* act
in alignment with best practices. However, following this 'best practice' is
certainly easier said than done and it would have huge implications. We
cannot see how this mobile telecom operator could follow this best practice
without slowing down its growth rate dramatically. When growing, they
had to put their most experienced people into the most important positions; slowing down the growth rate would imply that they were making
less money. It would also imply that their market share would decrease and
they would possibly be a loser in the market and in the end disappear. If we
look at the specific project reported, we see that there were so many risks
involved that they were beyond what could be managed. The solution to
this problem, again, would also be to slow down planned progress speed of
the project and reduce its ambitions. However, this solution would also have
potentially high costs. The operator embarked on the project in order to be
able to bill the new 3G services. They believed, like everybody in the business, that these services would be offered soon and consumed in huge
amounts. Not being able to bill these services would have huge negative
impacts on the market position and profits of the company. It turned out
that this prediction was false. However, when the project started, not being
able to bill 3G services in due time (that is, fast) was considered a more
serious risk than the risks related to the project. So we cannot see that
'best practices' have much to offer these projects. This leads us to the next

question: can better risk and project management techniques be developed so that the risks reported can be managed? Or alternatively, can the development and use of complex ICT solutions be turned into High Reliability Organizations? Or are risks inherent to these solutions so that we are in fact producing a Risk Society where accidents will be normal?

Most interesting to discuss here is the HRO hypothesis, in other words to what extent stronger focus on risks and learning from experience would make a difference. We have not collected our empirical material in order to test this hypothesis, so no firm conclusions can be drawn, but we do believe it would make a difference in some of the cases. A stronger focus on risks and learning from experience would first of all imply that organizations embark on less ambitious projects and plan to proceed at a slower speed, that is that they, in principle, take only one step at a time and a step no longer than previous experience would be valid for. In one case, however, this medicine does not work – the mobile telecom case. In this case the company had to move ahead fast to stay in business, or, at least, the possible gains of moving ahead fast were so big that the risks were worth taking. But in other cases slower project progress and lower ambitions would make sense. This was certainly the case for the hospitals involved in the ERP project. Slower progress makes sense for them if risks are substantially reduced. The same could perhaps have been said about the bank and ship classification cases. However, of these we think the mobile telecom case is the most relevant and interesting – at least if we take most of the business literature seriously. This literature is telling us that the business environment is continuously becoming more competitive – due in particular to globalization processes heavily fuelled by integrated ICT solutions, the fact that the future is becoming more unpredictable and that companies have to change faster and faster. So this case illustrates the central aspects of the Risk Society. Risks cannot be managed – they can only be transformed and distributed, that is when trying to managing risks, we just transform them into new ones which may pop up somewhere else (and then also possibly become someone else's risk).

The last case reported, the development of Intranets in a pharmaceutical company, sheds some new light on this issue. This case was a more successful one. Drawing upon Perrow's (1984) Normal Accidents Theory, we describe this as a case where the overall integration strategy was different from the other cases: the different Intranets (as well as other solutions mentioned) were more loosely coupled than the others reported in this book. And because they were only loosely coupled, the totality they created was less complex than if they were more tightly coupled. Accordingly each component (Intranet) could be managed and modified more independently without triggering cascades of side-effects. This is also in line with Perrow's recommendations for developing complex systems: do not build them! And, in fact, that is the only strategy we can recommend based on the research reported in this book. (And the assumptions about how risks can be reduced by reducing speed of change and growth also means, avoid making complex systems according to the definition of complexity presented at the beginning of this chapter.) But, in fact, we do not see this as a very realistic strategy. We do believe that, among other processes, globalization is making the world more complex, unpredictable and more rapidly changing. This will generate huge needs (or 'needs') for more integrated information systems – which still is the mantra of IS. Accordingly, we do believe that integrated ICT solutions will bring more fuel to the processes making the Risk Society and Reflexive Modernization more real and High Reliability Organizations more rare. Unfortunately.

REFERENCES

Arthur, W.B. (1994), *Increasing Returns and Path Dependence in the Economy*, Ann Arbor, MI: University of Michigan Press.

Axelrod, R.M. and M.D. Cohen (1999), *Harnessing Complexity: Organizational Implications of a Scientific Frontier*, New York: Free Press.

BCS/RAE (2004), 'The challenges of complex IT projects', British Computer Society and Royal Academy on Engineering Report, www.bcs.org/NR/rdonlyres/3B36137E-C5FE-487B-A18B-4D/281D88EF7/0/complexity.pdf, accessed 31 August 2005.

Beck, U. (1986), *Risk Society: Towards Another Modernity*, London: Routledge.

Beck, U., A. Giddens and S. Lash (1994), *Reflexive Modernization*, Cambridge: Polity Press.

Beniger, J. (1986), *The Control Revolution: Technological and Economic Origins of the Information Society*, Cambridge, Mass: Harvard University Press.

Berg, M. and S. Timmermanns (2000), 'Orders and their others: on the constitution of universalities in medical work', *Configurations*, 8(1), 31–61.

Ciborra, C., K. Braa, A. Cordella, B. Dahlbom, A. Failla, O. Hanseth, V. Hepsø, J. Ljungberg, E. Monteiro, K.A. Simon (2000), *From Control to Drift: The Dynamics of Corporate Information Infrastructures*, Oxford: Oxford University Press.

Douglas, M. and A. Wildavsky (1980), *Risk and Culture: An Essay on the Selection of Technical and Environmental Dangers*, Berkeley, CA: University of California Press.

Fitzgerald, B. (2000), 'System development methodologies: the problem of tenses', *Information, Technology & People*, 13(3), 17–185.

Hutter, B. and M. Power (2005), *Organizational Encounters with Risk*, New York: Cambridge University Press.

Kumar K. and J. van Hillegersberg (2000), 'ERP experiences and evolution', *Communications of the ACM*, 43(4) 23–6.

La Porte, T.R. (1988), 'The United States air traffic system: increasing reliability in the midst of rapid growth', in Renate Mayntz and Thomas P. Hughes (eds),

The Development of Large Technical Systems, Boulder, CO: Westview Press, pp. 215–44.

La Porte, T.R. (1996), 'High reliability organizations: unlikely, demanding, and at risk', *Journal of Contingencies and Crisis Management*, **4**: 63.

Lash, S., B. Szerszynski and B. Wynne (1996), *Risk, Environment and Modernity. Towards a New Ecology*, London, UK: Sage Publications.

Latour, B. (1999), *Pandora's Hope: Essays on the Reality of Science Studies*, Cambridge, MA: Harvard University Press.

Law, J. and A. Mol (2002), *Complexities: Social Studies of Knowledge Practices*, Durham, NC: Duke University Press.

Luhmann, N. (1993), *The Sociology of Risk*, Berlin: de Gruyter.

Perrow, C. ([1984]1999), *Normal Accidents: Living With High-Risk Technologies*, New Jersey, USA: Princeton University Press.

Schneberger, S.L. and E.R. McLean (2003), 'The complexity cross: implications for practice', *Communications of the ACM*, **46**(9), September, pp. 216–25.

Urry, J. (2003), *Global Complexities*, Cambridge, UK: Polity Press.

Weick, K.E. and K.M. Sutcliffe (2001), *Managing the Unexpected. Assuring High Performance in an Age of Complexity*, San Francisco, CA: Jossey-Bass.

PART I

Theory

2. Digital technologies and risk: a critical review

Claudio Ciborra

INTRODUCTION

The aim of this chapter is to study the multiple links between risk and digital technologies such as information and communication technology (ICT). It sets the ground for the empirical analysis of risks connected to the design and deployment of ICT infrastructures in a variety of settings: corporate, public organizations and government.[1]

The field of information systems (IS) offers a good point of departure for the study of risks connected to digital technologies, since it is populated by at least two different practices. First, there is the analysis of risk dedicated to complex projects involving software systems and methodologies of a mainly technical/mathematical nature. Second, there are managerial concerns that initially related to this kind of software-based project, but were later extended to a range of mainly strategic and operational business factors. Thus, in IS we find both the 'harder' quantitative techniques of risk management and 'softer' approaches to the handling of so-called operational risk aspects.

The management of large software projects was the earliest problem area out of which the ICT risk management discipline emerged; subsequently, this has become part of Software Engineering (SE). Building large software modules for big corporate applications, especially for the suppliers of US defence agencies, is exposed to a variety of risks: cost overruns, wrong specifications and usability characteristics, delays in delivery, and so on. Hence, in order to improve the planning and governance of such developments to mitigate the risks of major SE failures, there was a need to develop available risk management methods and techniques in ways that made them suitable for application to the ICT field. The cultural and professional milieu in which these methods and techniques had been originally tried out led to their emergence as strictly quantitative approaches based on a positivist, probabilistic definition of risk: probability of occurrence of a problem multiplied by the value of its impact. This naïve view of risk has dominated the SE discipline and practice since the 1980s. It is supported by a myriad of sub-techniques for identifying risks, measuring impacts and assessing probabilities. To be sure, the methods and techniques are accompanied by words of caution from senior software professionals who suggest that they should be applied with a grain of salt and situational common sense. Here, as often happens in the professional field, formal models seem to become gradually replaced by rules of thumb, prescriptions and war stories disguised as articulated experience.

With time and experience, managerial attention to ICT applications such as the study of organizational impacts, management of ICT strategy and redesign of business processes has crossed the boundaries of quantitative risk management and widened its scope. As a result, an organizational/managerial literature about information systems risks and their management in a business-wide perspective has emerged. This ranges from the more micro concerns about how to get the user requirements right (an issue that still overlaps with SE risk management) up to the strategic choice in selecting an application portfolio or an ICT infrastructure, where questions need to be asked about the risks of large ICT investments for a business as a whole. This literature, and its relative prescriptions, converges today in spirit and methodological approach with the field of operational risk. An example is the treatment of risk issues in the credit and financial sectors, as found in the 'Basel 2' documents (Basel Committee on Banking Supervision, 2001). In these, digital technologies are treated on the same grounds as other factors contributing to operational risk. Although the implicit underlying theory of risk used is the probabilistic one, the coexistence of many imponderable organizational factors makes the quantitative risk calculation largely beyond reach in practice. Hence, there has been a proliferation of double-entry tables aimed at qualitative classifications of situations, portfolios, instances and prescriptions on how to handle risks connected to systems and applications.

The technical and managerial perspectives share a basic belief in the powers of managerial and organizational control: it is believed that systematic assessment (as in the scientific study of work by F.W. Taylor) involving an orderly and rigorous study of risk can make its management more effective. Better control strategies are seen to be the paramount way of mitigating, reducing or annihilating risk. Typically, a linear reasoning prevails in these approaches, linked to rigid sequence identification, knowledge gathering, measurement (where possible) and plans for solutions and implementation.

With the advent of the Internet, network computing and inter-organizational systems, the boundaries of units of analysis – such as a 'software project' or a 'business firm' – seem to become too narrow for capturing all the various ramifications of the dynamics entertained by technology and risk. For example, consider recent developments in the ideas of 'democratizing finance' by transferring its sophisticated calculus techniques at the level of individual existence, so that life choices, change and innovation are devolved to the level of the individual armed with better knowledge and sophisticated financial tools. This new way of looking at, and practising, finance as a science for managing risk 'democratically' gives digital technologies an overarching importance and a new role. They become 'grid technologies', that is an information infrastructure that allows the calculation of indexes and units of accounts, so that risks are quantified and can be traded, pooled and shared on global markets by large numbers of individuals. Digital technologies diffuse and enmesh with the structure of markets under this encompassing grid infrastructure, creating virtual enterprise networks and affecting more than ever the personal lives of workers, managers and consumers. Any breakdown of these networks becomes potentially devastating for business and private lives, precisely because of the higher levels of integration and standardization achieved by the new technical platforms. On the one hand, grid technologies constitute the backbone of choice for the 'risk society', to the extent that they become the key coordination and communication infrastructure linking consumers, citizens, businesses and governments. On the other hand, as a powerful expert and calculating system, ICT becomes the paramount tool for running more and more sophisticated algorithms to quantify and manage risk at all levels, and for a greater number of economic agents. These far-reaching developments seem to elude the current discourses of software engineers as well as IS risk management consultants – but not for long.

Consider, further, the specificities that distinguish ICT as grid technologies from other modern technologies that create new risks, such as nuclear or chemical plants. Digital technologies are *technologies of representation* that can be used to augment other techniques of representation, such as risk calculation and management. Taken *all together*, these are powerful tools to represent, calculate, control, mitigate, reduce and transfer risk. The creation of new global markets for the reallocation of risk insurance contracts is enabled by digital capabilities such as large data warehouses; the collection, communication and recombination of huge volumes of data; and the ensuing possibility of building and updating complex indexes. ICTs appear to be able to reduce costs in two key areas. First, they can cut transaction costs on existing markets for goods and services, thereby making the whole economy more efficient, enterprises more global and governments more agile and responsive. Secondly, ICTs can decrease the costs of innovation, by allowing economic agents better to insure themselves against a richer variety of risks of (failure in) change. In this new financial order, the intertwining of digital technologies and risk is advancing further as the main instrument for the representation, quantification and sharing (through markets for risk and intermediaries) of hazards linked to the main life-choices of individuals.

The scope and reach (Keen, 1991) of grid technologies make the strait-jacket of the quantitative calculus of risk even more limited than it proved to be when moving from SE projects to the broader field of risk management for corporate ICT investments. However, it would be naïve to think that the technology-enabled way to a fully calculable life, in a fully calculable world, is going to be clear-cut. Most probably, instead, it is going to be punctuated by new and surprising risks. For example, a close analysis of how large ICT infrastructures are actually deployed within and between public and private organizations has begun to unveil a number of intriguing features. Despite the tight managerial control, careful planning, appropriate risk manage-ment, and so on, ICT infrastructures tend to have a life of their own: they basically *drift* as a result of improvised usages; unforeseen technical inter-dependencies between old (legacy) and new platforms; quirky design choices; surprising user resistance; and other unpredictable behaviours of both systems and humans. Here, the sociology of modernity (Beck, 1992; Giddens, 1990) turns out to be a useful reference to capture the runaway dynamics of man-made risks, unexpected consequences and proliferating side-effects. The facts are even acknowledged by Basel 2 recommendations, at least in the credit and finance industry. They see digital technologies as one of the factors causing the shift of the risk management agenda from low-impact/high-frequency incidents to high-impact/low-frequency events. Here, the sociology of modernity complements the technical and managerial perspectives by highlighting the non-linear nature of risk management. It also points to the fact that the risk management techniques and technologies for control can themselves be the source of new man-made risks.

ICT has the potential to extend the boundaries where the future can be ordered and calculated, hence 'colonizing' further the wild territory of uncertainty and transforming it into the cultivated land of calculable risk. In particular, grid technologies will dramatically decrease the costs and barriers to innovation, foster new behaviours and multiply those occa-sions of radical new learning and new life choices that have previously been abandoned because they were considered 'too risky'. On the other hand, the establishment of grid technologies, with their broadband com-munication channels and gigantic databases, would not solve possible infrastructure breakdowns; if anything, they will make such disruptions potentially more harmful. Security issues will multiply, as well as privacy concerns for the content of the databases. Compatibility problems with protocols and legacy systems are also destined to spread and cause unwanted side-effects.

In order to deal with all these new promising and puzzling developments, we submit that the economic and sociological analyses of digital technologies and risk need to be complemented by a phenomenological/existential one. Life, risk and technology are getting more intimate than ever. This is due to some subtler reasons than the hazards posed by GM crops or the thinning of the ozone layer. Paradoxically, the extension of the domain of quantifiable knowledge and representation exposes us to the danger of the further growth of ignorance generated by the mysterious new interdependencies and side-effects created by the very infrastructure deployed for the colonization of knowledge. The essence of such a 'reflexive' process needs to be captured by a new notion of risk, combined with a different perspective on the question of technology.

It is not just about us becoming dependent on the mobile phone/computer for our communication; it is not only about transactions passing through digital networks; it is not even about jobs being automated; or human reasoning being replaced by expert systems. Looking at the next developments in ICT platforms and risk management, the challenge emerging on the horizon is that the unfolding of our life (project) becomes simultaneously conditioned, constrained or enabled by grid technologies. The technology is already there, albeit in an indirect and hidden form, for instance when we apply for a loan or seek a life insurance scheme. In the next phase, it will be at hand in helping us compute whether we should engage in a house move or a career change; or whether we can afford one course of studies rather than another. For each choice, grid technologies will be able to offer a calculus of probabilities based on objective indexes, thus contributing to the quantification of our life projects to a greater extent. That is why only a fresh exploration into the intertwining of life, risk and technology could offer us some clues to help grasp such future developments. This latter goal will be pursued in a later chapter in this book.

In what follows, the first two sections deal with the technical and managerial approaches and their limitations. Institutional economic perspectives are introduced in the third section to tackle the issues of intersubjectivity and psychology of risk in two main settings: markets and hierarchies. Further economic perspectives, in particular from the finance domain, are then put forward to help enhance understanding of the implications of grid technologies and the creation of new markets for individualized risk management. Next, in order to capture the puzzling aspects of the ramifications of risks stemming from the new waves of technical applications, the sociology of risk is presented by discussing the duality of risk generated by digital technologies.

TECHNICAL APPROACHES

Risk management deals with risk exposure. According to the positivist definition adopted by Boehm (1991) to launch the field of software risk management, risk exposure is treated as the potential loss multiplied by the probability of loss. Potential loss is described by the components of the unsatisfactory outcome of a project, which leads management to identify lists of the risk factors that are seen as causes of overall negative outcomes. Risk factors have to be addressed, eliminated, mitigated or avoided, depending upon their probability of occurrence and the size of their impacts. Various techniques are used to carry out the analysis. For example, decision trees can provide a framework for analysing the role of risk factors and the sensitivity of final outcomes. Regression analysis allows the development of a cost model that relies on the data of past software projects (Fairley, 1994), which aims to elicit those factors that can explain the variation of the effort put into one particular project relative to the main trend identified by the regression curve. Simulation (for example Montecarlo methods) helps in identifying the behaviour of the intervening risk factors. Other approaches are based on disciplines such as statistics, mathematical modelling of decision making and graph theory.

A few aspects have been identified as limiting the scope of the technical approaches, such as these mentioned by Renn (1998):

- The quantitative combinations of variables, such as magnitude of impact and probabilities, assume equal weights. Low-probability/high-impact events may get the same weight as high-probability/low-impact ones, and this might distort the risk emerging in a given situation. On the other hand, attributing differential weights may prove to be an uncertain or impossible task.
- Probabilities tend to be extracted from the relative frequencies of past events. When this is not an adequate approach to anticipate future events, the calculation may have limited predictive power.
- People perceive the magnitude of impact and its probability differently, which leads to an appreciation of risk that may differ from the outcome of the algorithms.
- The desirability of effects may vary among different decision makers.
- The institutional and organizational contexts may influence the actual risk levels to which human agents are exposed, and may impact on the various risk-mitigating or risk-handling actions indicated by the purely technical calculus of risk outcomes.

Note that the last objection in the above list highlights the fact that the causes and consequences of risks, as well as risk-management actions, are embedded in institutional, organizational structures and are generally intertwined in social processes and networks of relationships. All the stages of effective risk management must take place within the constraints posed by such social and organizational contexts, and exploit and respect the opportunities offered by those constraints. A few practitioners of software risk management have stressed the importance of organizational processes to complement or support the quantitative techniques. For example, Boehm (1991) indicates that when uncertainty is high and no reliable estimates can be made of the key risk factors, engaging in prototyping the new system could be a way of reducing risks by acquiring knowledge and buying information and time; improved estimates can then be made to fit the quantitative models at a later stage.

Conversely, despite their promises, the adoption of structured design methodologies may increase risk precisely because they push forward the moment at which the actual project outcomes and their problems will be exposed in actual operation. Hence, some authors (for example Charette, 1996) suggest paying attention to the 'mechanics' of risk management: those organizational and process interventions that can transform an algorithm to calculate risk into an effective way of handling a project. The importance of processes such as planning for risk management is discussed below in this respect.

In summary, what is troubling in this first set of approaches is that the use of sophisticated formal models is accompanied by crude simplifications characterizing the risk situation. In particular, only one decision maker is identified (the management of the firm or the project) as being responsible for assessing the risks, evaluating them and formulating remedial policies based on the relevant calculus. The technical perspectives are therefore revealed as being too narrow, except in the simplest of situations, and adopting one as the single guide to risk identification and management may therefore constitute a risky option in itself. This indicates that a broader view that encompasses management and organizational processes is essential.

MANAGERIAL APPROACHES

The broader organizational perspectives on risk identified above address the issue of implementation within the concrete organizational or institutional setting that surrounds any risk-calculating algorithm. Not only do these approaches widen the scope of risk analysis and the range of risk factors taken into consideration, but they also point to the gap between models and their deployment. This often shows that managerial practice is at odds with the prediction of the models or methods themselves.

The literature focusing on the psychological, behavioural, institutional and organizational aspects of risk management is vast (for example see March and Shapira (1987) on the actual behaviour of managers facing risks and Perrow (1984) on the influence of organizational settings and routines). In comparison, the specific IS literature contribution is limited in terms of the quantity of published material, empirical research and, above all, its scope.

Lyytinen, Mathiassen and Ropponen (1998) address a range of organizational aspects by looking at various IS and software risk approaches. They highlight one important cognitive aspect in risk management: the scope of managerial attention towards the factors to be taken into consideration in any calculus or qualitative assessment. Thus, they find that various IS approaches to risk management may focus on different aspects, such as business strategy, rather than requirements analysis, since risks can be hidden in any of the multiple stages of the development and deployment of a system. In order to introduce structure into this potentially limitless field of interest, the authors propose a socio-technical framework for comparing various approaches, according to key domains defined by Leavitt's (1964) classic diamond diagram which connects four main variables: strategy, technology, structure and tasks. But such a commendable exercise aimed at reducing complexity proves to be of dubious use, since it is based on the presumed equivalence of the socio-technical notion of variance control to attain system equilibrium with the goals and scope of risk management in an organization. However, such equivalence is unwarranted. Within the socio-technical theoretical framework, variances are problems that need to be handled by an appropriate control system based on the coordination and communication of the members of the organization among themselves, usually involving the technical infrastructure. Control actions are based on feedback from a disturbance that *has occurred*. Risk, instead, is about *future* disturbances: immediate feedback from an occurred variance is not the only issue, nor is equilibrium necessarily a main feature. Risk management is all about uncertainty regarding future events, betting on their occurrence, buying insurance to mitigate their impact, and so on. In particular, all risk management contracts must be signed *before*, not after, a breakdown has occurred or before the information that would create a sense of urgency arises (Shiller, 2003, p. 30). Variance control in a socio-technical system is, instead, about detecting breakdowns *ex post* and taking counteractive, equilibrium-restoring measures (Herbst, 1974). Even the fact that socio-technical systems must engage in equilibrium seeking when dealing with variances is an idea that has been challenged

(Ciborra et al., 1984). Variances (and indeed risks) are sometimes the source of innovation and new order (or self organization) stemming from *disequilibrium*. Hence, reduction to a pre-existing order may constitute a repressive policy that kills innovation.

This is just one instance showing that, unfortunately, IS approaches do not distance themselves enough from the tenets of the engineering and technical perspectives, or at least do not challenge them. At the limit, they put forward a richer list of risk factors which are often overlooked by the practitioner who focuses on a particular project as opposed to a business perspective (McFarlan, 1981). On the other hand, the IS approaches rely on the same key fictions of the purely technical perspectives, such as that of the 'unbiased' decision maker. Thus, Keil et al. (1998) classify risks of software projects on the basis of their importance and perceived level of control, which they believe can prevent the risks from occurring. However, these authors fail to emphasize indications from the extensive behavioural literature pointing out that these perceptions can be heavily biased, depending upon a variety of psychological and contextual factors. The shape, values and enactment of a decision tree may differ according to the psychological and organizational context of the decision, since risk identification relies on cognitive aspects, such as problem framing (Tversky and Kahneman, 1974), and estimates are based on perceptions, attitudes and ultimately even feelings (Loewenstein et al., 2001) and moods.

Other managerial and behavioural aspects seem to remain elusive. Challenges have been made to the formulation of risk management that suggest there is a phase of calculation followed by the making of a choice among the risk-return combinations that are available. There is often denial of risk, or a causal relation is assumed between action and (risky) events. Also, real decision makers seem to be more impressed by the magnitude of any negative outcome, rather than the level of its probability: implicitly, they give more weight to the former. Even ranking risks on the basis of expected impact has not been empirically supported. March and Shapira (1987) report a vice-president stating, 'You don't quantify the risk, but you have to be able to feel it'. The same authors conclude that, although there is ample evidence that the risk-taking behaviour of managers is often far from optimal, such behaviour may indeed consist of accommodations of individuals and organizations to the 'subtle practical problems of sustaining appropriate risk-taking in an imperfectly comprehended world' (March and Shapira, 1987). Modelling and planning seem to possess, then, a limited scope; what matters in handling risk is 'situated action' (Suchman, 1987).

We conclude that the state of the art in the IS field concerning the management perspectives is rather uneven, if not lacking. For instance, it fails to take stock of the more sophisticated analyses of decision-making behaviour under uncertainty and knowledge distortion; does not acknowledge the plurality of decision makers; and does not challenge the main tenets of the engineering and technical perspectives.

ECONOMIC PERSPECTIVES

Given their narrowness of focus on technology, probability and control of the development process, we need to abandon the technical and managerial perspectives in the IS field in favour of a broader inquiry into the economic views on risk (following a similar broadening of perspective to that used by Ciborra and Hanseth (1998) when addressing the strategic alignment issues of ICT infrastructures in organizations). The agenda and the facets analysed from an economics viewpoint are multiple and can help us encounter a richer vision of the relationship between digital technologies and risk. This suggests that not only is the process of developing and applying a complex technological infrastructure punctuated by more or less computable risks, but technology itself can also be harnessed to reduce, mitigate or share risk. The economics of markets, transactions and organizations allow us to approach such a complex relationship in a way that the long, but rather flat, managerial lists of risk factors hardly make possible.

Information systems are about ICT embedded in organizations. The risks posed by digital technologies therefore need to be understood within an organizational framework, for which institutional economics and the economics of risk can be harnessed to understand the implications of key organizational/institutional contexts. To begin with, institutional economics indicates that there are two main organizational arrangements to be considered: markets and hierarchies (bureaucracies). We need to trace the risk factors of digital technologies within these two different contexts. In a market, risks can be shared or exchanged by creating markets for risks, measured in utilities or disutilities. The theory of social costs developed by Coase (1960) may provide further useful insights. What goes on in hierarchies is better framed by the notion of operational risk (Power, 2003). Here, many aspects of the managerial perspectives come to the fore again. But the boundaries between hierarchies and markets are not fixed (Williamson, 1975; Hart, 1995) and the different styles of handling risks regarding ICT projects may change over time, for example when the IS services are outsourced. The picture is further complicated when one considers that ICT is a factor that contributes to the change of boundaries between markets and hierarchies (Ciborra, 1981; Ciborra, 1983; Malone et al., 1987), thus impacting the styles of managing (trading) risk. If market risk can be better subjected to representation, calculation and exchange, and if digital technologies support the expansion and refinement of markets, the diffusion of ICT will not just be punctuated by risks, as for any other innovation, but will have a self-reinforcing effect. This means ICT diffusion will promote a special style of risk management, namely one based on the formal representation and calculation of risk, and the ensuing creation of specialized markets for trading risk.

Let us first look at risk in markets. The main difference between the economic and technical conceptions of risk is the possibility envisaged in economics of including a dimension of *intersubjective validity* through the notion of *utility*, which describes the degree of satisfaction or dissatisfaction with an event or an action among a variety of stakeholders (Renn, 1998). Harms and undesired effects can be framed as (social) costs (Coase, 1960) and thus become utilities or disutilities for different parties. Costs can be allocated by various mechanisms, market-like or non-market. Specifically, utilities can be traded; after all, utility can be measured by the amount of money one is willing to pay to avoid a potential harm. Economics thus introduces a social dimension, albeit in the narrow sense of a system of exchange of utilities/disutilities. Such a dimension is missing from the IS managerial perspectives, which are unable to deal with questions such as: risk for whom? Who is going to pay to avoid a certain risk? Also, a social dimension includes some of the psychological aspects of risk, by distinguishing risk-taking from risk-neutral or risk-averse attitudes of economic agents. Psychological and social effects can then find a common denominator to measure the degree of harm or utility: money.

Most of the techniques developed within the technical approaches, such as models of rational decision making, probability and discounted-value calculations, also apply to the economics approach. However, here they are supported by an economic framework that connects the individual and the social (intersubjective) dimension through the notion of utility. The economic perspectives open up various new domains of application, such as costs and benefits analyses and the possibility of sharing risk and social costs through trade. In addition, due attention is given to incentives; risk insurance, for example, can be used to influence individual behaviour by discouraging risky actions in order to save money. Finally, new models are added to the kit of techniques for representing risk quantitatively, such as the game-theoretic ones (Jaeger et al., 2001).

One limitation of the economic perspectives and their envisioning of markets to trade risks is that not all risks or social costs can be translated into money; for example, human life can be regarded as plainly incommensurable in some cases and for some individuals or communities. Another, as Coase (1960) has shown, is that there may be transaction costs involved in exchanging utilities and disutilities. This would bring in non-market institutions, such as courts and government agencies, to take care of the handling of risks, lest no trading occurs at all. The discussion of risk in the IS field has suffered from its implicit focus on ICT in non-market organizations, that is bureaucracies: hence any treatment of utilities or risk sharing is largely ignored, even by those authors who claim to transcend the narrow technical view (as seen in the previous section). This is a gap that needs to be filled to create a better understanding of the relationship between risk and digital technologies. We will address this below, after a short survey of the notion of operational risk and its relevance for hierarchical (non-market) organizations.

The notion of operational risk emerged in the banking environment as a residual category for those (mainly internally generated) risks not covered by the more common market and credit-risk management practices. It comes from the simple regulatory principle by which banks should hold some capital as a buffer against risks to their loans and credit operations (market-risk exposure). This buffer should be larger if it is to take account of the way banks can incur risks not only, say, in lending money to outside customers, but also if their internal ICT systems fail. Thanks to the so-called Basel 2 regulatory proposals in the last few years, especially in the banking sector, operational risk has become the encompassing concept and vision for the control and regulation of a wide range of risks that can be faced while operating a business. More precisely, Basel 2 consultative documents define operational risk as 'the risk of direct or indirect loss resulting from inadequate or failed internal processes, people and systems or from external events' (Basel Committee, 2001, par. 6). In this respect operational risk is an organizational concept that subsumes both the technical and managerial models and approaches which emerged in the discussion of IS and risk. However, the concept of operational risk has given rise in a deeper way to analyses and discussions that address the organizational dynamics of managing risks within hierarchies. In order to overcome the limitations of their narrow focus and naïve hypotheses about human behaviour and risk, it would be advisable for the managerial and technical IS literature to take notice of these developments, especially those occurring in critical accounting (Power, 1997).

The problems that emerge during the implementation of operational risk reflect themselves within the specific IS field. It is therefore useful to mention here the results of Power's (2003) analysis of the puzzles, dilemmas and contradictions of operational risk that point to the ramifications of lack of knowledge, the role of biased data when assessing risk in organizations and the influence of internal politics and impacts of negotiation. The issues raised by this concern include items such as:

- What data is relevant to operational risk? Historic losses? Expected or unexpected ones? What about sudden catastrophic events?
- Is this data reliable? Apart from rare events for which data is unavailable, as well as for the most frequent ones, there can be opportunistic massaging to hide errors.
- Effective learning and correction of mistakes since the negative event occurred can also make historic data irrelevant, because operations have been modified in the mean time.
- Collecting data from multiple organizations (a sort of best-practice exercise in reverse) is a possible solution, but requires the sharing of troubling and embarrassing information: hence one can expect to see pooled databases of this kind remain half empty.
- The 'key under the lamppost' effect. Data that is eventually collected systematically under existing internal auditing and information systems becomes the basis for measurement of operational risk. However, this gets to be defined by the databases available and not by the actual multiplicity of potential risks, which are not all covered by the existing systems when representing and recording historical risks.

Similar dilemmas affect the risk modelling stage, where Power (2003) notes that:

- The use of risk measurement techniques is not immune from organizational politics.
- Rational calculation of use in actual situations has to be marketed and sold internally, but this is not always accomplished successfully and so its scope is rendered, at best, fragmented and a matter of negotiation.

In general, the main approaches to the management of operational risk are of two different types, similar to the ones that emerged in our discussion of risk in IS development: a 'soft' calculative approach and a 'hard' approach. The first tends to rely on a variety of ranking and scoring techniques for qualitative variables, with the goal of directing attention to key risk drivers. The hard approach is based on the discipline of market risk management and the relevant quantitative techniques based on calculating costs and utilities. The problem with the latter approach is that it aims at enacting market techniques within a fundamentally non-market organizational setting.

GRID TECHNOLOGIES AND RISK

The economic perspectives are a good introduction to an inquiry into the reflexivity of grid technologies in relation to risk. As indicated earlier, by grid technologies we mean ICTs that increasingly have the characteristics of ubiquitous, mediating information infrastructures. Their hardware is characterized by the extension of the links (networks) to the individuals and organizations they support. Software guarantees the standardization of the linkages for the seamless transfer of data and to provide access to powerful databases that can track usage and produce profiles of users. By analogy with the electricity grid, ICT-based grid technologies can provide ubiquitous access to content and people, allow fast transfer or exchange of content and communication and enable more sophisticated processing of data in relation to various patterns of usage of the grid itself. The leading public example of grid technologies is the Internet, in its present and future forms (known as I2); but within narrower corporate boundaries there are also full-scale Enterprise Resource Planning (ERP) systems, web services and intranets that feature many elements of a grid technology. The economic perspectives highlight *contract enabling* as one of the significant potential uses of grid technologies because this kind of technology would provide the adequate information flows and databases to 'create, set up, control and maintain the network of exchanges and relevant contracts' (Ciborra, 1981) that build up the fabric of economic institutions such as markets and firms.

The infrastructure character of such technologies can contribute, on the one hand, to the generation of new, surprising risks (see Ciborra et al. (2000) and the next section); on the other hand it can be used to manage a growing variety of risks for which appropriate financial markets can be created. For instance, 'this new technology can do cheaply what once was expensive by systematizing our approach to risk management and by generating vast new repositories of information that make it possible for us to disperse risk and contain hazard' (Shiller, 2003, p. 2).

There are multiple ways in which grid technologies can act. First, there are the overall trends in formalization of transactions, and the pushing further away of the boundaries between markets and hierarchies in favour of markets (Ciborra, 1983; Malone et al., 1987). Thanks to ICT, 'buy' has extended its reach in relation to 'make': there will be more externalization or outsourcing of activities, regulated by market contracts. As a consequence, markets will be more efficient because of the decrease in transaction costs and will extend spatially and become closer to the functioning of a perfect market (always with the approximation determined by the initial state of a particular market).

Moreover, powerful grid technologies can have other effects on the costs of 'transition', or change and innovation, via their enabling of new opportunities for managing risk, as pointed out by Shiller (2003). In particular, grid technologies can have an impact on the realm of finance and become a powerful tool for the management of risks. Finance can reduce the harm on individuals by dispersing the negative effects among a large number of people. This already happens on the stock market, through the limited-companies arrangement, social security and some forms of individual insurance. But this could take place on a much broader scale and be tailored to the needs of individuals, way beyond their life insurance schemes, precisely thanks to grid technologies. Whenever people can mitigate their risks through new digital financial instruments, for example when changing a career or taking up an innovative course of studies (both high-risk personal choices), personal transition costs can be reduced and more individual and social innovation can be fostered: 'Financial arrangements exist to limit the inhibitions that fear of failure places on our actions and to do this in such a way that little moral hazard is created' (Shiller, 2003, p. 2).

Grid technologies would provide a new risk management infrastructure, by fostering the extension of the market and enhancing the possibilities for measuring utilities and introducing new units of account and measurement. Huge databases containing information on individuals (stemming from individual transactions like paying taxes or buying something with a credit card) allow for the construction of new powerful indexes against which everyone would be in the position to bet on the risk relating to a particular career, a profession, the house prices in a given area or the GDP of a certain country. All this would allow a person or a country to share on a global scale the risks of engaging in new ventures. In the past, complex financial arrangements such as insurance contracts were expensive to devise, and especially to tailor. Now, however, 'computer programs, using information supplied electronically in databases, can make complex financial contracts and instruments. The presentation of these contracts . . . can be fashioned by this technology to be user friendly' (Shiller, 2003, p. 10). To be sure, well-functioning markets for risk sharing require data for the effective estimation and pricing of risk. They can also reduce the transaction costs in the continuous negotiation of contracts, claims, adjustments and payments. Grid technologies can help to create 'a new financial order' by providing 'finely detailed, continuously-updated, widely available data on incomes and asset prices as well as aggregated data on these and other values relevant to the risk faced by individuals, organizations, and governments. Properly used, this new universe of information would allow better management of an ever wider spectrum of risks', and help to devise new risk management contracts across the globe (ibid., pp. 189–90). Risks will be objectified and quantified on an unprecedented scale, so that they can be bet against, traded, pooled and so on, and the activities to which they are attached will be carried out in a much more widespread and reliable way since the relevant risks can be shared among a broader consumer audience.

THE DUALITY OF RISK

As with any previous major revolutionary technology, ICT has impacts on work, employment, skills and organizations that can be disruptive, if not destructive. Technology is a major force in the process of creative destruction of capitalism (Schumpeter, 1976). Change and innovation create new risks at individual and societal level, and ICT is one of the culprits. But, as the last section has shown, ICT in the form of grid technologies can come to the rescue by allowing a 'democratization' of those financial tools that are today relegated to stock, market, derivatives and a restricted number of life insurance schemes: by encompassing a wide array of personal risks stemming from the relentless pace of change of technology-based capitalism. But it is here, perhaps, that Shiller's (2003) vision encounters its limits, creating a need to invoke sociological perspectives on risk and modernity.

Implicit in Shiller's (2003) advanced conception of ICT as grid technologies is an old and ubiquitous idea held by economists, according to which technology is a 'tool' that can be applied to good rather than bad ends in a contingent fashion (Ciborra and Hanseth, 1998). Thus, digital technologies represent a powerful tool for enhancing productivity as well as decreasing transaction costs; or, through the sophisticated sharing of risks on financial markets, for fostering change and innovation even at the micro-level of the individual economic agent. Of course, their application needs to be well governed, balancing costs and benefits for the various stakeholders through appropriate trade-offs. However, nowhere in the economist's conception can one trace the doubts observed by others that technology can be autonomous (Winner, 1977); behave as an actor with its own logic (Latour, 1999); or possess a far-reaching influence that affects how humans see reality and deploy technology according to patterns that are not purely instrumental.

In this respect, consider the notion of technology 'drift'. The drift of technical infrastructures has been identified as a ubiquitous phenomenon found in a variety of corporate large-scale ICT projects (Ciborra et al., 2000). When global companies engage in the launch of new ICT platforms to support new standardized and integrated business processes, they are immediately faced with the problem of deciding how to handle their existing and relatively successful legacy systems. Compromises need to be made with all the main actors on the stage, ranging from the angry orphans created by the substitution of the old standards, to the installed base and its autonomous dynamics. Compromises require time to be devised and implemented: some form of consensus needs to be gathered to align the new resources and processes and there will be a need to make adjustments on a continuous basis. This causes a main phenomenon: technologies and processes drift, so what one obtains at the end of the implementation process is not what the system was designed for originally. The models are not only corrupted, but are in a permanent state of redefinition. Implementation never ends. Time drifts too. The corporate timescape becomes more varied, with processes that are carried out at the speed of light running alongside others that are never really finished, or need to be painstakingly worked at to be completed. Management scholars, consultants and application vendors urge corporations, especially top management, to take action in this domain. Their prescriptions are straightforward. In order to overcome the present state of fragmentation, to avoid the widespread number of deals through which infrastructures are built, one needs to increase standardization and the integration of data, processes and businesses. These not-so-new top-down and control-oriented directives just accelerate technology drift.

In order to explain some of the paradoxical outcomes of ICT and the practical impossibility of maintaining a steady course during deployment, we submit that the basic assumptions of management models, old or new, may suffer from the following taken-for-granted assumptions:

- Linear reasoning prevails. Organizations and their management are seen as means–end chains. Goal directed decision-making, leadership and will are expected to enact and fix plans (Weill and Broadbent, 1998).
- Control and planning are regarded as key activities performed by organizations, and hence as essential design principles (Beniger, 1986).
- Evolution and change are seen as processes of improvement based on feedback that should be carefully monitored, and where possible measured and managed (Earl, 1996).
- Learning by mistakes is supposed to take place effortlessly.
- Private hoarding of knowledge and other key assets is both essential to gaining an advantage at the individual and organizational level and a source of potential opportunistic behaviour that requires to be kept in check. Again, control over key, unique resources becomes an increasing concern.

Instead, the sociological perspectives of Beck (1992) and Giddens (1990) would urge us (including the well-advised practitioners) to consider other important (and somewhat paradoxical) sources of risk, namely integration and standardization themselves, such as:

- The effort to create through ICT a lean, agile and standardized corporation takes too long a time in itself to be compatible with the rapidly changing requirements of the business and the market. The alignment of resources remains an elusive target precisely because of such efforts.
- Technical integration may bring with it a number of side-effects and unexpected consequences, for example interference between different standards or an infrastructure that is well tuned but too rigid.
- The control scope of organizations is bound to be limited, even if an enterprise invests heavily in digital technologies. Actually, huge investments in ICT may cause runaway dynamics (Arthur, 1994). Technology itself appears to evolve and diffuse along unexpected trajectories (Latour, 1999).
- Learning is not straightforward. Drift is the outcome of vicious circles where learning from mistakes fails to take place (Argyris and Schoen, 1996).
- Unpredictable knowledge-spillovers play a key role both inside and between organizations in triggering innovation and learning (Steinmueller, 1996). Learning is part of the more general phenomenon of reflexivity, by which institutions, organizations and individuals change, usually in unpredictable ways as a consequence of previous innovations and changes.

Digital technologies are contributing to both the generation of new side-effects and further reflexivity: digital organizations are simultaneously more controlled and more unpredictable. Unpredictability and increased runaway dynamics are also caused by the way the new risk management apparatus tends to show consistently the characteristics of higher levels of formalization, standardization and integration, which is an ideal landscape where side-effects can spread and diffuse at higher speed to provoke disrupting impacts. In particular, grid technologies, as with any infrastructural technology, may pose unforeseen hazards arising from collateral or systemic risks, which are typically not the ones the technical and engineering perspectives have in mind as risks that they should avoid when developing new computing and communication platforms. The collateral risks stem from the fact that, in order to function to mitigate individual and social risk, grid technologies involve a higher degree of interdependency between individual lives, the data they generate and the common databases, for example through the use of new identification and encryption technologies. Higher levels of transparency are required to ensure the trustworthiness of transactions, claims, and so on.

As mentioned above, only the pooling of individual data allows the construction of reliable indexes and units of accounts. If better indexes can mitigate moral hazard issues in individual or organization risk contracts, the establishment of such indexes enabled by grid technologies also requires the setting of standards and complex legal devices as an essential first step. Leaving aside the legal devices, standardization comes with a price of higher complexity and hidden new forms of fragmentation (Hanseth and Braa, 2001). Hence, every action, device or rule that sets out to reduce or mitigate risks may create side-effects of uncontrollable origin and manifestation, which can disrupt the newly-established control apparatus. Again, we encounter the phenomena that seem to elude the economic analysis but have been highlighted by the sociologists of risk society and modernity: those of reflexivity and runaway dynamics (Beck et al., 1994). Reflexivity refers to the fact that every new technology or regulative measure aimed at controlling risks, such as the grid technologies, inevitably creates new risks which originate from regions beyond the control of the new powerful platforms. In other words, the more we are able to extend the frontier of (formalized) knowledge thanks to technology, the more dangerous could be the events emerging out of the regions of our ignorance.

In the field of IS risk study, a sort of blindness to the phenomena of reflexivity and runaway risk dynamics has been created by an excessive fixation on notions of control and equilibrium, which characterizes even those authors who have put forward frameworks aimed at transcending the narrow focus of the more technical software engineering approaches (for example Lyytinen et al., 1998). The notable exception has been Mumford (1996) in a paper that identifies these phenomena very crisply and harnesses the relevant sociological literature for an IS audience. She applies the frameworks of Beck (1992) and Giddens (1990) to analyse in an anticipatory and penetrating way the devastating side-effects of Business Process Re-engineering as a tool to streamline and control organizational processes: 'Business process re-engineering was offered by its developers as a solution rather than a risk and managers only became aware of the risks when they tried to introduce it into their companies' (Mumford, 1996, p. 328). Unfortunately, this insightful but perhaps too little quoted analysis has not been extended yet to evaluate the deployment and the impacts of ICT infrastructures per se.

To be sure, the world of risk appears even more complex when further sociological, psychological and cultural dimensions are added to the analysis carried out so far (Jaeger et al., 2001). For example, it brings an awareness that risk is socially constructed and that the adoption of the technical or naïve perspective, or any narrowly positivistic methodology, is per se based on a choice of values regarding the definition of what risk is and to what extent it is acceptable. Cultural and institutional formative contexts (for example the managerial overarching mission of control) set the agenda and the problem of risk in a particular way, thereby shaping the perception of reality (Douglas and Wildavsky, 1982), even before there has been a situated framing of risk factors (Kahneman and Tversky, 1979).

We acknowledge the role of such ramifications, but we prefer to conclude the present survey of risk perspectives relevant for the IS field by honouring the role of technology and its dynamics as triggered by the learning of the actors and the counter-moves of the technical artefact, in the spirit if not the letter of Actor-Network Theory (Latour, 1999). A question we will address in chapter 3 is, accordingly, how the reflexivity in the dynamics of grid technologies when used as a tool to help us master risk can be related to the very human, or even existential, notion of risk.

CONCLUDING REMARKS

Information systems offer an interesting arena within which to study the complex and rapidly evolving relationship between digital technologies and risk. Given its intrinsic interdisciplinarity, such a field has hosted in the past decades both the technical and managerial perspectives on risk management. However, the IS literature on risk has not been particularly innovative or rich in scope. Economic perspectives can help overcome some of its major limitations. They also help to reflect on the emerging ramifications of the joining up between advances in grid technologies, on the one hand, and the democratization of financial tools on the other. The new financial order and its individualized risk management approach is a technology-based order, in which there is a reshuffling of the boundaries between the processes and activities that can be formally represented and the realm of ignorance. But the more sophisticated, integrated and standardized the technological platforms become, the more they tend to behave autonomously and drift. Sociological perspectives are needed to take into account the implications of emerging systemic risks, side-effects and runaway dynamics. Closer scrutiny is therefore required of the penetration and ubiquity of grid technologies and the opportunities they offer to manage a whole array of new risks surrounding the individual agent.

NOTE

1. This chapter is based in part on the Discussion Paper, 28 October 2004, published by CARR LSE.

REFERENCES

Argyris, C. and D.A. Schoen (1996), *Organization Learning II*, Reading, Mass.: Addison-Wesley.

Arthur, W.B. (1994), *Increasing Returns and Path Dependence in the Economy*, Ann Arbor: University of Michigan Press.

Basel Committee on Banking Supervision (2001), 'Operational risk', consultative document, Bank for International Settlements, Basel, January.

Beck, U. (1992), *Risk Society: Towards a New Modernity*, London: Sage.

Beck, U., A. Giddens and S. Lash (1994), *Reflexive Modernization: Politics, Traditions and Aesthetics in the Modern Social Order*, Cambridge: Polity Press.

Beniger, J.R. (1986), *The Control Revolution: Technological and Economic Origins of the Information Society*, Cambridge, Mass.: Harvard University Press.

Boehm, B.W. (1991), 'Software risk management: Principles and practices', *IEEE Software*, **8**(1) January, pp. 32–41.

Charette, R.N. (1996), 'The mechanics of managing IT risk', *Journal of Information Technology*, **11**, 373–8.

Ciborra, C. (1981), 'Information systems and transaction architecture', *International Journal of Policy Analysis and Information Systems*, **5**(4), 305–24.

Ciborra, C. (1983), 'Markets, bureaucracies and groups in the information society', *Information Economics and Policy*, **1**, 145–60.

Ciborra, C., K. Braa, A. Cordella, B. Dahlbom, A. Failla, O. Hanseth, V. Hepsø, J. Ljungberg, E. Monteiro and K.A. Simon (2000), *From Control to Drift – The Dynamics of Corporate Information Infrastructures*, Oxford: Oxford University Press.

Ciborra, C. and O. Hanseth (1998), 'From tool to Gestell', *Information Technology and People*, **11**(4), 305–27.

Ciborra, C., P. Migliarese and P. Romano (1984), 'Analysing organizational noise', *Human Relations*, **37**(8), 565–88.

Coase, R. (1960), 'The problem of social cost', *Journal of Law and Economics*, **15**(1), 1–44.

Douglas, M. and A. Wildavsky (1982), *Risk and Culture: The Selection of Technological and Environmental Dangers*, Berkeley, CA: University of California Press.

Earl, M.J. (ed.) (1996), *Information Management: The Organizational Dimension*, Oxford: Oxford University Press.

Fairley, R. (1994), 'Risk management in software projects', *IEEE Software*, **11**(3) May, 57–67.

Giddens, A. (1990), *The Consequences of Modernity*, Cambridge: Polity Press.

Hanseth, O. and K. Braa (2001), 'Hunting for the treasure at the end of the rainbow. Standardizing corporate IT infrastructure', *The Journal of Collaborative Computing*, **10**(3–4), 261–92.

Hart, O. (1995), *Firms, Contracts, and Financial Structures*, Oxford: Oxford University Press.

Herbst, P. (1974), *Socio-Technical Systems*, London: Tavistock.

Jaeger, C.C., O. Renn, E.A. Rosa and T. Webler (2001), *Risk, Uncertainty, and Rational Action*, London: Earthscan.

Kahneman, D. and A. Tversky (1979), 'Prospect theory: An analysis of decision under risk', *Econometrica*, **47**, 263–91.

Keen, P.W. (1991), *Shaping the Future: Business Redesign through Information Technology*, Boston: Harvard Business School Press.

Keil, M., P.E. Cule, K. Lyytinen and R.C. Schmidt (1998), 'A framework for identifying software project risks', *Communications of the ACM*, **41**(11), 76–83.

Latour, B. (1999), *Pandora's Hope: Essays on the Reality of Science Studies*, Cambridge, MA: Harvard University Press.

Leavitt, H.J. (1964), 'Applied organization change in industry: structural, technical and human approaches', in W. Cooper et al. *New Perspectives in Organization Research*, Chichester: Wiley, pp. 55–71.

Loewenstein, G.F., C.K. Hsee, E.U. Weber and N. Welch (2001), 'Risk as feelings', *Psychological Bulletin*, **127**(2), 267–86.

Lyytinen, K., L. Mathiassen and J. Ropponen (1998), 'Attention shaping and software risk: a categorical analysis of four classical risk management approaches', *Information Systems Research*, **9**(3), 233–55.

McFarlan, F.W. (1981), 'Portfolio approach to information systems', *Harvard Business Review*, **59**(5), 142–50.

Malone, T.W., R.I. Benjamin and J. Yates (1987), 'Electronic markets and electronic hierarchies', *Communications of the ACM*, **30**, 484–97.

March, J. and Z. Shapira (1987), 'Managerial perspectives on risk and risk-taking', *Management Science*, **33**, 1404–08.

Mumford, E. (1996), 'Risky ideas in the risk society', *Journal of Information Technology*, **11**, 321–31.

Perrow, C. (1984), 'Normal accidents: living with high-risk technologies', New York: Basic Books.

Power, M. (1997), *The Audit Society: Rituals of Verification*, Oxford: Oxford University Press.

Power, M. (2003), 'The invention of operational risk', discussion paper 16, CARR-LSE, June.

Renn, O. (1998), 'Three decades of risk research: accomplishments and new challenges', *Journal of Risk Research*, **1**(1), 49–71.

Schumpeter, J.A. (1976), *Capitalism, Socialism and Democracy*, London: Routledge.

Shiller, R.J. (2003), *The New Financial Order: Risk in the 21st Century*, Princeton: Princeton University Press.

Steinmueller, W.E. (1996), 'Technology infrastructure in information technology industries', in M. Teubal, D. Foray, M. Justman and E. Zuscovitch (eds), *Technological Infrastructure Policy: An International Perspective*, Dordrecht: Kluwer.

Suchman, L.A. (1987), *Planning and Situated Action*, Cambridge: Cambridge University Press.

Thompson, J. (1967), *Organizations in Action*, New York: McGraw-Hill.

Tversky, A. and D. Kahneman (1974), 'Judgement under uncertainty: heuristics and biases', *Science*, **185**, 1124–31.

Weill, P. and M. Broadbent (1998), *Leveraging the New Infrastructure: How Market Leaders Capitalize on Information*, Boston: Harvard Business School Press.

Williamson, O.E. (1975), 'Markets and hierarchies: analysis and anti-trust implications', New York: The Free Press.

Winner, L. (1977), *Autonomous Technology: Technics-out-of-control as a Theme for Political Thought*, Cambridge, Mass.: The MIT Press.

3. Information technology, contingency and risk

Jannis Kallinikos

1 INTRODUCTION

Over the last two decades or so, the concept of risk has experienced a remarkable renaissance. Traditionally, risk analysis has been a delimited and, in some respects, sterile (though very useful) field, closely associated with the deployment of a variety of quantitative, probability-based techniques for predicting the distribution of future occurrences and dealing with them. It has predominantly been applied to the operation of technical systems as a means of mitigating the outbreak of failures and the undertaking of economic ventures whereby returns have been tied to risks taken (Renn, 1998). However, the relatively recent redeployment and development of the term suggests that risk analysis is no longer confined to those narrow domains to which it has traditionally been applied. The term has indeed become a central concern in the wider field of social theory (for example Adam et al., 2000; Beck, 1992; Beck et al., 1996; Douglas, 1985; Luhmann, 1990; 1993). Conceptual expansion of this sort often takes place at the expense of precision encountered in narrowly defined fields and this would seem to apply to the case of risk as well. But there are gains too. Older phenomena are reframed and new domains are brought under the scrutiny of ideas and techniques that have survived the test of time.

The ideas put forth in this chapter seek to explore the relationship between *risk* and *information technology*. More specifically, the chapter draws on accounts on risk that derive from the wider field of social theory, with the view of understanding the subcategory of risks that are associated with the growing involvement of information systems in economic and organizational life. Prior to that, however, the chapter attempts to retrace the recent interest in risk and risk management, by placing it into the wider social context to which it belongs. Rather than being accidental, the central significance that risk analysis has been acquiring is closely tied to fundamental premises upon which modernity is constructed as a distinctive social order. Risk analysis is a systematic body of techniques and methods for dealing with emergent events (that is contingencies) in a world (the modern world) in which the future has been instituted as an open future (Luhmann, 1993; 1998).

The prospective orientation of risk analysis suggests that the relationship between risk techniques and the future reality such techniques seek to manage is not an exogenous one. The more elaborate the risk techniques and the knowledge on which they are based, the greater or more prolific the risks that are 'discovered' in a future yet to come. This claim is simple and elusive at the same time and ultimately recounts the reflexive relationship between knowledge and reality (Beck et al., 1996). Rather than simply being out there, the distinctions of reality on which perceptions of risk are based are constructed by recourse to elaborate systems of knowledge. Many of the nutritional or ecological risks currently 'discovered' would have been impossible to capture without access to sophisticated scientific theories and the technological measurements they enable. Risk analysis is, however, not simply an epistemic phenomenon. It often furnishes the means for intervening and acting upon the world. Technological regulation is one of those central domains of modern society in which knowledge and forms of intervening upon the world are superimposed upon one another. The common assumption is that technology is a major means for constructing manageable domains and a powerful instrument for calculating and controlling the inherent unpredictability of contemporary life. Less evident is the fact that technology maintains a reflexive relationship to risk. Deployed to control future uncertainties, technology reshuffles the balance between high-frequency/low-impact and low-frequency/high-impact risks, often giving rise to novel contingencies that occasionally emerge as more risky and intractable than the risks it initially addressed.

This chapter attempts to deal with some facets of this reflexive and, to a certain degree, paradoxical relationship between technology and control. The next two sections explore the ties between knowledge, risk and time orientation in an effort to lay out the foundations upon which this relationship between technology and control (and hence risk) is predicated. Such a relationship is then further explored by laying out the bare bones of a theory of technology as a distinctive form of regulation in which control is accomplished through the construction of functionally simplified and insulated domains. However, as a strategy of control, functional simplification and closure are, at least partly, at odds with the current orientation towards large and interoperable information infrastructures in which traditionally standing apart systems and technologies are brought to bear upon one another. Three broad sets of issues are singled out and discussed. The first relates to the increasing *self-referentiality* of information technologies and the concomitant issue of relevance versus irrelevance of the reality (and the risk profiles) thus constructed. The second takes up the double face of integration. *Interconnectedness* of operations is a complex choice that opens new possibilities but also constructs new risks and fragilities. Finally the issue of lost accountability is discussed as the result of the de-sequencing of time that the growing involvement of information systems and electronic trans-activity bring about, and the *quasi-instantaneity* thus arising.

2   RISK, UNCERTAINTY AND KNOWLEDGE

The observations set forth in the introduction provide the overall context for appreciating the centrality which the concept of risk has recently assumed. The reflexive and mutually reinforcing relationship between, on the one hand, the development of knowledge and technology and, on the other hand, the perception and documentation of risks are reflected on the growing awareness of the negative *ecological* and *health effects* associated with the expanding involvement of technology and technological artefacts in contemporary life. A number of serious technological disasters, the growing indicators of the negative nutritional effects of the food industry and other technology-related developments (for example car fumes, offshore oil, climatic changes) have made increasingly evident that technology is not as clearly a univocal ally to humans as safety experts, engineers, governmental representatives and commercial interests want us to believe (Stirling, 1998). The complexity and the interdependent character of the current world further aggravate some of the problems, associated with the mitigation of risks and the management of undesirable effects. In an interdependent world, local incidents propagate rapidly along multifarious and ramified paths and their effects may multiply in ways that are difficult to predict in advance and to restrain (Beck, 1992; Beck et al., 1996).

The sharp ecological awareness of the current age and the widespread belief in the limited controllability of complex interdependent technologies coincides with a wider cultural turn. The current concern on issues of risk could be understood as being closely associated with contemporary society's receding confidence in the major ideals nourished by modernity, that is control, predictability, welfare, equality and progress (Bauman, 1992; Lyotard, 1978/1984). Modernity's promise of a life, elucidated by reason and conducted according to the firm principles laid out by the transparency of scientific knowledge, has been delivered but partly. From the present horizon, it seems rather unlikely that this condition will come to change in the future (Heller, 1999). The decline of what Lyotard referred to as the *grand narratives* of modernity has given way to scepticism and sustained institutional questioning. Increasingly, the ecological and nutritional crisis has been interpreted as an integral component of life modernity helped to bring about, rather than an aberration.

The reassessment of the modern condition is undeniably the outcome of a variety of forces that reflect the cumulative experience of modernity across a broad spectrum of domains (Heller, 1999). However, the decline of the certainty once promised can be interpreted as the inevitable consequence of the fundamental and frequently overlooked (or underestimated) fact that knowledge is not related to certainty, predictability and control in a simple and straightforward fashion. Counter-intuitive as it may seem, *knowledge*, as defined in modernity (that is secular, empirically justified belief), is often related in an *inverse fashion* to *certainty*, a condition, I believe, that Beck et al. (1996) include in the term *reflexive modernization*. Scientific knowledge undeniably participates in the understanding and control of specific domains of the world by providing detailed accounts of cause–effects relationships and the processes by which causes are tied to effects. This is a clear and hardly contestable fact. However, in so doing, scientific knowledge helps shed light on an even greater zone of states and processes that had so far remained either obscured, or were construed as being the outcome of a much simpler reality. New factors are discovered (or assumed) with uncharted characteristics and causal connections. Such discoveries often distort rather dramatically the balance between the known/unknown, certainty/uncertainty. Knowledge and reality are thus intrinsically tied to one another and the expansion of the former as a rule leads to the expansion of the latter. Rather than being accidental, this expanding region of what is not yet known, as the outcome of the growth of knowledge, reflects the basic form by which the modern game of knowing is constituted (Lyotard, 1978/1984). The psychic life, the human body, the natural environment, represent some typical domains in which scientific research has set out an ever-expanding process of discoveries, statements and propositions that have at the same time revealed a growing array of factors and domains about which very little is known.

The receding horizon of certainty/security is also related to the increasing awareness (based often on regretful experience) of the adverse effects of human actions caused by an incomplete understanding of patterns and causal relations. *Human intervention* in society and life that is predicated on a partial understanding of the domains upon which such an intervention is exercised (which in the case of society and life is the rule), may lead to side-effects of largely varying magnitude (Beck, 1992). The current environmental sensitivity provides again a good example of bitter learning from experience,[1] which illustrates both the recursivity of the effects of human actions and the reflexive character of the game of knowledge. Unwarranted interventions on the natural ecology are discovered a posteriori. Strange as it may seem, a considerable part of such interventions are documented, in their essential effects, through the deployment of a complex ecology of technologies, themselves the outcomes of both scientific and technological progress. In this respect, technology and knowledge could be said to participate in their self-criticism, as Kenneth Burke (1981) felicitously observed some time ago.

As already indicated, there is no way to deny that the pursuit and acquisition of knowledge often leads to deeper insight and control of specific domains of life. But this, as suggested above, is only part of a more complex and ambiguous picture. Despite spectacular scientific discoveries and the accumulation of knowledge in many fields, no other society has ever been as sharply aware as ours of its steadily receding horizon of certainty. The journey of knowledge is not simply without end. As it proceeds, the process of knowledge acquisition branches out towards an increasing number of directions yet to be pursued. Particular aspects of life may be predictable and controllable, but the overall outcome of the huge project of knowledge accumulation and technological progress is to increase rather than reduce uncertainty. This, I would like to insist, is the outcome of the complex constitutive bond between what is to be known and the means through which it is getting known. The more complex the categories, concepts and cognitive relations of a knowing structure (that is a theory or a model) the more reality is discovered within reality (Kallinikos, 1996b; 2006). Ignorance knows nothing about itself.

Therefore, the perception and documentation of risks is not often a posterior response to a pre-existing reality, as it is commonly assumed. Modern society is certainly involved in the construction of risks through its intervention in natural and biological processes or through the less direct, culture-shaped ways of defining domains of relevance and levels of risk tolerance (Douglas, 1985; Renn, 1998). What counts as risk varies substantially across contexts and cultures. But the implications of the complex and constituting bonds underlying knowledge and uncertainty suggest that modern society participates in the construction of risks in a more fundamental fashion. The pursuit of knowledge raises the awareness of the complex interactions between underlying social, cultural and natural processes and often creates more uncertainty than it helps to alleviate. It steadily introduces new aspects of reality (that is factors, causal processes, and so on) that harbour risks or hazards and could thus be amenable to risk analysis. The *social construction of risk* owes more to this complex, non-linear relationship of knowledge to uncertainty than to the cultural modes that define the relevant factors to be taken into consideration and the specific levels of tolerance, as Renn (1998) for instance, seems to assume.

The significance attributed here to knowledge as the basic matrix out of which risk and risk analysis are constituted as meaningful domains of the modern world must undeniably be understood as part of the wider context of the technological and cultural changes that mark late modernity. As indicated above, ecological sensitivity, the decline of scientific legitimacy as a moral guide and the growing awareness of the open status of societal processes are crucial factors in the understanding and appreciation of the centrality that risk analysis is currently assuming. But it is also crucial to understand that these changes have been long in the making (Giddens, 1990; Heller, 1999). They are part and parcel of the modern world picture, being closely associated with the specific forms by which science is constituted as a societal game (Heidegger, 1977; Lyotard, 1978; 1984). They are also inextricably bound up with the central place that contingency assumes in the contemporary world, and the consequent framing of the present in terms of a *more or less probable future* (Luhmann, 1982; 1993; 1998). These claims make necessary the careful examination of the concept of risk and the crucial role that time and contingency assume in the contemporary world.

3 RISK, CONTINGENCY AND TIME

The understanding of the world as more or less risky is inextricably bound up with the modern *time ontology*, that is the conception, instrumentation and eventual institutionalization of a specific temporal order in modernity. Risk, as already indicated, is a prospective concept. It is predicated upon the distinction between *actuality* and *possibility* (Renn, 1998), a distinction that partly overlaps with that between present (that is actuality) and future (that is possibility). While certainly interpretable, the present is what it is, the actualization of just one of the many options that once constituted the open future of a present that is now past. The future is always pregnant with several possibilities and the transformation of possibility to actuality always implies the passage from the plural and open states of the future to the singular state that constitutes the present. As soon as risks are realized, they cease to refer to the future, that is they are not risks any longer but actual states of the world that are regrettable to one or another extent.

Placed against this context, James Bradley's contention on time must be understood as coinciding with a radical change in the time semantics of his age that marks the hesitant advent of modernity. Bradley claimed that time does not flow from the past through the present to the future, as most people would be inclined to think, but on the contrary runs from the future to the present, only to vanish in the shadows of the past (Borges, 1979). As the cultural and social principles of modernity became institutionally embedded, the future came increasingly to acquire a primacy, both as a *way of understanding* (that is semantics) time and the world, and also as a *set of social practices for dealing with reality* (Heidegger, 1985). Older theocratic semantics collapsed and the future was increasingly understood and construed as contingent, that is a future that is neither necessary nor impossible (Luhmann, 1982; 1993; 1998). Both necessity, in the sense of pre-destined causal change (theological or scientific), and impossibility deny the open and contingent character of the world. In so doing, they deny as well a set of crucial social and human conditions that are constitutive of humanity and that we tend to take for granted. The exercise of choice, the making of decisions and the scanning and grasping of opportunities are as fundamental to contemporary life as the air we breathe.

It is in this respect that risk is closely associated with the open character of the world and the possibilities/opportunities such openness helps bring about. Thus conceived, risk is to action what a shadow is to a human figure. It is the inevitable and shifting accompaniment of a world that is consti-tuted as open and plural, amenable to initiatives and interventions that could possibly render it different from the present. In a more mundane lan-guage, these claims should be taken to imply that without risk there would be no opportunities and therefore no profit, and without profit no eco-nomic initiatives either, an interpretation not discordant with Knight's seminal work on risk, uncertainty and profit (Knight, 1921).[2] The crucial significance of the open character of the world in the constitution of human action is reflected too in the widespread belief that excessive concern with order has stifling effects on humans. Excessive order tends to rule out alternative ways of understanding and acting upon the world. 'Men act, things but move' as Kenneth Burke used to say (Burke, 1966).

A case therefore could be made, on the basis of the aforementioned claims, for the fact that risk analysis and risk techniques are part of the wider project of managing the vast complexity of the modern world, which is so organized and constituted as to make *contingency its defining attribute* (Luhmann, 1995; 1998). Future events cannot be predicted/constructed with certainty, even though some of these events may have more than a random chance to occur. Uncertainty and unpredictability are intrinsic characteristics of the cultural order of modernity that institutes its future as an open future, and makes science one of its major institutions. Contingency therefore coincides with the making of the probable to an inherent attribute of contemporary life.

Contingent events are further closely associated with the very principles underlying the social (as opposed to cultural) organization of modernity. The decline of the status-based stratification of the pre-modern world was increasingly replaced by a framework of social rules that rendered the relationships of individuals to institutions (state, bureaucracies, family) selective, mobile and revocable (Kallinikos, 2004a; 2006). All social relationships (that is work, family or community) in modernity are in principle, though less in practice, *renegotiable* and *revocable* or *reversible*. Contingency therefore coincides with the interplay of these cultural and social forces in modernity and becomes a basic source of social change that drives the perpetual adaptation of expectations and social structures to emergent situations. Instability is the only stability modernity knows (Lyotard, 1991; Knodt, 1995).

Thus conceived, contingency is neither a fatalistic nor a theocratic belief. It is, on the contrary, modernity's secular credo that causal sequences, though perhaps knowable, are not always known. The interplay of a huge array of factors and processes, which are but partly known and controlled, and the timing of events do not follow pre-destined regularities. They are therefore bound to create surprises and unexpected outcomes. The belief in contingency and the social practices stemming from it coincide thus with the pervasive role played by events in contemporary life. Contingency is furthermore associated, as suggested above, with the multi-centric organization of modern society and the distribution of widely divergent motives and expectations across the social fabric. In principle, if not in practice, every individual can act on the basis of preferences or expectations that reflect his or her own personal condition or the institutional arrangements within which the individual finds herself/himself embedded. This is another way of claiming that cultural orientations, the social institutions and the organization of modern society make the perpetual parade of events an intrinsic characteristic of it. Contingency is thus a *cultural belief*, a *social attitude* and a fundamental *institutional trait* combined.

Modernity's preoccupation with control and order, of which risk management is but one aspect, is just the mirror image of the basic role accorded to contingency in modern life. *Risk*, *contingency* and *future orientation* are all manifestations of a cultural and social organization that got rid of many of the social and cultural constraints that produced a closed world. While premodern societies were undeniably engaging in mitigating what they perceived as unfavourable and threatening outcomes, it is only modern society that made risk analysis and risk techniques integral and increasingly vital practices of its institutions (Luhmann, 1993). The interplay of the cultural, social and institutional forces described above quite understandably made the problem of order (that is, control of contingencies) a major concern of the modern society (Giddens, 1990) and a vital practice of its institutions.

All this said, it is crucial to point out that possible events are not *randomly distributed* over the future timescape. Contingency as a defining characteristic of modernity by no means implies that all future events have an equal chance to occur. Randomness defies human purpose (and meaning) as much as necessity does. Past events, choices and commitments leave traces that often cumulate to create structures that give some events a greater chance to occur than others. An inevitable corollary is that future events depend, at least partly, on *decisions* made in the present or decisions that have been made in the past (Luhmann, 1993; 1998). Risks in this respect are not *subject-independent* possible occurrences and must be perhaps distinguished from threats or hazards, if by these last terms are meant prospective dangers that are independent of human actions and decisions made in the past or the present. The many terms tied to risk analysis and the indiscriminate use of them is indicative, Luhmann (1990) suggests, of the conceptual confusion prevailing in the field. Following his suggestion, I also tie risks to decisions. Risks are always the risks of someone, even though that 'someone' may be the entire society or humanity. To avoid or take risks always implies a choice on the part of social actors or groups even though such choices may be, and not infrequently are, made unwittingly.[3]

Risks are thus tied to decisions and the rationale of risk analysis is to make informed decisions that would reduce future risk exposure, mitigate or moderate the effects of unfavourable outcomes. Probability, game theory (the decisions of others are taken into account in the form of conjectures) and other techniques of forecasting represent efforts to chart the future and, in the light of the forecasts, make decisions that either increase the likelihood of prospective gains or reduce the likelihood of prospective losses. Contingency planning, on the other hand, involves the preparation of a response in the case of failures caused by unfavourable outcomes of one's actions. Predicting/constructing the future has, however, proved to be a complex enterprise. The limitations (and the merits) of traditional techniques of forecasting have been well documented in the literature, especially under conditions where information over past events is irregular or unreliable (Holler, 2002; March, 1988; Renn, 1998), and it would be superfluous to repeat these criticisms here.

A few things are, however, worth mentioning in the light of the confusing experience late modernity offers (Beck et al., 1996). The lack of information does impede projections into the future. This seems quite obvious. In many other cases, though, it is the very availability of information that may impede, and perhaps more radically, the predictability of the future and the transformation of the present future into future present (Luhmann, 1982; 1998). Availability of information may cause cognitive overload in the system, provide evidence that invalidates older beliefs and cause–effects sequences, and introduce new factors with uncharted effects on behaviour. In other cases, newly generated information joins other already available information sources to produce novel versions of reality out of the sheer combinability of information of diverse information items (Ciborra, Chapter 2 in this volume; Hylland-Eriksen, 2001; Kallinikos, 2006; Shiller, 2003). The overall implications of these processes are often the increase rather than the reduction of uncertainty. As suggested in more general terms in the preceding section, the relationship of knowledge to certainty is complex and far from linear. It is thus of paramount importance to understand that the contingent constitution of the contemporary world could possibly be influenced and handled but not undone.

4 TECHNOLOGY, CONTROL AND CONTINGENCY

There is a widespread understanding of technology according to which it is predominantly perceived as a productive force, that is an ensemble of designed processes and devices that vastly increase the effectiveness of human operations and the input/output ratio. Technology extends/ improves human skills and raises the sensorimotor and manipulative capacities of humans. In other cases, it imitates, expands or accelerates natural processes, and not infrequently invents new ones. Hardly contestable as it may be, such an understanding of technology predominantly derives from engineering or economics and is based on the very functions or goals technology accomplishes (Simon, 1969). It tends to conceal, however, the distinctive form or forms by which technology is involved in the making and regulation of human affairs. In analysing the prospects of managing contingencies through technology, it is crucial to understand not simply what technology does but also how it is getting involved in the construction of predictable worlds.

Placed in the overall context of relations outlined in the preceding two sections, technology is here conceived as a *structural form* for dealing with the contingent character of the modern world. It does so through the twin strategy of *functional closure* and *simplification* of the very processes it constructs and regulates (Luhmann, 1993). Technological regulation coincides with the building of functionally simplified sequences and causal patterns which are abstracted from the wider social and natural complexity to which they may be initially embedded. Functional simplification implies the reduction of an initial complexity, not the construction of simple technical systems. Technology is technically complex and the knowledge it is based on elaborate. It is functionally simplified in the sense of embodying specific functionalities whose *recurrent order* is safeguarded through the exclusion of known or unknown events or forces (that is functional closure) that may have disruptive effects on its operations (Kallinikos, 1996a; Mumford, 1934; 1952). The predictable forms by which technology often (but not always) operates are precisely due to the construction of causal patterns and sequences, whose recurrent unfolding is ensured through the exclusion of unforeseen factors. Functional simplification and closure, in this sense, coincide with the controlled reduction and insulation of causal interactions. In so doing, however, technology compresses and *intensifies* these interactions and magnifies both their power and their disruptive force. Nuclear power stands as the epitome of technology's distinctive way of constructing/regulating reality but most technologies make use, albeit in varying intensity, of the same strategy of control and regulation (Kallinikos, 2006).

It is easy to conjecture that contingent (external) events that manage to intrude the closed circuits of technological interactions may have disruptive effects that ride on the intensified or magnified nature of these interactions. Most significant perhaps, is technology's incapacity to deal with the occurrence of unexpected events that may cause large-scale disruptive effects. Technology deals with the unexpected by excluding it, but does not know what to do with it once it has managed to intrude the technological system. It is imperative to point out that the reverse side of technological simplification is the *loss of flexibility* and emergent response. Technology cannot handle (that is absorb, creatively react, ignore, forget or dissimulate) unforeseen incidents, even though technologists attempt to construct systems that respond to emergent events on the basis of learning from experience (neural networks).[4]

The rule so far is that security mechanisms must be added on the system to take care of unforeseen incidents. But these secondary technologies cannot but be themselves based on the principles of functional simplification and closure (Luhmann, 1993). Secondary technologies are constructed on the basis of conjectures about possible incidents and dysfunctions. By definition, they entail a *fixed set of responses* that could cope with disruptive effects, as these last have been envisaged at the moment technology was built. The problem is therefore pushed further into a constructed hierarchy of technologies, where secondary technologies control primary processes, tertiary technologies control security mechanisms of the secondary order and so forth. But this technological edifice must be constructed in advance and 'spot' responses pre-specified. This strategy of handling and averting risks recounts in a way the paradox of knowledge/ignorance. Risks are compressed into a complex net of technologies through a complex architecture of control, trading off low-impact/high-frequency with high-impact/low-frequency risks. The inevitable consequence of this strategy is thus the possibility of the occurrence of large-scale disruptive effects following the failing of these mechanisms to deal with unexpected contingencies. Luhmann (1993: 92–3) refers to the great German romantic poet Hölderlin to make the point that the quest of control may end up increasing rather than reducing risks.[5]

How does information technology (IT) fit into this context? In the current debate, perceptions of risk are heavily shaped by the fears and expectations of human intervention upon nature and life. Ecological, nutritional and genetic issues seem overwhelmingly to determine the profile of risks in the contemporary world. Placed against these developments, IT appears as innocent environment-friendly technology, far removed from the natural or biological involvement of materials and genetic technologies. However, the picture is considerably more complicated than this observation may initially suggest. To begin with, many of the operations of materials and genetic technologies are heavily dependent on information systems of considerable complexity. Varying assemblages of hardware/software monitor the smooth operations of complex technological systems like air jet navigation or nuclear power stations. Biotechnology is also variously dependent on the capacities of the variety of information systems and technologies involved in genetic research and the production of biogenetic products. In most of these cases, IT emerges as crucial, ancillary (secondary or tertiary) technology of control.

The distinctive contribution of IT emerges, however, more straightforwardly in the context of the aforementioned matrix of relations constituted by the partly overlapping distinctions of knowledge/ignorance, certainty/uncertainty and control/contingency. Information processing assumes a crucial role in the prediction/construction of future events, and the monitoring of the institutions and organizations of the contemporary world. The idea of information processing, as the central mechanism underlying complex behaviour, occupies a central place in Simon's (1969) celebrated meditations on *The Sciences of the Artificial*. Perception, active information search and processing, data storage and transmission are at the heart of those activities that allow complex systems to scan their surroundings adequately, and shape and monitor their own operations to control their relationship with the environment in which they find themselves embedded. Seen in this light, IT appears, as Beniger (1986) suggests, as a control device *par excellence*.

Contemporary technologies of information and communication represent the electronic expansion of mankind's invention and utilization of a variety of sign systems and technical conventions by which information is generated, processed and cumulated, but also transmitted and communicated (Ong, 1982; Borgmann, 1999). Pre-electronic information systems based on writing and specialized systems of notation (for example accounting, statistics) were essential to political and economic institutions (Cooper and Kallinikos, 1996; Goody, 1986) and the control of human/ organizational operations across time and space. The partial automation and the objectification of processing algorithms into systems run by digital machines are a powerful indicator of the growing importance which information processing and storage activities assume in the management of the current world. They are also a clear expression of the aforementioned strategy of functional closure and simplification and the prospects and problems associated with it.

IT could thus be construed as a system of cognitive/semantic closure and simplification manifested in clear rules of reality representation and automated procedures of information processing and inference making (Zuboff, 1988). Information gathering and processing in the electronic age is an essential means for reducing uncertainty, predicting and ordering future states, and managing an organization's or system's relationships to its environment. However, there are two major limitations to such a claim. First, the understanding of information technologies in terms of control overlooks, nonetheless, the complex relationship of knowledge to uncertainty and risk as analysed above (Hanseth and Braa, 2000). It is predicated upon a foundationalist understanding of reality (Lyotard, 1978; 1984; Rabinow, 1996; Rorty, 1979), and the assumption that knowledge of the world is a large yet *finite quantity* that can one day be exhaustively mapped and used for instrumental or other purposes. Most significantly, perhaps, the framing of complex behaviour and information processing in terms of control fails to notice the crucial fact that uncertainty and risk are not *aberrations* from a normal state (that is certainty), but the very *stuff* of which the reality of modernity is made. A world without risk and uncertainty is a static, immobile and initiative-less universe, in which the final word has already been uttered. All-embracing determinism is characteristic of theology and magic, not of science (Levi-Strauss, 1966).

Secondly, IT pushes the handling of contingencies at a more comprehensive level. It does so as a *meta-technology*, controlling other technologies either in the form of providing security arrangements or through the planning and monitoring of material processes (for example process industries, power generation). In other instances, IT emerges as a primary technology, restructuring, regulating and monitoring processes that were previously performed in various, loosely coupled settings with a variety of technologies (for example bank and insurance offices, tax authorities, and so on). This strategy gestates, however, higher risks. In all these circumstances, IT becomes a central medium for compressing risks and transporting them to a comprehensive level. It is commonly assumed that the superior information processing and controlling capacity of IT furnishes the means for spotting and adequately handling intruding contingencies. In so doing, however, IT increases the possibility of disruptive incidences with wide-ranging and far-reaching consequences. Single incidences (for example local disruptions, hacker attacks) may jeopardize a much broader range of operations than might otherwise be the case (Hanseth and Braa, 2000). Let us, however, turn to a more detailed consideration of these effects.

5   THE TWISTS OF LARGE-SCALE INFORMATION SYSTEMS

It should have become evident by now that risk is employed in the present text with a much broader semantics than the one identified with the calculable probability distribution of future events. In one sense, it becomes identical with uncertainty as the unknown, though varying, probabilities of future events (Holler, 2002). In another sense, it differs from the standard notion of uncertainty as it focuses primarily on the regrettable outcome of current decisions. It is to such a broader conception of risk that I will refer, when discussing the vagaries and twists that the growing organizational and economic involvement of information technologies seems bound to give rise to.

If what has been said so far makes sense, then the role of information technologies in rendering transparent the present, and predicting or constructing the future ought to be reframed, and the established wisdom changed in several ways. As already suggested, standard views on IT consider it as an ordering and controlling mechanism and such a view is reinforced by major and seminal works in the field, for example Simon (1969) and Beniger (1986). It would be meaningless, indeed futile, to question the contribution of information technologies to the construction of predictable, organizational worlds, and to the consequent management of disruptive contingencies. True as such a relation may be, it is only part, as I have repeatedly stressed, of a much more complex and ambiguous picture. It is my contention that unless this wider picture is brought to the fore and analysed, the evaluation of the role played by the technologies of information as instruments of manageability and control is destined to remain essentially incomplete.

The identification of the risks associated with making IT the major instrument of control in contemporary institutional life finds its point of departure on the paradoxical relationship between knowledge/certainty, control/risk sketched above. Employed to control contingencies, IT gives rise to new contingencies by being involved in the construction of a new architecture of control. In the rest of this chapter, three broad sets of issues are singled out and the risks they gestate are discussed at some length. All three are seen as being associated with the growing organizational and economic involvement of IT and the emergence of organizational information infrastructures (Ciborra et al., 2000). These are the following:

- The *self-referentiality* of IT and the production of information along lines that reflect the very logics and the structure of information systems often tied together to large interoperable infrastructures. In this broader sense, information systems construct rather than copy reality. Self-referentiality and particularly the spectacular growth of information that is produced by large and interoperable information infrastructures inevitably impinge on the relevance of the information thus produced and, by extension, with the suitability of risk profiles, based on that information.
- The *interconnectedness* of systems and operations. The integration of organizational operations provides new possibilities but at the same time increases the frailty of large-scale information platforms, as risks are compressed and adverse local outcomes may rapidly propagate across the entire system.
- The declining accountability brought about by the *instantaneity/ simultaneity* that the diffusion of IT promotes. The future as a major organizing principle for sequential ordering and control of prospective outcomes declines as information systems saturate organizational reality and electronic transactivity gains momentum.

Let's turn to the somewhat detailed examination of these issues.

5.1   Self-referentiality and Relevance

The growing involvement of information systems in organizations contributes, by definition, to the expansion of mechanisms that record, process and store information. Taken in its entirety, information made available by contemporary technologies of information covers a large and expanding area of organizational operations and the surrounding conditions in which they are embedded. An increasing number of organizational tasks are currently monitored by having recourse to IT-based applications. But the *scope* of organizational operations thus covered is only one consequence of the organizational involvement of IT. In providing the possibility of bringing together and juxtaposing previously unconnected or missing items of information, IT-based applications increase substantially the *depth and scope of information*. A new visibility into causal processes and mechanisms is thus gained by the comparison and juxtaposition of information items that were previously unavailable, and new aspects of reality are constructed or illuminated (Borgmann, 1999; Zuboff, 1988). In this respect IT is unique and incomparable in the new possibilities it provides.

However, information produced and proliferating in that way is bound to have important and, in some respects, adverse consequences. For one thing, sheer information availability may induce the expansion of the range of alternative courses of actions to be considered, and increase the activities directed towards the adequate depiction and evaluation of these courses of action. All this could, and often is thought to, raise the organizational intelligence, and provide organizations with essential insights into their operations. Reality is nevertheless substantially more insidious. The growing involvement of IT in the monitoring of organizational operations implies that information becomes available and outdated on the basis of an *information mechanics* that reflects the logic or logics of the information systems by which it is produced, without immediate consideration for the underlying realities of the organization. 'Information, made abundant and disposable by technology, can lose its bearing on reality, and signs proliferate without regard to things', says Borgmann (1999: 211). Black-boxed into a complex system of procedures and algorithms, the mechanics of information generation works in unobtrusive ways that evade the inspection and understanding of the average user and the expert alike (Turkle, 1995). In such a context, the attribution of meaning or purpose as to why and how such data and information items are generated becomes increasingly difficult to make, and relevance is easily lost (Weick, 1985). Let us examine this claim in some detail.

Contrary to the business rhetoric of IT vendors and consultants, large-scale information systems cannot but be characterized by strong elements of *self-referentiality*.[6] Systems of this sort are reified cognitive structures of considerable complexity. They are made of extensive series of items, rules and procedures that are attuned to one another, in ways that ensure consistency, and the adequate functioning of the system as a whole (Kallinikos, 1999; 2006).[7] Most information systems have a particular and, in some cases, rather long history, and a learning curve that reflects the methods, techniques and problem-solving procedures as they have developed and became crystallized over time. All these structural factors coalesce to prevent the one-to-one correspondence of the system (for example representations, data items, procedures and rules) to the field of reality to which it applies. Little wonder that the information system in its entirety addresses a particular domain of organizational operations (for example finance and accounting, materials management). And yet it does so in a generic, context-free fashion that recounts the constraints of digitization, automation, the developmental trajectory of the technology/software package (early or mature stage), other technologies already in use and many other similar constraints of structural character (Hanseth, 2000; Hanseth and Braa, 2000; Kallinikos, 2006).

In view of a widespread misconception, conveyed by the terminological mystifications of IT vendors and academics alike,[8] it is of paramount importance to make clear that reality can enter the organization only through the oblique forms created by the structural grid, which the information system provides. In one way or another, reality must be pressed into the structure and logic of the information system/s. Data must be fed into the system in particular forms and in sequential patterns that conform to the procedural logic of the system. Input data are then processed according to the functional simplification of processing algorithms and output data produced and organized in accordance with the cognitive standardization of the software package (Kallinikos, 1999; 2006). Such a stance does not imply that individuals are passively obeying the 'ghost in the machine', as neophyte constructivists/interpretivists, in information systems and organization studies, might seem prone to suggest.[9] It does though claim that human action, in the context particularly of intricate technologies, is subject to polyvalent constraints that reflect the status of *technology as a distinctive domain* of reality regulation (Borgman, 1984; 1999; Mumford, 1934; 1952; Winner, 1986; 1993).

Issues of this sort were of course always present in organizations. However, they currently become increasingly problematic, as the growing involvement of information systems in organizations establishes a model of reality and an information mechanics that tend to push into the background the *tangibility of referential reality* (Kallinikos, 1996a; 1999; Sotto, 1990; 1996; Zuboff, 1988). The conception of IT as cognitive structural grid suggests that information systems are key factors in the making of organizational worlds. IT-based systems and artefacts invent and arrange items, separate adjacent or dependent processes and bring together distant ones, decompose and reconstruct reality and institute relations with the elements thus created. Once again, the criteria for doing so do not derive from problems exterior and anterior, which technology seeks to address in an immediate correspondence to reality. Rather problems are fabricated (which does not mean that they are unreal) by technology itself, in accordance with its own premises and then are addressed in technology's distinctive way.

As all technologies, IT brings standardization across contexts. But the very constitution of software packages as cognitive structures makes them particularly susceptible to *de-anchorage from the immediacy of reality*

(Cassirer, 1955). A huge space of a certain type of freedom and improvization is thereby opened (Borgmann, 1999; Kallinikos, 1996a; Zuboff, 1988). But there is a long shadow, cast by the *lack* of tangible references. While releasing technology from the bounds of imitation and indexical signification, the withdrawal of reality that IT promotes may end up as a self-propelling, runaway process of meaningless information generation and endless information accumulation (Kallinikos, 2006). The risks of being driven away in irrelevant directions, without being able to control this process and validate information, are indeed high. The explosive growth of information over the last two or three decades (see, for example, Lyman et al., 2003) suggests that the problem of 'being driven away', as referential reality becomes increasingly vague and distant, will grow in significance and become perhaps acute.[10]

Secondly, the depth of information technology and the insights it may offer to causal relations may reveal novel relationships within and outside the organization. Some of these relationships may not be well understood and may therefore trigger further processes of information search and clarification. As far as these processes are kept within reasonable limits, they can make a positive contribution to the mitigation of risks and the management of organizations. And yet, self-referentiality may be at work here as well. Given the ambiguity of the world and the decontextualized character of information, the process of information search and evaluation may easily end up as a *deviation-amplifying loop*. Again, the spectacular growth of information that has taken place over the last decades is quite indicative of this self-propelling character of information growth dynamic. In the absence of clear standards and rules as to how to go about, and where to stop further information search and evaluation (and few organizations have been able to work out such rules), this process may deplete substantial organizational resources and lead, as suggested in the preceding section, to more rather than less uncertainty. In the very end, it may construct risks that could never have been envisaged prior to the availability of information, and whose relevance may remain questionable from the point of view of the referential reality and the organization as a whole.

Organizations have often established routines and standard operating procedures that guarantee response relevance, external adaptation and various forms of intersubjectively assessing and validating information (Weick, 1985). Routines are inherently conservative and exhibit their own degree of self-referentiality. Perhaps routines and standard operating procedures are conditioned by the recognition of the inexhaustible diversity and variability of the world. But routines and standard operating procedures do not simply reflect the cognitive limitations of human beings (Simon, 1957). They recount a considerable practical wisdom at the same time (March and Simon, 1958; March, 1988; Sennett, 2000) that helps individuals and organizations keep away from irrelevant information search and evaluation, and avoid exaggerated or any other kind of unsuitable responses. The systemic self-referentiality of software packages as analysed above does not offer any guarantee that this practical wisdom will be reasonably accommodated. Indeed, it could be conjectured that the opposite may take place (Ciborra, 2002; Goranzon, 1992; Kallinikos, 2004b; Zuboff, 1988), even though new routines and procedures of information search may develop, along with the use of particular packages and the experiential learning thereby accruing (Orlikowski, 1992; 2000).

5.2 The Double Face of Interconnectedness

The problems associated with the withdrawal of referential reality and the meta-risks of escalating information search and evaluation procedures are aggravated by the considerable environmental and technological complexity, under which most organizations are currently operating. A clear indication of technological complexity is the disparate ecology of information systems and hardware devices encountered in many organizations. Such ecology of technologies is not the rational or deliberate outcome of a single decision (Ciborra et al., 2000). It usually reflects a series of decisions, not necessarily compatible with one another, made in periods with widely divergent, organizational, technological and market conditions. Each decision may be itself rational but the overall outcome is a jumble of technologies. Organizational information infrastructures echo an amazing array of factors that resist deliberate manipulation in advance, and mock the ideal of rationality and the so-called management of technological portfolios when looked upon a posteriori. Such factors include path-dependent patterns of development dictated by technological interdependencies, standardization and interoperability, and other factors such as the state of the art of the available technology at each moment or the different conditions facing the organization at various time intervals (Hanseth, 2000).

Dispersed information systems and technologies of this sort in organizations gestate various problems that are, in one way or another, associated with the cardinal issue of *fragmentation*. As far as risk management is concerned, there could be several questions that seem to be related to this situation. Perhaps the most important is that of an unreasonable and, in many respects, misleading profile of risks and time projections, constructed upon information made available by information systems with different rationalities and domains of application. Lack of organizational-wide information, too much selectivity and local priorities may all contribute to the construction of risk profiles that may be irrelevant or unrepresentative from the point of view of the organization as a whole. In a sense this is a manifestation of the well-known problem of sub-optimization (March and Simon, 1958), which, however, acquires its distinct identity in the current economic and technological environment. A crucial consequence is the lack of an overall nexus of references on to which to anchor risk policies. The probability that the organization is dragged along courses of action that result in the construction of an irrelevant profile of future events is indeed high, and is intimately related to the changing context of information search and validation analysed in the preceding section.

There have lately been technological developments of large, organization-wide information platforms, such as Enterprise or ERP Systems, that attempt to deal with the issue of fragmentation. It would seem reasonable to conjecture that the diffusion and organizational embeddedness of such information platforms will allow organizations to overcome fragmentation and avoid the problems and inconsistencies associated with it. This is at least the commercial argument for motivating the use and selling of such off-the-shelf software packages. At one level, this is undeniably true but again it reflects only part of a much wider and ambiguous picture. Such a picture recounts the fundamental argument of this text that knowledge and information may increase rather than reduce risk and uncertainty. But there are other reasons as well that make integration a risky strategy. Some of these reflect the specific state of the art created by *the integration* of organizational operations and the particular forms by which integrated information platforms of this sort both reduce but also increase organizational complexity.

Integration achieved through organization-wide information platforms increases the *interconnectivity* of organizational operations (Hanseth and Braa, 2000). Most of these information infrastructures exhibit a modular architecture that seeks to combine functional or local adaptation with organization-wide information sharing. One basic reason, though, behind the rationality of these systems is the cross-functional coordination of organizational operations at the most elementary level of everyday tasks and processes. An inevitable consequence is the rise of organizational connectivity and the construction of information/communication paths along which information/messages/orders can travel across the organization. In his renowned work *The Architecture of Complexity*,[11] Simon claimed that dense interconnectivity is usually a major factor of inefficiency (and risk), under conditions of frequent environmental disturbances of the organization. Disturbances in tightly coupled systems, entering the organization at a certain point or locally generated, can easily propagate across the entire system and cause adverse effects of various kinds. The solution, according to Simon, is hierarchy, or perhaps more correctly *segmentation* (local containment of information) which is coordinated through *hierarchy*, an argument that has further been developed by Jay Galbraith (1973), just at the beginning of the information age.[12]

The most interesting application of these thoughts that bears on the present work is perhaps Perrow's (1984) analysis of the risk of serious failures, facing the operations of highly complex systems. The thrust of Perrow's argument is that a complex system – operating under conditions that are not adequately understood, and involving, in addition, causal connections of a non-linear type – is bound to experience, sooner or later, adverse incidents. Loose coupling, when it is possible, may be an organizational response to manage complexity and ambiguity of this sort, as it may isolate local incidents and impede their propagation throughout the system. Now, loose coupling is not the same as fragmentation, and the conditions analysed by Perrow, and perhaps Simon, cannot without qualification be applied to large information systems or organizational information infrastructures. Also more recent conceptual and technological developments, influenced by the investigation of the human brain and the development of neural networks, make interconnectivity, non-hierarchy and distributed information the *sine qua non* of complex behaviour (see for example Fetzer, 1991; Kallinikos, 1998).[13] If there is a lesson to be learned from those conceptual avenues, once opened by Simon, this would presumably be that interconnectivity does not easily pay off. It has advantages and drawbacks that must be carefully weighed. As suggested above, the quest for control transports possible risks at a more comprehensive level and creates favourable conditions for disruptive effects of a large scale.

The issue of interconnectedness becomes even more insidious when it is placed in the wider context of the strong ties organizational information infrastructures are capable of maintaining to external information sources and the Internet. Interconnectedness is, of course, a major and often inexorable characteristic of the contemporary world. Yet the distinctive nature of the interconnectedness constructed through IT is its *continuous* and *homogeneous* (interoperable) status which makes it quite different from the connections entertained by other technologies, let alone the sort of ties allowed by cultural and institutional rules, practices and conventions. Interconnected information systems resemble numbers in this respect, reducing the diversity (and the extension) of the world to one scale or medium (Cline-Cohen, 1982; Introna and Nissenbaum, 2000). Industrial technologies are usually discontinuous and self-contained. There is no way of connecting at the level of operations, different, say, assembly lines. Even extended networks (that is roads, railways, gas or electricity systems) are not often interoperable. In this respect, the diffusion of IT weakens substantially the classical technological control strategy of functional closure and simplification.

The discontinuity of operations is often more radical in the wider domain of softer 'technologies' that rely heavily on institutionally embedded rules, procedures or practices (for example public bureaucracies, banks) to accomplish their operations. Despite the many and serious problems of interoperability (Hanseth, 2000) and security arrangements, information systems (specifically those that are web-based) provide multiple avenues for the travel of information across organizational divisions, and interorganizational, institutional and geographical boundaries. Not only 'an ill will . . . can become potent and destructive', as Borgmann (1999) puts it, under these conditions, but any unintended consequences, failures, mistakes or secrets can rapidly propagate across extended regions of the information world that contemporary technology participates in constructing. Let us quote Borgmann (1999: 196) more fully:

> Cultural information is by its nature scattered and refractory. It can be stolen and destroyed, but only with exertion and a piece at a time. The information in cyberspace, however, is so tightly interconnected and so quickly, if not always easily, that ill will has become more potent and destructive.

Integration could presumably acquire forms that would make it both a more flexible and less risky strategy of control. Non-centralized architectures and distributed information processing are assumed to combine the advantages of integration (that is sharing of information and visibility into causal patterns) at the same time as they distribute risks throughout the system and allow for local adaptation. Non-centralized architectures could therefore bypass the problems of rigid integration. Nevertheless, the issues identified in the two preceding paragraphs remain. Cognitive standardization and the syntactic/semantic homogeneity brought about by the diffusion of IT-based artefacts, systems and processes cannot be undone by distributed architectures. The problem is of another order. Cultural reality is scattered and refractory, as Borgman suggests, but scattered in a way that is radically discontinuous. Cognitive models of distributed information processing operate at a considerably simpler reality (Lackoff, 1995). The homogeneous status of the cognitive processes on which such models are based undoes or bypasses the discontinuity of cultural reality. In so doing cognitive homogeneity and information standardization express the twin strategy of functional closure and simplification, compressing and transporting risks at a more comprehensive level (Kallinikos, 2006).

5.3 Quasi-instantaneity: The De-sequencing of Time

The significance the future has acquired in modernity as the starting point for the instrumentation of the present is ultimately related, as I have repeatedly suggested, to the growing awareness of the contingent character of the contemporary world. Future orientation is a way of dealing with and managing the open status of modern reality. If the future is populated by contingencies and cannot thus be clearly predicted, it would be possible, at least, to construct it along quasi-predictable lines. By projecting a picture of 'what will be' on the future, and proceeding from it backwards, step by step, into the present, organizations become able to construct accounts of quasi-predictable worlds that work as mantras for action, responsibility allocation and eventually control.

Sequential ordering of events and actions is essential to the *attribution of cause–effects relationships* and the construction of a *legible world* into which the contributions of individuals, units or groups could be placed with clear and articulated demands and held *accountable* thereby. The meticulous partitioning of standardized time, and the concomitant place-ment of actions and operations into this detailed and legible grid, represent basic forms for constructing human agency in modernity. This way, modern organizations separate individual actions from one another to render them inspectable and accountable, and segment tasks and operations to ensure legible causalities and measurable relations (Cooper, 1989; March and Olsen, 1989). Time and motion studies may seem distant reminders of this project but reflect, nonetheless, a mundane practice of a much wider philosophy of action and uncertainty control.

It is thus crucial to point out the significance of sequential time in the construction of organizational legibility and the management of organiza-tions. The tracing of causes, the attribution of outcomes to particular actions, the construction of means–ends chains all presuppose a sequential time upon which the world can be laid out in legible forms that promote manipulability, inference making and learning from experience (March and Olsen, 1976; 1989). These cardinal characteristics of the modern, bureau-cratic age, and the sequentialization of operations brought about by indus-trial technology, are currently undergoing significant modifications by the quasi-simultaneity of electronic transactions that organizational informa-tion infrastructures promote. The present swells and expands, as more transactions can take place in real time. Organization roles (and persons) are 'decentred' as people find themselves torn or challenged between the demands or seductions of an incessant flow of information stimuli, on the one hand, and the serial and focused requirements imposed by the accom-plishment of organizational tasks, on the other.

There is a seeming paradox here that is worth mentioning. IT-based work patterns are structured sequentially. Like writing, IT-based work bypasses the simultaneity of oral interaction and constructs reality in sequential patterns (Ong, 1982). The requirements of information automation make necessary the meticulous segmentation of organizational tasks and their reconstruction as extensive series of procedural steps (Kallinikos, 2004b). In this respect, the organizational involvement of Enterprise or ERP or other large-scale systems participates in the sequentialization of organizational operations. Sequential ordering furthermore applies to the domain of organizational or inter-organizational communications. Each transaction is often a response to preceding ones or involves the taking of an initiative that is itself expected to generate responses.

However, while promoting sequential ordering at one level, large unified information platforms participate in the *compression of time* by the construction of a different timescape. The time frames of responses become increasingly shorter, rendering projections into the future, as an ordering strategy, increasingly difficult, often superfluous and perhaps unproductive. Transactions follow one another in short time intervals that challenge the premises of control and causal attribution, essential to the accountability ideal of modern formal organizing. There is, as H.G. Wells (1942) prophetically claimed, 'interstitial squeezing . . . It is the intervals between events that are dwindling to nothing . . . (while) the crowding together of events goes on.' In this electronically produced quasi instantaneity, the promise of managing contingencies and averting risks through proactive strategies of reality construction and sequentialization gets increasingly lost.

Electronic transactivity is furthermore tied to the proliferation of unpredictable events and the loss of accountability in the way it was described in the preceding section. Interconnectedness and the reduction of the diversity of the forms of human signification/communication (Borgman, 1999) create a unified platform (that is the web, the Internet) that invites or at least enables participation from diverse and often hardly foreseen sources. Even though the crossing of institutional boundaries is subject to multiple constraints and organizational security policies, it is often difficult to predict initiatives in a connected world. It may seem ironic, yet the world becomes increasingly multi-centric (perhaps fragmented) by the IT-based connectedness that was initially assumed to overcome the fragmentation of earlier stages. Financial markets stand as the epitome of these developments but events of this sort, perhaps of a less dramatic nature, are part of the everyday reality that IT helps to construct. The 'de-sequencing' of time as the outcome of the diminishing distance between future and present and the decentring of human agency are assumed to be major characteristics of the late modernity of the information age (Castells, 1996; 2000; Chia, 1998; Heller, 1999). And yet, the effects of organizational web-based information infrastructures on the construction of this electronic simultaneity have not been carefully studied and need further research and documentation.

It can be conjectured that the inflation of the present, which electronic transactivity promotes, impinges even upon the conception of the past, and the role that past events play as a guide to the future. Institutional memory is a basic means by which collective entities like organizations maintain a sort of consistency and continuity between past commitments and modes of operating, on the one hand, and present or prospective choices, on the other. The loosening of the past upon the making of present and future actions is bound to produce a situation where organizations get increasingly saturated by data and information, whose significance cannot properly be assessed. It is obvious that, under these conditions, the information upon which the construction of accountability relies becomes hampered. Most crucially perhaps, intention (and prospective action and risk mitigation) is getting lost in the ever-growing ebb of information, devoid of causal attributions, relevance and reliability. Organizations may exhibit symptoms usually associated with the psychopathology of memory loss.

NOTES

1. This does not of course deny that unwarranted interventions are in many cases motivated by powerful economic and political interests.
2. See Holler (2001) for the problematic distinction between risk and uncertainty.
3. The coupling of risks to decisions by no means implies that risk is a psychological concept. Individual perception of risk occurs in a social and institutional context, mediated by cultural beliefs and institutional patterns.
4. For a summary see Hayles (2005), Kallinikos (1998; 2006).
5. *Wo aber Kontrolle ist/Wachst das Risiko auch* (But where there is control/Risk grows as well).
6. This is an expression itself of the mentioned principles of functional closure and simplification.
7. The existence of so-called bugs or the issue of interoperability do not contradict the claim of the internal consistency of information systems. Consistency is a graded concept.
8. Such mystifications are often conveyed by a bunch of terms such as customization, parametrization, configuration, implementation, organizational adaptation and others.
9. This issue cannot be dealt with here. See Winner (1993), Searle (1995) and Kallinikos (2002) and the comments on this issue developed in the preceding section.
10. This is undeniably a long process of socio-cultural evolution. The first de-anchoring from the immediacy of things occurs presumably with the development and institutionalization of verbal language and signs. See for example Cassirer (1955) and Cooper and Kallinikos (1996).
11. Included in his *The Sciences of the Artificial.*
12. See also Weick (1976) for a somewhat similar argument.
13. See Vera and Simon (1993) for a response to connectionism.

REFERENCES

Adam, B., U. Beck and J. van Loon (eds) (2000), *The Risk Society and Beyond*, London: Sage.

Bauman, Z. (1992), *Intimations of Postmodernity*, London: Routledge.

Beck, U. (1992), *Risk Society: Towards a New Modernity*, London: Sage.

Beck, U., A. Giddens and S. Lash (1996), *Reflexive Modernization*, Cambridge: Polity.

Beniger, J. (1986), *The Control Revolution: Technological and Economic Origins of the Information Society*, Cambridge, Mass: Harvard University Press.

Borges, J.-L. (1979), *Borges Oral*, Madrid: Allianza.

Borgmann, A. (1984), *Technology and the Character of Contemporary Life*, Chicago: The University of Chicago Press.

Borgmann, A. (1999), *Holding On to Reality: The Nature of Information at the Turn of the Millennium*, Chicago: The University of Chicago Press.

Burke, K. (1966), *Language as a Symbolic Action*, Berkeley: The University of California Press.

Burke, K. (1981), 'The interactive bind', in C. Wilder-Mott and J. Weekland (eds), *Rigor and Imagination: Essays on the Legacy of Gregory Bateson*, New York: Prayer.

Cassirer, E. (1955), *The Philosophy of Symbolic Forms, Vol. 1: Language*, New Haven: Yale University Press.

Castells, M. (1996), *The Rise of Network Society*, Oxford: Blackwell.

Castells, M. (2000), 'Materials for an explanatory theory of the network society', *British Journal of Sociology*, **51**(1), 5–24.

Chia, R. (ed.) (1998), *Organized Worlds: Explorations in Technology and Organization with Robert Cooper*, London: Routledge.

Ciborra, C. (2002), *The Labyrinths of Information*, Oxford: Oxford University Press.

Ciborra, C., K. Braa, A. Cordella, B. Dahlbom, A. Failla, O. Hanseth, V. Hepsø, J. Ljungberg, E. Monteiro and K.A. Simon (2000), *From Control to Drift: The Dynamics of Corporate Information Infrastructures*, Oxford: Oxford University Press.

Cline-Cohen, P. (1982), *A Calculating People: The Spread of Numeracy in Early America*, Chicago: The University of Chicago Press.

Cooper, R. (1989), 'The visibility of social systems', in M. Jackson, P. Keys and S. Cropper (eds), *Operational Research and the Social Sciences*, New York: Plenum, pp. 51–7.

Cooper, R. and J. Kallinikos (eds) (1996), 'Writing, rationality and organization', *Scandinavian Journal of Management*, **12**(1), Special Issue.

Douglas, M. (1985), *Risk Acceptability According to the Social Sciences*, London: Routledge.

Fetzer, J. (ed.) (1991), *Epistemology and Cognition*, Dordrecht: Kluwer.

Galbraith, J. (1973), *Organization Design*, Reading, Mass: Addison-Wesley.

Giddens, A. (1990), *The Consequences of Modernity*, Cambridge: Polity Press.

Goody, J. (1986), *The Logic of Writing and the Organization of Society*, Cambridge: Cambridge University Press.

Goranzon, B. (1992), *The Practical Intellect: Computer and Human Skills*, London: Springer Verlag.

Hanseth, O. (2000), 'The economics of standards' in C. Ciborra (ed.), *From Control to Drift: The Dynamics of Corporate Information Infrastructures*, Oxford: Oxford University Press, pp. 56–70.

Hanseth, O. and K. Braa (2000), 'Globalization and "Risk Society"', in C. Ciborra (ed.), *From Control to Drift: The Dynamics of Corporate Information Infrastructures*, Oxford: Oxford University Press, pp. 41–55.

Hayles, K. (2005), 'Computing the human', *Theory, Culture and Society*, **22**(1), 131–51.

Heidegger, M. (1977), *The Question Concerning Technology and Other Essays*, New York: Harper.

Heidegger, M. (1985), *The History of the Concept of Time*, New York: Harper.

Heller, A. (1999), *A Theory of Modernity*, London: Routledge.

Holler, M. (2001), 'Classical, modern and new game theory', available at http://www.law.yale.edu/documents/pdf/holler.pdf.

Hylland-Eriksen, T. (2001), *The Tyranny of the Moment: Fast and Slow Time in the Information Age*, London: Pluto Press.

Introna, L. and H. Nissenbaum (2000), 'The politics of search engines', *Information Society*, **16**(3), 169–85.

Kallinikos, J. (1996a), *Technology and Society: Interdisciplinary Studies in Formal Organization*, Munich: Accedo.

Kallinikos, J. (1996b), 'Mapping the intellectual terrain of management education', in R. French and C. Grey (eds), *Critical Essays in Management Education*, London: Sage.

Kallinikos, J. (1998), 'Organized complexity: posthumanist remarks on the technologizing of intelligence', *Organization*, **5**(3), 371–96.

Kallinikos, J. (1999), 'Computer technology and the constitution of the work', *Accounting, Management and Information Technologies*, **9**(4), 261–91.

Kallinikos, J. (2002), 'Reopening the black box of technology: artefacts and human agency', in L. Applegate and R. Galliers (eds), *Twenty-third International Conference on Information Systems*, Barcelona, Spain, pp. 287–94.

Kallinikos, J. (2004a), 'The social foundations of the bureaucratic order', *Organization*, **11**(1), 13–36.

Kallinikos, J. (2004b), 'Deconstructing information packages: organizational and behavioural implications of ERP systems', *Information Technology and People*, **17**(1), 8–30.

Kallinikos, J. (2006), *The Consequences of Information: Institutional Implications of Technological Change*, Cheltenham, UK and Northampton, MA, USA: Edward Elgar.

Knight, F. (1921), *Risk, Uncertainty and Profit*, Boston: Houghton.

Knodt, E. (1995), 'Foreword', in Niklas Luhmann, *Social Systems*, Stanford: Stanford University Press.

Lackoff, G. (1995), 'Body, brain and communication', in J. Brook and I.A. Boal (eds), *Resisting the Virtual Life*, San Francisco: City Lights, pp. 115–19.

Levi-Strauss, C. (1966), *The Savage Mind*, London: Weidenfeld & Nicolson.

Luhmann, N. (1982), *The Differentiation of Society*, New York: Columbia University Press.

Luhmann, N. (1990), 'Technology, environment and social risk: a systems perspective', *Industrial Crisis Quarterly*, **4**, 223–31.

Luhmann, N. (1993), *The Sociology of Risk*, Berlin: de Gruyter.

Luhmann, N. (1995), *Social Systems*, Stanford: Stanford University Press.

Luhmann, N. (1996), 'Complexity, structural contingency and value conflicts', in P. Heelas, S. Lash and P. Morris (eds), *Detraditionalization*, Oxford: Blackwell, pp. 59–71.

Luhmann, N. (1998), *Observations on Modernity*, Stanford, CA: Stanford University Press.

Lyman, P., H.R. Varian and Associates (2003), *How Much Information*, www.sims.berkeley.edu:8000/research/projects/how-much-info-2003/index.htm.

Lyotard, J.-F. (1978), *La Condition postmoderne: rapport sur le savoir*, Paris: Minuit.

Lyotard, J.-F. (1984), *The Postmodern Condition: A Report on Knowledge*, Manchester: Manchester University Press.

Lyotard, J.-F. (1991), *The Inhuman*, Cambridge: Polity Press.

March, J. (1988), *Decisions in Organizations*, New York: Free Press.

March, J. and J. Olsen (1976), *Ambiguity and Choice in Organizations*, Oslo: Universitetsforlaget.

March, J. and J. Olsen (1989), *Rediscovering Institutions*, New York: Free Press.

March, J. and H. Simon (1958), *Organizations*, New York: Wiley.

Mumford, L. (1934), *Technics and Civilization*, San Diego, CA: HBJ.

Mumford, L. (1952), *Arts and Technics*, New York: Columbia University Press.

Ong, W. (1982), *Orality and Literacy: The Technologizing of the Word*, London: Routledge.

Orlikowski, W.J. (1992), 'The duality of technology: rethinking the concept of technology in organizations', *Organization Science*, **3**(3), 398–427.

Orlikowski, W. (2000), 'Using technology and constituting structures: a practice lens for studying technology in organizations', *Organization Science*, **11**(4), 404–28.

Perrow, C. (1984), *Normal Accidents: Living with High Risk Technologies*, New York: Basic Books.

Rabinow, P. (1996), *Essays in the Anthropology of Reason*, Princeton, NJ: Princeton University Press.

Renn, O. (1998), 'Three decades of risk research: accomplishments and new challenges', *Journal of Risk Research*, **1**(1), 49–71.

Rorty, R. (1979), *Philosophy and the Mirror of Nature*, Princeton, NJ: Princeton University Press.

Searle, J. (1995), *The Construction of Social Reality*, London: Penguin.

Sennett, R. (2000), *The Corrosion of Character: The Personal Consequences of Work in the New Capitalism*, New York: Norton.

Shiller, R.J. (2003), *The New Financial Order*, Princeton: Princeton University Press.

Simon, H. (1957), *Administrative Behavior*, New York: The Free Press.

Simon, H.A. (1969), *The Sciences of the Artificial*, Cambridge, Mass.: The MIT Press.

Sotto, R. (1990), *Man Without Knowledge: Actors and Spectators in Organizations*, PhD. Thesis, Stockholm: School of Business, Stockholm University.

Sotto, R. (1996), 'Organizing in the cyberspace: the virtual link', *Scandinavian Journal of Management*, **12**(1), 25–40.

Stirling, A. (1998), 'Risk at turning point', *Journal of Risk Research*, **1**(2), 97–109.

Turkle, S. (1995), *Life on the Screen. Identity in the Age of the Internet*, New York: Simon & Schuster.

Vera, A. and H. Simon (1993), 'Situated action: a symbolic representation', *Cognitive Science*, **17**(1), 7–48.

Weick, K. (1976), 'Educational organizations as loosely-coupled systems', *Administrative Science Quarterly*, **21**(1), 1–19.

Weick, K. (1985), 'Cosmos vs chaos: sense and non-sense in electronic contexts', *Organizational Dynamics*, **14**, 51–64.

Wells, H.G. (1942), *The Conquest of Time*, London: Watts & Co.

Winner, L. (1986), *The Whale and the Reactor: In Search of Limits in the Age of High Technology*, Chicago: University of Chicago Press.

Winner, L. (1993), 'Upon opening the black box and finding it empty: social constructivism and the philosophy of technology', *Science, Technology and Human Values*, **18**, 362–78.

Zuboff, S. (1988), *In the Age of the Smart Machine*, New York: Basic Books.

4. Complexity and risk

Ole Hanseth

As said in the introduction, an important motivation for the research presented in this book is Ulrich Beck's development of the theory of the (World) Risk Society and the research that this theory has inspired or at least influenced heavily. Accordingly, this theory, and its more mature and general version, the theory of Reflexive Modernization, will be presented in the first section of this chapter. In parallel with the development of these theories, the 'Complexity Science' field has emerged. As this book focuses on risks related to complexity, an overview of this field will also be given. In the following sections we will inquire deeper into the relations between these theories, arguing that they have a common core.

1 WORLD RISK SOCIETY AND REFLEXIVE MODERNIZATION

Beck builds his theory of (World) Risk Society on a distinction between what he calls first and second modernity. First modernity is based on nation-state societies, where social relations, networks and communities are understood in a territorial sense. He argues further that the collective patterns of life, progress and controllability, full employment and exploitation of nature that were typical in this first modernity have now been undermined by five interlinked processes: globalization, individualization, gender revolution, underemployment and global risks. The kind of risks he primarily focuses on are those related to the ecological crises and global financial markets. Among the first we find various risks related to pollution, side-effects of drugs, substances included in industrialized produced food, and so on. Of particular interest in research communities have been possible long term risks related to genetically modified organisms. Many of the issues related to the environment add up to risks related to global warming. Another kind of risks are those related to accidents in modern technological systems ranging from leakages of poisonous material from chemical plants like the Bhopal case or from nuclear power plants like Chernobyl, or accidents in transportation systems like collisions between trains, aircrafts, ships, and so on. Another category of risks are those related to financial markets. Famous examples of such risks are the Asian crises in the late 1990s and 'Black Monday' in October 1989. 'New' risks are also found in working life regarding job security. There are, for instance, increased risks for unemployment because your employer files bankruptcy or closes down the office you are working in to transfer the jobs to a low-cost country, or your education has become irrelevant.

These risks are all related to globalization. This is true for the globalization of risk in the sense of its intensity – for example, the threat of nuclear war. Another example is the globalization of risk in the sense of the expanding number of contingent events that affect everyone or at least large numbers of people on the planet – for example, changes in the global division of labour. In a similar way the risks related to financial markets stem from their global integration achieved through truly global ICT networks. Pollution is also becoming a global issue. This is partly illustrated by the transfer of polluted material all over the world by wind, birds, and ocean streams, documented by the high values of such materials in Arctic areas. The best illustration of this is – of course – global warming.

At the same time as the risks are becoming global, their origin is also – according to Beck and Giddens – globalization (Beck, 1986; 1999; Giddens, 1990; Beck et al., 1994). And, further, they see both ongoing globalization processes as well as the outcome – that is increased risks – as fundamentally related to modernity. Globalization is the form modernization has taken today, and risks are increasing because of the changing nature of modernity. The very idea of controllability, certainty and security – which was so fundamental in the first modernity – collapses in the transfer to second modernity (Beck, 1999, p. 2). Modernity's aim has been to increase our ability to control processes in nature and society in a better way through increased knowledge and improved technology. The concept of 'world risk society' draws our attention to the limited controllability of the dangers we have created for ourselves. And the Reflexive Modernization argument (at least in Beck's version) says that while it has been the case that increased modernization implied increased control, in second modernity, modernization, that is enhanced technologies and an increase in bodies of knowledge, may lead to less control, that is higher risks.

1.1 The Essential Dynamics of Modernity

We will now look more closely at the essence of modernity and how increased modernization in terms of globalization leads to increased risks. Here we will follow Giddens' (1990) distinction of three dominant, interdependent sources of the dynamism of modernity:

The separation of time and space, which has in particular been possible through the invention of various technologies such as the clock, the standardization of time zones, calendars, and so on. These tools are essential to the coordination of activities across time and space. (See for example Yates (1988) on the importance of standardization of time (zones) and the invention of timetables for the development of railroad traffic.) Powerful tools for coordination across time and space are preconditions for the rationalization of organizations and society as well as the development of more powerful control technologies (Beniger, 1986).

The development of disembedding mechanisms. These mechanisms enable the 'lifting-out' of social activity from localized contexts and the reorganization of social relations across large time–space distances.

Giddens describes two main disembedding mechanisms: symbolic tokens and expert systems. He does not define symbolic tokens but presents money as a paradigm example. Other examples are 'other forms of money' – stocks, bonds, funds, derivatives, futures, and so on. 'Expert systems' means systems of experts and expert knowledge. Expert knowledge – under modernity – is developed under regimes underlining universality and objectivity. Expert – and scientific – knowledge should be built up of facts, theories and laws that are universal and not linked to specific contexts or subjective judgements. The fact that expert knowledge is free of context implies, of course, that it can be transported anywhere and applied to anything. Both forms of disembedding mechanisms presume as well as foster time–space distantiation.

The reflexive appropriation of knowledge. Modernity is constituted in and through reflexively applied knowledge. This means that social practices are constantly examined and re-examined in the light of incoming information about those very practices, thus constitutively altering their character. The production of systematic knowledge about social life becomes integral to systems reproduction, rolling social life away from the fixities of tradition.

1.2 Modernization as Integration

Integration is a central theme of this book. And the essence of modernity as outlined above can also to a large extent be seen as integration. Time–space distantiation is largely about enabling the integration of processes across time and space. The same is the case for the development of disembedding mechanisms. Symbolic tokens and expert systems can be established as common for communities otherwise distinct and separated. By sharing disembedding mechanisms, communities are becoming more equal; they have more in common which makes interaction and collaboration easier, that is they are becoming more integrated.

Modernization and globalization are closely connected. Actually, the most visible form of modernization is globalization. Globalization means modernization on the global level. And, as a part of this, modernity itself is inherently globalizing.

Seeing globalization as modernization also illustrates the links between integration and modernity. Globalization in the intuitive sense is an integration process going on at many levels: integration of nations, business organizations, markets, technological systems, cultures, and so on – and, indeed, the integration of all these. Globalization also includes, as a side-effect, the increased integration of the social and the natural which is probably best illustrated by the ongoing climate change.

The essence of modernity also links directly to the integration of ICT solutions. Such solutions, like the Internet, are also mechanisms that substantially contribute to the separation of time and space through their power to help coordinate processes across time and space. ICT solutions are also powerful disembedding mechanisms. 'Symbolic tokens' can be interpreted as any kind of *formalized information*. Computer technologies greatly enhance our capabilities to process, store and distribute such information. For this reason, computer technologies have also stimulated the development of wide ranges of new formalisms from new financial instruments like 'futures' and 'derivatives' to new systems of classification and coding (see for instance Bowker and Star, 1999). And finally, if we take ideas about ICT-based knowledge management systems seriously, computer technologies are also enhancing the development of new 'expert systems' and the 'reflexive appropriation of knowledge'. So, just as we should expect, we can conclude that ICT solutions in general, and the integration of such, are at the heart of modernity and ongoing modernization processes.

1.3   Consequences of Globalization and Modernization: From Control to Risk

Globalization and modernization are closely related to control. Both Giddens and Beck see increased control as the key motivation behind modernization efforts and, further, integration as a key strategy to obtain more control.

Increased risk means decreased control. In this respect, current modernization and globalization processes represent a break from earlier modernization. Traditionally, modernization implied more sophisticated control according to the tenets of the 'control revolution' (Beniger, 1986). More knowledge and better technology implied sharper and wider control. In the age of high modernity and globalization, however, more knowledge and improved control technologies may just as well lead to *more unpredictability*, *more uncertainty*, and *less controllability*, in other words – *more risk*.

This is what lies at the heart of the 'reflexivity' argument. In particular, the theory of reflexive modernization contradicts the instrumental optimism regarding the predetermined controllability of uncontrollable things: 'the thesis that more knowledge about social life . . . equals greater control over our fate is false' (Giddens, 1990: 43), and 'the expansion and heightening of the intention of control ultimately ends up producing the opposite' (Beck et al., 1994: 9).

This shift, which may appear contradictory, can be explained by *the ubiquitous role of side effects*. Modernization means integration. At the same time, all changes and actions – new technologies introduced, organizational structures and work procedures implemented, and so on – have unintended side-effects. And, the more integrated the world becomes, the longer and faster side-effects travel, and the heavier their consequences. Globalization, then, means globalization of side-effects. In Beck's (Beck et al., 1994: 175, 181) own words: 'It is not knowledge but rather non-knowledge that is the medium of reflexive modernization . . . we are living in the age of side effects . . . The side effect, not instrumental rationality, is becoming the motor of social change.'

If risk is so closely related to side-effects of our actions, we might assume that more and better knowledge about the worlds we are living and acting within will enable us better to predict the effects of actions and accordingly reduce risks. But both Giddens and Beck argue that this strategy does not work. Even though it may be a bit counter-intuitive, they argue that new knowledge might even decrease control/increase risk. Giddens (1990) says that this happens because knowledge applied to social activity is filtered by four sets of factors:

- *Differential power*. The appropriation of specialist knowledge does not happen in a homogeneous fashion, but is often differentially available to those in power positions who are able to place it in the service of sectorial interests.
- *The role of values*. Changes in value orders are not independent of innovations in cognitive orientation created by shifting perspectives on the social world. If new knowledge could be brought to bear upon a transcendental basis of values, this situation would not apply. But there is no such rational basis of values, and shifts in outlook deriving from inputs of knowledge have a mobile relation to changes in value orientations. Values and empirical knowledge are connected in a network of mutual influence. This implies, for instance, that different pieces of knowledge about how to solve a specific problem

may be inconsistent and even contradictory because of the different 'value systems' they are based upon. As globalization unfolds, more problems become shared by 'all' of us, for example, environmental problems. And, as long as we believe in different value systems, we will generate knowledge about such problems, which may – and often certainly will – further lead to conflicting strategies for solving the problems, which may make them more serious and difficult.

- *The impact of unintended consequences.* No amount of accumulated knowledge about social life could encompass all circumstances of its own implementation. Knowledge about social life transcends the intentions of those who apply it to transformative ends.
- *The circulating of social knowledge in the double hermeneutic.* Knowledge claimed by expert observers rejoins the subject matter, and accordingly changes it. This may further invalidate the specific knowledge generated as well as other stocks of knowledge.

Taken together, the three features of modern institutions (time–space distantiation, the development of disembedding mechanisms, and the reflexive appropriation of knowledge) explain why living in the modern world is more like being aboard a juggernaut than being in a carefully con-trolled and well-driven motor car. Giddens uses the juggernaut as an image to illustrate modernity as a runaway engine of enormous power that, col-lectively as human beings, we can drive to some extent but that also threat-ens to rush out of our control, which could render it as being torn asunder. The juggernaut crushes those who resist it and, while it sometimes seems to have a steady path, there are times when it veers away erratically in direc-tions we cannot foresee. The juggernaut of modernity is, in Giddens' perspective, not all of one piece. It is not an engine made up of integrated machinery, but one in which there is a push-and-pull of tensions, contra-dictions and different influences.

The theories of Risk Society and Reflexive Modernization can be seen as complexity theories in the sense that complexity is at their core. Seeing globalization as an integration process, for instance, can very well lead to it also being seen as a process of making the world more complex exactly through this integration process. That process creates a world of more elements and links, but certainly also a world of more types of elements and more types of links, which is changing more rapidly – exactly as complex-ity was defined in Chapter 1. The role attributed to side-effects also links naturally to complexity. The role of side-effects is increasing exactly because the 'system' is becoming so complex. Because of its complexity we cannot know how all components are interacting; accordingly the outcomes of those interactions will be more unpredictable. We will now look deeper into issues related to complexity as analysed within 'Complexity Science' and how key concepts from this field are related to the theories of Risk Society and Reflexive Modernization.

2   COMPLEXITY SCIENCE

Over the last couple of decades the field called Complexity Science has emerged. It has emerged primarily from the study of phenomena within physics (like thermodynamics and biology). But contributions are also made from studies of more social phenomena, in particular within the economy, like financial markets and also, an issue central to this book, standardization (David, 1986; Arthur, 1994). Complexity science is made up of a broad range of disciplines such as chaos theory and Complex Adaptive Systems (CAS). CAS are concerned with the dynamic with which complex systems evolve through adaptation and are increasingly used in organizational studies, for example in health care. CAS are made up of semi-autonomous agents with the inherent ability to change and adapt to other agents and to the environment (Holland, 1995). Agents can be grouped, or aggregated into meta-agents, and these can be part of a hier-archical arrangement of levels of agents. Agents can respond to stimuli – they behave according to a set of rules (schema).

Adaptation is the process whereby the agent fits into the environment and the agent as well as the CAS undergoes change. Adaptation – and cre-ativity and innovation – is seen as being optimal at 'the edge of chaos' (Stacey, 1996), or more generally, adaptation occurs within the zone of complexity which is located between the zone of stasis and the zone of chaos (Eoyang, 1996; Plsek and Greenhalgh, 2001; Wilson et al., 2001). Dooley (1996) suggests that CAS behave according to three principles: order is emergent, the system's history is irreversible, and the system's future is unpredictable.

Overall, complexity science investigates systems that *adapt* and *evolve* as they *self-organize* through *time* (Urry, 2003). In particular, attention has been directed at how order within such systems is created without a 'designer', rather *emerging* like, for instance, the order among cells in an organism, molecules in a fluid or other material, a beehive – or the emer-gence of a standard. Central to the emergence of orders are *attractors*, that is a limited range of possible states within which the system stabilizes. The simplest attractor is a single point. There are also attractors with specific shapes which are called 'strange attractors', that is unstable spaces to which the trajectory of dynamical systems are attracted through millions of iterations (Capra, 1996).

Orders emerge around attractors through various *feedback* mechanisms, and through *path-dependent* processes of many small steps that may end in *lock-in* situations (David, 1986). Some steps may be crucial in the sense that they may force the process in radically different (unexpected) directions. Such points are called tipping or bifurcation points (Akerlof, 1970). The existence of such points makes the evolution of complex systems *non-linear* in the sense that small changes in a system at one point in time may lead to hugely different consequences at a later point in time.

A de facto, or emergent, standard, like MS Windows or QWERTY, is a typical example of an attractor. The feedback mechanism in play is what W. Brian Arthur (1994) calls *increasing returns* which define demand-side economies of scale: the more a product or service is produced, sold, or used, the more valuable it becomes. Increasing returns play crucial roles in the adoption and diffusion of standards and IT artefacts that form key components in IIs – telecommunication protocols, data exchange protocols, operating systems, programming languages. The value of a compatibility standard, for example, the http protocol, is largely determined by the number of users deploying it, that is, the number of users with whom one can communicate when one adopts the standard. Increasing returns result from positive *network externalities*, which arise when one participant joining the network affects others' extracted value without additional compensation being paid. A large installed base attracts complementary products and thereby makes a standard indirectly more attractive, for example plug-ins that can be added to HTML documents (Shapiro and Varian, 1999). A large base increases the credibility of the standard and reduces risks of forgone investments. Together these features make a standard more attractive to users and expand the II based on that standard through additional adoptions that further increase the size of the installed base, which in turn results in the *positive feedback* loop (Grindley, 1995, p. 27). Increasing returns then lead to *lock-in*. A lock-in means that, when a technology has been adopted over a certain threshold, called momentum point, it will be very hard or impossible to propose competing technologies due to accrued investments in the installed base and technological capability (Arthur, 1988). *Path dependency* also implies that past events – early adoption decisions or correctly timed designs – can have a huge and unexpected impact on the future actions of other actors. Events deemed irrelevant and innocent can affect history by having tremendous effects later on (David, 1986).

Network externalities are side-effects, that is the path-dependent processes just described are driven by side-effects just like the processes Beck is interested in. Path-dependent processes take place when one component behaves unpredictably and then triggers unpredicted behaviour of a new component, which again triggers unpredicted behaviours of others, and so on. Thus Beck's concept of reflexivity describes a form of path-dependent processes.[1] The theories of Reflexive Modernization and Complexity Sciences, therefore, are similar in the sense that they both focus on complexity and both see side-effect driven path-dependent processes as the core of these phenomena. But they are certainly different as well. They are different when it comes to ontological, epistemological and method-ological issues. They are also different when it comes to what issues they want to highlight and understand. Complexity Science studies self-reinforcing processes while Beck looks at self-destructive processes. Both are looking at global financial markets: members of the Complexity Science field try to understand why it works, while Beck is more interested in studying why it does not work (in the sense of producing risks, uneven distribution of resources, and so on). This can partly be explained by a different focus. Beck's theory is more on the macro level of society, while Complexity Science addresses the mechanics at a more micro level. In this sense we can combine them by using (some of) the concepts from Complexity Science to study the processes creating the Risk Society at a more micro level. And that is what we aim at with this book. To do that we will move one step further towards the micro level. We will look at (some aspects of) Actor-Network Theory to get a more detailed model of how side-effects are created and propagate.

3 ACTOR-NETWORK THEORY

Actor-Network Theory has so far primarily been linked to the study of scientific research and the development and adoption of new technologies. The focus of ANT and ANT-based research has been the complex inter-actions and tight coupling of social, human, organizational, technological, material, political elements, and so on, in the development of scientific the-ories and technological solutions (Latour, 1999). For a presentation of ANT as a theory of complexity, see Law and Mol (2002). The unpredictable behaviour of complex systems is, then, the result of interactions and the propagation of side-effects between components of a technological, social, political, as well as an organizational nature.

Central concepts (in early ANT studies) are closure (Law and Bijker, 1992), stabilization (for example Bijker, 1993) and enrolment and align-ment (for example Callon, 1991). Specifically, closure indicates a status where a consensus emerges around a particular technology. Closure stabil-izes the technology by accumulating resistance against change. It is achieved through a negotiation process and by enrolling actors/elements of various kinds into a network and translating (re-interpreting or changing) them so that the elements are aligned (fit together) in a way that supports the designers' intentions.

The early ANT studies can be said to have focused on complexity. They spelled out the rich and complex relations between the scientific and the technological on the one hand and the social on the other, related to the making of scientific theories and technological solutions. This also covers the complex relationships between the local and the universal. ANT has been used in research on the negotiation of IS standards and their embedding of their local context of development and use (Bowker and Star, 1994; 1999; Timmermans and Berg, 1997; Star and Ruhleder, 1996; Hanseth and Monteiro, 1997; Fomin et al., 2003).

Since their emergence in the early 1980s, ANT and ANT research have evolved and left their (so-called) 'managerial' approach which focused on how one single actor-network was aligned by a dominating central actor (Law, 2003b). Complexity has been addressed more explicitly as the focus turned to the dynamics unfolding when independent actors try to align different but intersected actor-networks (Latour, 1988; Star and Griesemer, 1989; Law and Mol, 2002; Law, 2003a; Law and Urry, 2003). This happened as attention moved towards more complex cases where order and universality could not be achieved in the classical way.[2] These cases are described as 'worlds' which are too complex to be closed and ordered according to one single mode or logic. There will only be partial orders which are interacting in different ways, or interconnected and overlapping subworlds which are ordered according to different logics. The interconnectedness of the subworlds means that when one is trying to make order in one subworld by imposing a specific logic, the same logic is making disorder in another – an order also has its dis-order (Law, 2003b; Berg and Timmermans, 2000). Rather than alignment, stabilization and closure, the keywords are now multiplicities, inconsistencies, ambivalence, ambiguities (Law, 2003a; Law and Mol, 2002). Mastering this new world is not about achieving stabilization and closure, but rather about more ad hoc practices – 'ontological choreography' of an ontological patchwork (Cussins, 1998). This approach has been applied to studies of cases such as train accidents (Law, 2003a), a broad range of hi-tech medical practices (Mol and Berg, 1998), interdisciplinary research (from which the concept of 'boundary objects' was developed (Star and Griesemer, 1989)). This approach to complexity has also been applied to analyse the challenges, not to say impossibility, of achieving closure and stabilization in relation to complex IS and IS standards (Aanestad and Hanseth, 2000).

The evolution of ANT has brought it close to the theory of 'reflexive modernization' as well as Complexity Science. The change in focus away from networks that are managed or controlled from a centre is a change towards a focus on the creation of order in self-organized networks which is the centre of attention in Complexity Science. The similarities between ANT and reflexive modernization are strongly expressed by Bruno Latour. Referring to the theory of Ulrich Beck, he states that a

> perfect translation of 'risk' is the word network in the ANT sense, referring to whatever deviates from the straight path of reason and of control to trace a labyrinth, a maze of unexpected associations between heterogeneous elements, each of which acts as a mediator and no longer as a mere compliant intermediary (Latour, 2003, p. 36).[3]

From Beck's perspective, the change of focus within ANT is a move from the first modernity to a second reflexive modernity.[4] This is a reflexive modernity in the sense that modern society itself is modernized: the change is happening not within social structures but to them, which leads to a 'pluralization of modernities' (Beck et al., 2003, p. 2). 'This *"meta-change"* of modern society results from a critical mass of unintended side-effects [. . .] resulting from [. . .] market expansion, legal universalism and technical revolution' (ibid., p. 2, emphasis in original) – what we normally refer to as globalization. Beck describes the term side-effect more precisely as 'effects that were originally intended to be more narrow in their scope than they turned out to be' (ibid., p. 2).

The term 'reflexive' means, in Bruno Latour's interpretation, that 'the unintended consequences of actions reverberate throughout the whole of society in such a way that they have become intractable' (Latour, 2003, p. 36). In other words, side-effects may be reflexive in the sense that they may propagate through large networks and finally be reflected (hence the term reflexive) back on what initially triggered them. Thus, the end result of one act may be the opposite of what was intended.[5] In ANT terms, the propagation of side-effects is the dis-ordering created by an ordering action.

4 COMPLEXITY AND TECHNOLOGY IN ORGANIZATION STUDIES

We will now look at studies of complex technologies and how they relate to the theoretical framework presented so far. In his book *Autonomous Technology* Langdon Winner (1977) discussed different ways in which technology is seen as autonomous or out of control within various political theories from Karl Max to Jacques Ellul. Complexity is a present feature of technology in all theories he discusses, and in some it is the feature which makes technology appear as autonomous. This autonomy is created by the unpredictable propagation of side-effects perfectly in line with the theories presented above.

Complex technological systems have also been focused on within the Organization Studies field. We will here present two theories that have been developed: the theories of Normal Accidents and High Reliability Organizations.

4.1   Normal Accident Theory

Normal Accident Theory (NAT) was originally developed by Charles Perrow (1984), based on studies of complex technological systems where failures could lead to disasters. The focus has been on real disasters, or 'near-disasters', caused by complex technological systems like the Three Mile Island and Bhopal accidents. Technological systems studied include various petrochemical plants, nuclear power plants, aircrafts and air traffic control, nuclear weapons, hydro power dams, mines, and so on.

At the centre of NAT is what is called *interactive complexity* of *tightly coupled* systems. In such systems accidents are normal. Interactive complexity, or complex interactions, is defined in contrast to what Perrow calls linear interactions. The latter covers interactions among a sequence of components where output from one is input to the next. On the other hand, interactions are complex when there are branching paths, feedback loops, jumps from one linear sequence (Perrow, 1999, p. 75). Components are tightly coupled when there are no slack or buffers in between so that change in one immediately causes change in the other (ibid., p. 90).

Any component of a system might sometimes behave in unanticipated ways. Such unanticipated behaviour may then interfere with the unanticipated behaviour of other components, triggering unanticipated behaviour of even more components, and so on. Perrow argues that systems that have high degrees of (interactive) complexity are found to have higher chances of producing unexpected interactions. These unexpected interactions can produce failures in the system. The relative severity of these failures depends on the coupling of the system. That is, systems that have many interdependent interactions, or that are tightly coupled, are more at risk of producing a grave failure than systems that are loosely coupled. Thus, NAT describes that the more complex and tightly coupled a system is, the higher risk that system has to produce a severe failure. In this sense, systems with certain characteristics, such as complex interactions and tight coupling, will *inevitably* produce a failure. Thus, it could be said that it would be normal for that type of system to have an accident (thus the title Normal Accidents). Perrow (1999) argues that commissions analysing serious accidents tend to search for one single element that can be blamed; either this element is an operator, a manager, or a single component within the technological system. He argues further that attaching the cause of a failure to an individual element is in most cases a serious misunderstanding. He concludes that disasters and serious accidents related to complex technologies are as a rule caused by unanticipated behaviours and interactions involving a huge number of components of various kinds – technological as well as 'non-technological'.

NAT is pessimistic about the possibilities for managing and controlling the technologies studied so that accidents can be avoided. Better tools for controlling these technologies can lead to improvements, but only marginal ones. Because the accidents and failures are an inherent consequence of the complexities of the technologies, accidents can only be avoided by reducing the complexity of the systems. In the case of some systems, Perrow (1999) argues, the risk of serious accidents can only be brought down to an acceptable level by destroying the technology. This is the case, in his view, for nuclear technologies, because of the potential dramatic consequences of failures.

We see Perrow's theory in harmony with those presented above. He sees the complex technological systems he is studying like a sort of 'risk society' – at least in the sense that it is complexity in itself that is the source of unpredictability and that such complex systems are inherently beyond control. Further, it is side-effects and their propagation and interaction that cause accidents.

4.2 Normal Accidents or High Reliability Organizations?

Another group of researchers have studied similar organizations and addressed similar issues to Perrow. Through studies of safety critical organizations that are all complex and faced with tight coupling, like air traffic control, they claim to have identified organizations with a very high degree of reliability (La Porte, 1988; La Porte and Consolini, 1991; La Porte, 1996; Weick and Sutcliffe, 2001). These different high reliability organizations all faced complexity and tight coupling, but achieved outstanding safety records by applying similar strategies. These strategies can be summarized as follows:

1. Organizational focus on risk and intense training and socialization to make sure employees can respond to hazardous contingencies swiftly and adequately without being guided by a manager.
2. When complexity gets too tough for an individual to handle, informal networks, consisting of senior officials, technical specialists and

advisors step in. Together they form the organization's collective mind that can look at the situation from every angle before deciding on the proper course of action.

3. Use of redundancy to back up failing parts and persons in the organization.
4. HROs (High Reliability Organizations) learn to comprehend the complexities of the technology and the production process from errors and other experiences.

These strategies taken together, characterize the ideal typical HROs (La Porte and Consolini, 1991).

The fact that different groups have addressed the same issues yet arrived at almost opposite conclusions has triggered a quite extensive debate (Perrow, 1994; 1999; Sagan, 1993; Rijpma, 2003; La Porte, 1994; La Porte and Rochlin, 1994; Clark, 1993).

The NAT supporters are not convinced by the general applicability of the HRO strategy (Perrow, 1994; 1999; Sagan, 2004). Their key arguments are:

1. Learning is easier said than done (Edmonson, 1996).
2. Group interest decreases the concern for risks and possibilities for learning. Complex organizations produce accidents because official safety goals are rendered obsolete by production pressures and parochial interests. Organizations are poor at learning from incidents, partly because they tend to blame individuals for making mistakes, rather than addressing the underlying causes of accidents.
3. Adding redundancy may introduce new sources of errors, and, accordingly, increase risk just as much as it reduces it (Sagan, 2004).
4. The inherent unpredictability of complex systems implies that they will never be error-free. Sooner or later accidents will happen. In the long run NAT wins, Rijpma (2003, p. 40) concludes.

The question for us, then, is whether the complexities created by integrated ICT solutions will be, or may become, HROs or rather, if accidents will be normal. Of these two positions, it is obviously Perrow that is closest to Beck's and Giddens' position. And the critical question is whether we can obtain necessary knowledge, that is complete, knowledge about a system so that we can know that we will operate it in a safe manner.

If we relate the cases studied by the HRO community, like air traffic control, to the definition of complexity presented in Chapter 1, we can see that they only partly match. Intuitively we agree that air traffic control is a complex socio-technical system, but the speed of change in that system is moderate compared to other areas where ICT are crucial and that are central to globalization (like the media sector, mobile telecommunication, and so on). Speed of change is also indeed crucial when we are discussing possibilities for and the limits of learning. Regarding complex systems, one might argue, as Beck, Giddens and Perrow do, that our knowledge about the components and their interactions will always be incomplete. But over time we might learn quite a lot about them – as long as the system stays stable. Yet every time it changes, our knowledge about how it works becomes invalid – or at least incomplete. Over time our knowledge about it will grow again – until it changes again. And the more complex the system is (in terms of number of components and links), the slower the learning processes. If the speed of change of the system grows, at some point it may change faster than the learning process of those involved. (More on this in Kallinikos' chapter, Chapter 3, this volume) In cases like air traffic control, it is also quite obvious what kind of risks need to be managed. In other areas, that is not the case. A typical example here is biotechnology. What kinds of risks are related to the development of genetically modified organisms? In particular – what are the long term risks? It is obvious that learning from experience is not easy in such cases when we are dealing with 'unknown unknowns', that is when we do not know what to worry about, we cannot know how to deal with or control it either.

In addition, possibilities of learning how a complex system works are constrained, according to Giddens and Beck, by the fact that when systems get complex, more knowledge may lead to decreased control, that is increased risks. Whether this will be the case for integrated ICT solutions is an empirical question that remains to be answered.

Challenges related to learning in organizations are also studied under the label 'learning myopia'. Levinthal and March (1993) point to three kinds of myopia: temporal, spacial and failure. This means that learning in organizations is constrained by the fact that organizations (or their members) tend to overlook events that are distant either in time (past experiences, future threats or opportunities) or space, and that they tend to focus more on successes and overlook the lessons to be learned from failures.

Learning myopias are indeed highly present in the development of ICT solutions (Lyytinen and Robey, 1999). Lyytinen and Robey identify three main reasons for this. First, organizational intelligence is insufficient to deal with the complexity of the ICT solutions and projects. This problem is enhanced by high turnover in ISD (Information System Development) organizations and inappropriate pre-existing institutional arrangements and related patterns of thinking, what Ciborra and Lanzara (1994) call formative contexts. The formative contexts shape both the plans and actions taken and the interpretation of events. Existing formative contexts lack scientific bases. For this reason they appear, according to Lyytinen and

Robey (1999) not as theories-in-use, but rather as myths-in-use. Additional barriers to learning identified by Lyytinen and Robey are disincentives for learning and inappropriate organizational design.

Increased globalization and complexity also increase the role of all these three factors leading to learning myopias identified by Levinthal and March (1993) and the learning barriers in ICT projects identified by Lyytinen and Robey (1999). The more complex and global a system becomes, the harder it becomes to see the relevance of events distant in time or space at the same time as the role of such distant events increases. At the same time, the more severe will the limitations of ISD organizations' organizational intelligence become, and the more inappropriate their formative contexts.

NOTES

1. The concept of path-dependence has more recently diffused from economics and into other scientific fields – first historical sociology (Mahoney, 2000), then sociology and social sciences more broadly (Urry, 2003).
2. John Law and Annamarie Mol (2002, p. 1) define complexity as follows: 'There is complexity if things relate but don't add up, if events occur but not within the process of linear time, and if phenomena share a space but cannot be mapped in terms of a single set of three-dimensional coordinates.' This definition is very brief and rather abstract.
3. The most substantial difference between the two is maybe the status they attribute to theories. Reflexive Modernization is presented as a theory in the classical sense which describes the world 'as it is', while ANT has adopted the ethnomethodological position and sees itself just as one 'ethnotheory' having the same status as other such theories (Latour, 2003).
4. According to Beck two processes of modernization of our society can be distinguished: a first one called first or simple modernization characterized by a stable system of coordinates as for instance the nation state, the gainful employment society, a concept of rationality that emphasizes instrumental control; a second one called reflexive modernization characterized by a fundamental societal transformation within modernity which revolutionizes its very coordinates and calls into question its own basic premises (Beck, 1999).
5. Reflexivity may be seen as a form of path-dependence. This concept has more recently emerged as influential within broader discussions of complexity theory. It has diffused from economics into other scientific fields – first historical sociology (Mahoney, 2000), then sociology and social sciences more broadly (Urry, 2003). Path-dependency in terms of self-reinforcing processes leading to lock-ins have been widely studied in relation to standards.

REFERENCES

Aanestad, M. and O. Hanseth (2000), 'Implementing open network technologies in complex work practices. A case from telemedicine', in *Proceedings from IFIP WG 8.2 International Conference. The Social and Organizational Perspective on Research and Practice in Information Technology*, 10–12 June, Aalborg, Denmark.

Akerlof, G.A. (1970), 'The market for "lemons": quality, uncertainty and the market mechanism', *The Quarterly Journal of Economics*, **84**(3), August, 488–500.

Arthur, W.B. (1988), 'Competing technologies: an overview', in G. Dosi et al. (eds), *Technical Change and Economic Theory*, New York: Pinter Publishers, pp. 590–607.

Arthur, W.B. (1994), *Increasing Returns and Path Dependence in the Economy*, Ann Arbor, MI: University of Michigan Press.

Avison, D., D. Wilson and S. Hunt (2003), 'An IT failure and a company failure: a case study in telecommunications', in *Proceedings from the 8th AIM Conference*, 21–23 May, Grenoble, France.

Beck, U. (1986), *Risk Society: Towards Another Modernity*, London: Routledge.

Beck, U. (1999), *World Risk Society*, Cambridge: Polity Press.

Beck, U., W. Bonss and C. Lau (2003), 'The theory of reflexive modernization: problematic, hypotheses and research programme', *Theory, Culture & Society*, **20**(2), 1–33.

Beck, U., A. Giddens and S. Lash (1994), *Reflexive Modernization*, Cambridge: Polity Press.

Beniger, J. (1986), *The Control Revolution: Technological and Economic Origins of the Information Society*, Cambridge, Mass: Harvard University Press.

Berg, M. and S. Timmermans (2000), 'Orders and their others: on the construction of universalities in medical work', *Configurations*, (8), pp. 31–61.

Bijker, W.E. (1993), 'Do not despair: there is life after constructivism', *Science, Technology & Human Values*, **18**, 113–38.

Bowker, G. and S.L. Star (1994), 'Knowledge and infrastructure in international information management: problems of classification and coding', in L. Bud (ed.), *Information Acumen: The Understanding and Use of Knowledge in Modern Business*, London: Routledge, pp. 187–213.

Bowker, G. and S.L. Star (1999), *Sorting Things Out. Classification and its Consequences*, Cambridge, MA: MIT Press.

Callon, M. (1991), 'Techno-economic networks and irreversibility', in J. Law (ed.), *A Sociology of Monsters: Essays on Power, Technology and Domination*, London: Routledge, pp. 132–61.

Capra, F. (1996), *The Web of Life: A New Scientific Understanding of Living Systems*, London: HarperCollins.

Ciborra, C. and G.F. Lanzara (1994), 'Formative contexts and information technology: understanding the dynamics of innovation in organizations', *Accounting, Management and Information Technologies*, **4**(2), 61–86.

Ciborra, C., K. Braa, A. Cordella, B. Dahlbom, A. Failla, O. Hanseth, V. Hepsø, J. Ljungberg, E. Monteiro and K.A. Simon (2000), *From Control to Drift: The Dynamics of Corporate Information Infrastructures*, Oxford: Oxford University Press.

Clark, L. (1993), 'Drs. Pangloss and Strangelove meet organizational theory: high reliability organizations and nuclear weapons accidents', *Sociological Forum*, **8**(4), 675–89.

Cussins, C. (1998), 'Ontological choreography: agency for women patients in an infertility clinic', in M. Berg and A. Mol (eds), *Differences in Medicine: Unravelling Practices, Techniques and Bodies*, Durham and London: Duke University Press, pp. 166–201.

David, P.A. (1986), 'Understanding the economics of QWERTY', in W.N. Parker (ed.), *Economic History and the Modern Economist*, Oxford and New York: Basil Blackwell.

Dooley, K. (1996), 'Complex adaptive systems: a nominal definition', www.eas.asu.edu/~kdooley/casopdef. html (last accessed 21 October 2005).

Edmonson, A.C. (1996), 'Learning from mistakes is easier said than done: group and organizational influences of the detection and correction of human error', *The Journal of Applied Behavioral Science*, **32**(1), 5–28.

Eoyang, G. (1996), 'Complex? Yes! Adaptive? Well, maybe. . .', *Interactions*, **3**(1), 31–7.

Fomin, V., T. Keil and K. Lyytinen (2003), 'Theorising about standardization: integrating fragments of process theory in light of telecommunication standardization wars', *Sprouts: Working Papers on Information Environments, Systems and Organizations*, **3**(1), 29–60.

Giddens, A. (1990), *Consequences of Modernity*, Cambridge: Polity Press.

Grindley, P. (1995), *Standards, Strategy, and Politics. Cases and Stories*, New York: Oxford University Press.

Hanseth, O. and E. Monteiro (1997), 'Inscribing behaviour in information infrastructure standards', *Accounting Management & Information Technology*, **7**(4), 183–211.

Hanseth, O., C. Ciborra and K. Braa (2001), 'The control devolution: ERP and the side-effects of globalization', *The Database for Advances in Information Systems*, Special Issue: *Critical Analysis of ERP Systems: The Macro Level*, **32**(4), Fall, 34–46.

Holland, J. (1995), *Hidden Order*, Reading, MA: Addison-Wesley.

Hopkins, A. (1999), 'The limits of normal accidents theory', *Safety Science*, **32**(2), 93–102.

La Porte, T.R. (1988), 'The United States air traffic system: increasing reliability in the midst of rapid growth', in Renate Mayntz and Thomas P. Hughes (eds), *The Development of Large Technical Systems*, Boulder, CO: Westview Press, pp. 215–44.

La Porte, T.R. (1994), 'A strawman speaks up: comments on the limit of safety', *Journal of Contingencies and Crisis Management*, **2**(4), 207–11.

La Porte, T.R. (1996), 'High reliability organizations: unlikely, demanding, and at risk', *Journal of Contingencies and Crisis Management*, **4**, p. 60–71.

La Porte, T.R. and P. Consolini (1991), 'Working in practice but not in theory: theoretical challenges of "High-Reliability Organizations"', *Journal of Public Administration Research and Theory*, **1**, pp. 19–47.

La Porte, T.R. and G. Rochlin (1994), 'A rejoinder to Perrow', *Journal of Contingencies and Crisis Management*, **2**(4), 221–27.

Latour, B. (1988), *Science in Action*, Cambridge, MA: Harvard University Press.

Latour, B. (1999), *Pandora's Hope: Essays on the Reality of Science Studies*, Cambridge, MA: Harvard University Press.

Latour, B. (2003), 'Is re-modernization occurring – and if so, how to prove it? A commentary on Ulrich Beck', *Theory, Culture & Society*, **20**(2), 2003, 35–8.

Law, J. (2003a), 'Ladbroke Grove, or how to think about failing systems', Manuscript, www.comp.lancs.ac.uk/sociology/papers/law-ladbroke-grove-failing-systems.pdf (last accessed November 2004), December.

Law, J. (2003b), 'Traduction/Trahison: Notes on ANT', Manuscript, www.comp.lancs.ac.uk/sociology/papers/law-traduction-trahison.pdf (last accessed November 2004), November.

Law, J. and W.E. Bijker (1992), 'Postscript: technology stability and social theory', in W.E. Bijker and J. Law (eds), *Shaping Technology/Building Society*, Cambridge, MA: MIT Press, pp. 290–308.

Law, J. and A. Mol (2002), *Complexities: Social Studies of Knowledge Practices*, Durham, NC: Duke University Press.

Law, J. and J. Urry (2003), 'Enacting the Social', Manuscript, www.comp. lancs.ac. uk/sociology/papers/law-urry-enacting-the-social.pdf (last accessed November 2004).

Levinthal, D.A. and J.G. March (1993), 'The myopia of learning', *Strategic Management Journal*, **14**, 95–112.

Lyytinen, K. and D. Robey (1999), 'Learning failure in information systems development', *Information Systems Journal*, **9**, pp. 85–101.

Mahoney, J. (2000), 'Path-dependence in historical sociology', *Theory and Society*, **29**, pp. 507–48.

Mol, A. and M. Berg (eds) (1998), *Differences in Medicine: Unravelling Practices, Techniques and Bodies*, Durham, NC and London: Duke University Press.

Perrow, C. (1994), 'The limits of safety: the enhancement of a theory of accidents', *Journal of Contingencies and Crisis Management*, **2**(4), 212–20.

Perrow, C. ([1984]1999), *Normal Accidents: Living With High-Risk Technologies*, New Jersey, USA: Princeton University Press.

Plsek, P.E. and T. Greenhalgh (2001), 'Complexity science: the challenge of complexity in health care', *British Medical Journal*, **323**, 625–8.

Plsek, P.E. and T. Wilson (2001), 'Complexity science: complexity, leadership, and management in health care organisations', *British Medical Journal*, **323**, September, 746–49.

Rijpma, J.A. (2003), 'From deadlock to dead end: the normal accidents – high reliability debate revisited', *Journal of Contingencies and Crisis Management*, **11**(2), 37–45.

Sagan, S.D. (1993), *The Limits of Safety: Organizations, Accidents, and Nuclear Weapons*, Princeton, NJ: Princeton University Press.

Sagan, S.D. (2004), 'The problem of redundancy problem: why more nuclear security forces may produce less nuclear security', *Risk Analysis*, **26**(4), August, 935–46.

Shapiro, C. and H.R. Varian (1999), *Information Rules: A Strategic Guide to the Network Economy*, Boston, MA: Harvard Business School Press.

Stacey, R.D. (1996), *Complexity and Creativity in Organisations*, San Francisco: Berrett-Koehler.

Star, S.L. and J.R. Griesemer (1989), 'Institutional ecology, "translations" and boundary objects: amateurs and professionals in Berkeley's museum of vertebrate zoology, 1907–39', *Social Studies of Science*, **19**, pp. 387–420.

Star, S.L. and K. Ruhleder (1996), 'Steps toward an ecology of infrastructure: design and access for large information spaces', *Information Systems Research*, **7**(1), 111–34.

Staw B.M. and J. Ross (1987), 'Behavior in escalation situations: antecedents, prototypes and solutions', in B.M. Staw and L.L. Cummins (eds), *Research in Organizational Behavior*, Greenwich, CT: JAI Press.

Timmermans, S. and M. Berg (1997), 'Standardization in action: achieving local universality through medical protocols', *Social Studies of Science*, **27**, pp. 273–305.

Urry, J. (2003), *Global Complexities*, Cambridge, UK: Polity Press.

Weick, K.E. (1995), *Sensemaking in Organisations*, London: Sage Publications.

Weick, K.E. and K.M. Sutcliffe (2001), *Managing the Unexpected: Assuring High Performance in an Age of Complexity*, San Fransisco, CA: Jossey-Bass.

Wilson, T., T. Holt and T. Greenhalgh (2001), 'Complexity science: complexity and clinical care', *British Medical Journal*, **323**, September, 685–8.

Winner, L. (1977), *Autonomous Technology: Technics-out-of-control as a Theme in Political Thought*, Cambridge, MA: MIT Press.

PART II

Cases

5. When 'perfect' integration leads to increasing risks: the case of an integrated information system in a global company

Knut H. Rolland and Eric Monteiro

INTRODUCTION

In order to accommodate the dynamics of globalization with increased competition and an unpredictable environment, the management literature often recommends companies to increase 'global integration' and enhance 'local responsiveness' (Bartlett and Goshal, 1998; Devinney et al., 2000). Given the complex dynamics of processes of globalization (Beck, 1994; Urry, 2003), however, the actual implementation of such generic strategies is certainly not obvious.

Closely linked to such strategies is often the introduction of various kinds of integrated information systems (IS). For example, perfectly in line with the recommendations in management literature, many international companies are implementing so-called Enterprise Resource Planning systems (ERPs) to standardize local work practices by providing shared and seamlessly integrated platforms for controlling and disseminating information flows throughout the company. Another well-known application of information technology is the current trend of comprehensive IS for managing customer relations (CRM systems). Other examples of integration technologies include service-oriented architectures (SOA), Intra- and Extranets, component-based systems, and XML, to name a few.

Although technically different, these technologies typically all aim at integrating existing heterogeneous collections of more or less incompatible systems and work practices (for example Hanseth and Braa, 2001; Rolland et al., forthcoming). In this way, they appear as a compelling technological fix to the problem of managing global business. Likewise, 'perfect' integration through standardizing interfaces between components and underlying infrastructure is also perceived as 'best practice' in both management (Weill and Broadbent, 1998) and more technical (Chari and Seshadri, 2004) literatures.

In this chapter we critically examine these assumptions, and propose that such systems and technologies that aim for seamless integration, more often than not tend to re-produce new forms of fragmentation and heterogeneity. For sure, we are not arguing that increased integration per se is a poor strategy for global businesses. What we are aiming for is a more nuanced understanding, building on the premise that integrated IS intrinsically involve 'double-bind effects' (Kallinikos, 2004). Thus in this chapter we argue that precisely because of the inherent socio-technical complexity of integration itself, as soon as integrated IS are 'worlded' in a context of organizational practices and existing technologies, they tend to *re-produce the very fragmentation they were developed to overcome*.

As a 'critical case' for this line of argument we present a longitudinal case study of a globally integrated IS (dubbed GSIS) in a major maritime classification company (dubbed MCC). Used by more than 1500 users across more than 150 offices worldwide and integrated with a highly standardized corporate-wide IT infrastructure, the GSIS offers a highly relevant case for providing insights on the nature of implementing and managing integrated IS in global companies. Inspired by Perrow (1999), we suggest that the GSIS increasingly becomes a complex rather than linear system producing 'tight couplings' and 'complex interactions' with components and work practices across a wider infrastructure. Because of tight coupling between the GSIS and a heterogeneous installed-base (Ciborra et al., 2000), new fragmentation in terms of local databases for storing audits and local work arounds were produced. More importantly, however, whenever management tried to accommodate this kind of fragmentation with corrective actions and new software releases this evoked new complex interactions, which again produced new forms of fragmentation, and so on.

The practical as well as the more analytical implications of this dynamics are indeed multifaceted.[1] In this chapter, in relation to the theme of this book we zoom in on two interrelated issues of risk. Firstly, we focus on the inherent cycles of *integration and fragmentation* in implementation of integrated IS. Tracing the trajectory of five different versions of the system, we see that the more 'perfect' the integration in terms of the completeness of the information architecture and the number of actors incorporated, the more risks tend to be generated. This is because, we argue, with a larger number and wider range of different involved components and actors the more likely it is for complex interactions to occur.

Secondly, as a consequence of complexity, an inherent risk in implementing the system is the risk of failing to learn from past experience. To paraphrase Perrow (1999), the learning curve in complex systems seems to be flat. As seen in the case of the GSIS in MCC, since the type and sources of the fragmentation are different each time, it becomes problematic to learn directly from past experiences and implementations. Similarly, learning failure has long been an issue in IS research (Lyytinen and Robey, 1999), and our analysis aims at furthering this literature with special regard to implementing integrated IS. Here we submit that due to the inherent socio-technical complexity of integrated IS, despite iterative prototyping and systematic testing *the risk of non-learning* is greater compared to other less integrated IS.

THE MARITIME CLASSIFICATION COMPANY (MCC)[2]

MCC is an international ship classification company with 6000 employees located in over 300 offices in more than 100 countries worldwide. As a classification company, MCC is part of an extensive network of institutions, international treaties and regulations, established over the past 150 years or so that together regulate and distribute risks in the maritime industry in order to minimize loss of life and damage to the environment and vessels. Classification companies apply expert knowledge in assessing the conditions of the ships, and typically act as a brokering agency between ship owners, insurance companies, and national and international regulating institutions.[3] This traditional role of classification companies has during the last decade been put under growing pressure as a consequence of an ongoing transformation from being typically semi-autonomous and geographically defined, to becoming truly global corporations (Bartlett and Ghoshal, 1998). In addition, a string of serious accidents involving classified oil tankers has recently threatened classification companies' reputation as neutral and well-functioning certification institutions.

The auditors in MCC carry out various annual, intermediate and renewal audits (that is surveys) on ships according to a complex set of rules and instructions set by MCC themselves, insurance companies, national and international regulating institutions. During an audit, an MCC auditor conducts a detailed technical inspection of a ship, and if it is found to be in satisfactory condition, and in accordance with the rules, the ship's certificate is endorsed or a new certificate is issued. Otherwise, a 'Condition of Class' (CC) is issued, and if the problem is not fixed within a few days the ship's certificate can be withdrawn. This is a particularly critical situation for the ship owner involving potential economical losses, sanctions from ports and authorities, getting a poor reputation, and insurance problems.

A key juridical and informational artefact in auditing is the so-called 'final audit report'. After an audit onboard a ship two important documents are typically prepared. First, the auditor writes up a 'quick report'

that contains a brief summary of what has been conducted and the preliminary results of the audit mainly for providing feedback to the crew on
the ship. Then, typically a few weeks after the actual audit, a complete audit
report is handed over to the owner of the ship (and in some cases to the
authorities). This is an extensive document that explains all the details of
the auditor's findings and conclusions in addition to more informal comments and recommendations.

However, as is the case with other kinds of audit work (Power, 1997), this
is a complex undertaking involving experience-based enactment of many
rules and issues in various contexts and situations. Conducting an audit is
often a delicate act of balancing. On the one hand, auditors must be suspi-
cious of the ship's condition and focus on the things that he or she might
think are in poor condition,[4] and on the other hand, the auditor must avoid
to appear unjustly rigid and arrogant. Given that the crew often consists of
people with different educational and cultural backgrounds, this can be
challenging. A key issue is the varying competence and spoken language of
the crew since many aspects of an audit simply cannot be completed
without their cooperation and active participation. Moreover, it is not
unusual to undertake more than one audit at a time. This makes the reporting more complicated since the same physical artefacts – for example,
rudders, tanks and engines on the ship – can be involved in several audits.
To make this event more intricate, MCC auditors also, not unusually,
conduct audits on behalf of national authorities and other classification
companies. Numerous types of audits having different requirements, and
crews with different backgrounds can make it especially difficult to structure and write up audit reports since it is of a profound importance that the
crew can actually make sense of the report in case any improvements on the
ship are required.

THE GSIS: A STRATEGY FOR GLOBAL INTEGRATION AND LOCAL RESPONSIVENESS

Over the years from its inception in 1994, the GSIS project evolved into a
high-profiled, prestigious effort with ambitious scope and a budget of more
than USD 100 million. In its early formative phases, however, it started out
as relatively narrow and confined. It grew from modest to ambitious
through a sequence of conscious, strategic moves as well as more circum-
stantial events. The GSIS project was born out of the growing frustration
with the unwieldy access to and structure of essential business information
for MCC. In the business of MCC, accurate, updated and complete information of 'hull damages' on vessels is crucial. An influential group of

HQ-based senior ship engineers, deeply fascinated by the potentials of ICT, argued for the problematic aspects of the existing situation: relevant information on 'hull damages' existed, but only in fragmented, partial and overlapping forms on paper and in numerous databases. The paper-based archives at HQ, second only to the National Library in size, were neither updated nor complete at all times as documents were kept in local offices world-wide, or in electronic form in one of the many local or HQ-based databases. A manifestation of this was a huge map of MCC's 110 fragmented IS and documents relevant for the topic of 'hull damage', occupying the entire wall of one of the senior engineer's spacious office. This was, he wryly commented, 'to remind everybody that something had to be done to create order in the prevailing chaos of information'.

The decisive push forward for the GSIS project was in 1994 when top management supported the initiative politically and economically. In doing so, the GSIS project was simultaneously transformed into a dramatically more ambitious effort than the initial focus on 'hull damages'. Top management's motivation was driven by a growing recognition of the implications of the global restructuring of the business sector of maritime certification, from semi-autonomous, geographically defined actors to truly global ones. This, they argued, implicated tighter and more streamlined work procedures – and corresponding information systems:

> We are distributing our work processes . . . we want to be as close as possible to the customer. The system [GSIS] represents a common database – thus it will not matter where the actual work is done . . . This implies that we have to standardize our way of working – design new processes – but they have to be accepted by the entire organization. (Manager)

The underlying mechanism for integrating the fragmented, incomplete and partly overlapping information sources into a coherent whole was through a so-called *product model* (see Figure 5.1). A product model would be a logical backbone around which to structure the information elements for all types of vessels as well as the relevant work routines. The underlying principles for a product model are thus exactly as for information architectures: to provide an accurate model of all relevant information and its relations for a specific domain of interest. Formulating a product model as the core of the future GSIS was given largely by the fact that several of the HQ-based ship engineers had prior knowledge of product models from an earlier, research project aimed at working out specifications for such a product model. The vision emerged of developing a complete product model covering all phases of a vessel's life as the principal means to eliminate the perceived chaos created by the plethora of existing information sources. Moreover, the idea was that the product model would ensure not

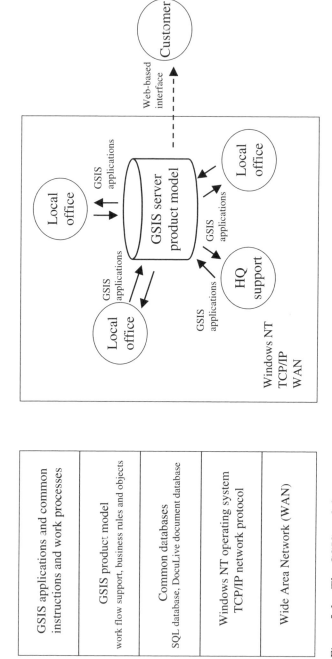

Figure 5.1   The GSIS and the integrated infrastructure in MCC

only interoperability between a suite of applications, but also a common vocabulary for the entire company:

> [It] was part of the vision to have an [Information architecture] because we had to develop various applications that will be using the same data within the same domain – it's just logical that they should speak the same language. Like TCP/IP is the standard on the Internet, the [Information architecture] is the standard for the domain knowledge of MCC. (Software developer)

Consequently, the existing legacy system for handling audits, the current paper-based checklists, calculation tools, hull damage databases, local databases, and paper-based achieves – all had to be phased out and substituted by the new GSIS.

In terms of technology, the GSIS project wanted to avoid making a large inflexible system that was impossible to maintain and extend. Therefore, the software developers argued, it was essential to build the software system by using self-contained components and state-of-the-art object-oriented design and programming techniques to facilitate evolutionary development. In close collaboration with a consulting company, the project decided to design the system from scratch using Microsoft's COM technology – the latest trend in component-based software engineering in the mid-1990s, which at the time was envisioned to become a de facto standard for component-based and distributed systems. However, for this to be possible, GSIS managers had, from the inception of the project in 1994, run a campaign for standardizing on Microsoft technologies against the central IT department and the R&D department who had a huge installed base of competence and IT systems on UNIX, and therefore tended to favour UNIX-based solutions. On the other hand, for strategic reasons, some of the top managers wanted to implement Windows NT across the entire corporation. Luckily for the GSIS project they saw GSIS as an important ally against the UNIX proponents. For management, then, the GSIS surfaced as an opportunity, not only for making local work processes related to auditing more efficient, but also for integrating and standardizing the entire IT infrastructure of the firm. For the initial mobilizing and legitimizing of the GSIS project this was a prerequisite, but as we shall see, this also made the GSIS a complex undertaking having a long string of surprising and unintended effects.

The software project itself involved over 30 experienced developers including experts from a local consultant company and MCC software engineers, and the development process was highly iterative and followed a 'spiral model approach' (Boehm, 1988) combining a prototyping approach with a traditional document-driven approach. As an additional strategy for mitigating risks and to avoid repeating historical failures and near misses in in-house software development, three of the largest offices in Norway, Singapore and Holland were selected to participate in prototyping sessions and early trials of the latest versions of the GSIS system. A worldwide network of super-users was also established to ensure that auditors, managers and secretaries had local experts available on the GSIS system. In addition, a team of experienced engineers was given the task of preparing the local offices for implantation of the new system by giving regional workshops, hands-on user learning, and preparing necessary documentation and guidelines for local IT people.

In early 1999 the GSIS project was two years behind the initial plan. After heated discussions on the reliability of the existing GSIS software solution, version 1.0 of GSIS was implemented in one Scandinavian office during January 1999 (see Figure 5.2). To everybody's surprise, the system was used in 'real' reporting after only two weeks, rapidly taking over from the old way of producing ship inspection reports.

However, in immediate need of IT support for producing and submitting audits electronically, numerous locally developed solutions were quickly spread among local offices. Given increasingly heated global competition with their competitors radically cutting their prices, top management also considered it critical to implement a common standardized IT solution to reduce the costs of producing audits. The GSIS project was thus under constant pressure to implement a working software solution beyond the initial pilot sites. Consequently, it was decided to implement the next version of the GSIS across all relevant local offices. This strategy, however, implied increasing complexity in terms of complex interactions between the GSIS and a legacy system, which in turn had unanticipated outcomes in local usage and appropriation of the GSIS.

EXAMPLES OF COMPLEXITY IN IMPLEMENTING GSIS

Re-producing Software Bugs and Failure Situations

The initial rollout plan for GSIS v 1.5 in the spring of 1999 aimed for a simultaneous 'big-bang' implementation across the remaining local offices worldwide. This strategy was, however, quickly abandoned. It was recognized as highly unrealistic by the implementation project due to the dramatically uneven distribution of technical (bandwidth for local communication) and organizational (IT competence and training capacity) resources. This forced a phased, regional rollout with the emergent strategy of running the old, HQ-operated database on the mainframe system in parallel with GSIS.

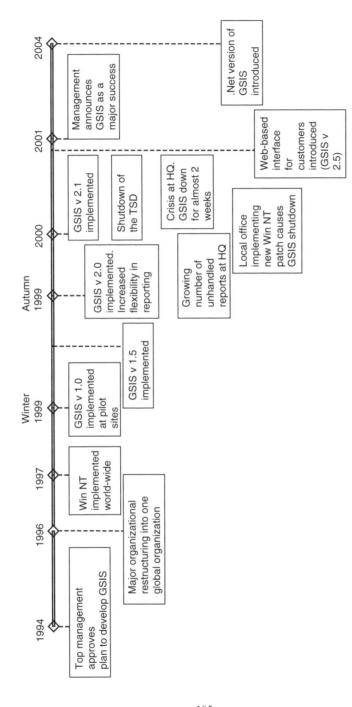

Figure 5.2   Major events in implementing GSIS

The database referred to as the 'Technical Ship Database' (TSD) was developed in the early 1970s and had been extended and maintained by a small group of engineers at HQ ever since. Thus a prerequisite for maintaining global consistency of audit information was to integrate the two systems by developing a software component to translate between the TSD database and the GSIS. The basic idea was to synchronize the two systems automatically every 24 hours, so that audits reported in the GSIS were accessible in the TSD, and, vice versa, whenever audit information was updated at HQ in the TSD it was visible in the GSIS system the next day. In this way, the unplanned integration appeared as the only feasible approach for diffusing the GSIS into real production beyond pilot sites. However, this 'solution' turned out to be an uncontrollable problem as the GSIS v 1.5 was introduced across entire regions (for example Scandinavia and Southern Europe).

First, the integration of the old TSD system and the GSIS introduced *tight coupling* in the audit work process. A central feature in the paper-based scheme was the informal practice of experience-based filtering and validating of audit information done by HQ engineers when manually entering information into the TSD. This was quite flexible and provided, in Perrow's words, 'loose coupling' in the sense that decisions regarding the structure of the audit report were decentralized, as well as giving the content a last quality check before going into the master database. In the new production infrastructure this was transformed through a tighter coupling between practices of writing the report (through the GSIS) and the formal publication and spreading of audit information to other auditors, customers and HQ engineers alike. Consequently, the HQ engineers' ability to filter information and to perform a last quality check on the content of the audit report was limited by the software component's ability to translate from the state-of-the-art product model used by GSIS to the ancient data model of the TSD.

Second, the integration of the two systems implied *complex interactions* between the old system and the GSIS. These two systems had very different information architectures that were never intended to co-exist – not to say interact. Although the functionality of the GSIS improved, the software component produced complex interactions with the old TSD system that continuously introduced new errors in both the old system and the new GSIS system. Consequently, users suddenly discovered that recent information was deleted or inaccessible. This problem was not merely caused by a poorly designed software component. Rather it was related to the heritage of the old mainframe platform, the information architecture implemented, and the ways in which its users had, over nearly three decades of use, added various codes, scripts and local administrative information to the initial columns and data cells in the database. For example, users of the TSD had over the years added different codes to the initial tables in the database for the purpose of generating specialized reports for local engineering departments at HQ. A different problem was that the new GSIS information architecture in many cases required much more detailed information regarding audits. Moreover, the date formats in the TSD database were often inconsistent and different from the ones used in the GSIS. This caused many misunderstandings since the GSIS was designed to automatically generate dates for new inspections of ships. It was simply not possible to report an audit through the system if it was not recognized by the systems as a 'due audit' at the present time. Obviously, since the software component shuffled information between the systems every 24 hours, even if errors as in the examples above were discovered, it became a race against time to correct the software component before the next update took place. As a consequence, even more errors were often introduced while attempting to correct known errors:

> We had problems with data quality that had increased since the first version. This was, to a large extent, caused by the migration from [TSD] to [GSIS] – which we never managed to control, and that we always underestimated the seriousness of. We managed to correct some errors – but while doing that, we also introduced new errors . . . (Implementation manager)

This situation underscores a 'double bind effect' (Kalinikos, 2004) in the diffusion of GSIS. At the same time as the integrated solution provides access to more information and connects a larger number of previously incompatible systems, integration simultaneously generates new failure situations and unpredictability.

Improving Functionality, Increasing Risks

During the autumn of 1999 the problems with the (unintended) integration and the inflexible reporting system became acute. At this point, the project was under growing pressure to come up with a more flexible and largely improved system. In the new version of GSIS the project managed to come up with an innovative solution to the reporting problem. The solution involving a checkbox where the user could simply state what different versions of reports existed and where the originals were stored, made it easy to store a digital version of the report locally and then to send a link or a copy of this document by email to the HQ. Furthermore, the users were allowed to modify the generated reports by importing them in Microsoft Word where users could add pictures, comments, and re-structure their contents.

This increased flexibility by allowing different types of reports in local offices and made the auditors more satisfied with the GSIS. However, as more local offices adopted the long-awaited version of GSIS, it turned out to have unintended side-effects at HQ. At HQ they had trouble handling reports arriving in various forms and formats from which information needed to be verified and integrated by a team at HQ. Together with the software developers, this maintenance team were desperately trying to manage all these reports with various hacks and temporary solutions. Still, however, they did not manage to reduce a rapidly growing backlog of audit reports: 'We [at HQ] faced tremendous problems where an extensive backlog had been growing – on top of all the frustration in local offices' (Manager).

The initial 'local problem' of reporting momentarily solved by a flexible design aligning the practices of the local offices with the technology, backfired as an out-of-control and rapidly growing backlog at HQ. After several months, only by hiring seven new consultants to the maintenance team, the backlog was eventually reduced. Paradoxically, a system that was supposed to decentralize the work of producing audits from the HQ to the local offices unintentionally produced a side-effect that centralized it.

This example shows that adding new functionality can indeed imply new and increased complexity in terms of unintended side-effects at other levels. Thus, as Perrow (1999) argues, new fixes can indeed increase complexity, rather than reduce it. Arguably, it also underscores the limited value of using prototypes and prototyping techniques in reducing risk, since the sources of uncertainty and risk first manifest themselves on a global level. Here the sources of unintended outcomes tend to be distributed across a great number of different actors, components and events that cut across different contexts, that only together at a specific moment in time, through their unintended interaction produce a certain (often) unintended effect. Thus, these unintended consequences are not only difficult to predict, but they are also difficult, not to say impossible, to trace and consequently to learn from.

Re-introducing Fragmentation

The time-consuming task of developing the software component and handling its unintended consequences left other critical development tasks pending. In particular, along with a long string of less critical software bugs, the first version of GSIS imposed an exceedingly rigid way of producing audit reports. Users had to go through a step-by-step procedure that often differed from the particular type of audit, local division of labour, and auditors' iterative style of working, shifting back and forth between an overall focus on certificates and a focus on more technical details and practical problems. As explained by one of the managers of the GSIS project this had various unintended consequences:

> Since the system did not support modification of reports – as for instance including digital images in reports as some auditors tended to do, a second copy of the report was stored outside the [GSIS] database. This turned out to become a serious problem – and we saw many different solutions to this problem popping up everywhere . . . (Project manager)

Thus, because of the extensive pilot testing of the GSIS, the software developers were aware of this problem, but due to the critical situation with the unintended integration between two very different systems this could not be prioritized. A striking unintended consequence of this was that local offices started to use their own locally designed systems for storing reports digitally:

> I know it's not part of the official procedure – but we store all reports electronically anyway. We have developed an automatic document handling system that gives a report an index and stores it in a database. I think most regions use this or similar systems . . . (Super-user, Denmark)

In short, one can say that the GSIS as an integrated information system, at least at this stage, had the contradictory and highly unanticipated outcome of establishing a more fragmented IT infrastructure where digital documents were stored in many different formats and digital archives throughout the global company. In retrospect, this can be traced back to the relatively tight coupling and frequent complex interactions between the GSIS and the old mainframe system. However, the temporary solution, as the example referred to above, was perceived by both project management and local actors as an efficient way of dealing with the rigidity of the present GSIS version. Simultaneously, in the long run, this added to the complexity of an already complex IT infrastructure where the GSIS was an emergent strategy for coping with the present problems, connected to a large number of local systems. In this way, a corporate-wide diffusion of GSIS established tighter couplings between different local offices, their local information management practices and solutions, and more centralized IT initiatives at the HQ.

Integrating a Larger Infrastructure and Customers

In early 2000, although the software quality in terms of number of bugs and user satisfaction increased along with the implementation of new and improved versions of GSIS, the socio-technical complexity was not reduced. On the contrary, with the inclusion and integration of a number of other corporate-wide IS and external actors, the socio-technical complexity of the GSIS tended to increase by each new version. For example, it was discovered that to avoid further local fragmentation of audit information and to standardize practices there was an urgent need for integrating information and systems for managing customer information and accounting. In this way, the GSIS became closely intertwined with other components of a corporate-wide IT infrastructure. Precisely because of this standardized infrastructure (that is both GSIS and the underlying infrastructure were based on Microsoft technologies) they tended to produce complex interactions when parts of it were extended or redesigned:

> How Windows NT is configured locally is very important for how [GSIS] works. For example, if we don't adjust and test [GSIS] before a new service pack is implemented – we can get problems of compatibility. Microsoft can have modified one DLL – or for some reason a library may have been replaced. In those cases, if those components are not replaced in [GSIS] applications or in the [GSIS] architecture – we get failure situations. (IT manager)

Such complex interactions between components of the GSIS and the Windows NT infrastructure became all too clear when a local office had to upgrade with the newest 'service pack' from Windows NT, which was a prerequisite for running the new accounting application. The new service pack also happened to involve a new and incompatible version of the DLL that was used for the GSIS client to communicate with the GSIS transaction server. Eventually, the consequence was that this caused a breakdown of the central GSIS server, and henceforth the entire global GSIS system went down.

As part of a strategy for improving the services for customers, the GSIS was also integrated with a web-based system where customers could browse audit information on their ships. Compared to the paper-based work process where the HQ acted as an important intermediary providing the auditor with slack and giving the report an added quality check, the process was not much more tightly coupled. With the new version, an auditor's reporting in an office in, for example, Denmark was immediately accessible for a customer. A consequence of this was that local auditors now spent more time on handling customer calls directly:

> [We] get phoned up and they're [the customers] saying there was somebody onboard my ship on Friday, but the status hasn't changed. He did the job; he probably did not report it over the weekend. If he does it this morning, and give it to me and I verify it this afternoon – it will be there on Wednesday. They

[the customers] have got red, yellow and green dots on their screen and they expect it to change instantly as soon as we've been onboard the ship. So that has raised the expectations. (Manager, UK)

This was not only time consuming for auditors, but also risky to send the report instantly without any time for double-checking. The report was still verified through a review system among colleagues, but the auditors perceived the lack of time to be problematic since not more than one other colleague had seen the report before the customer received it. As an unintended consequence, the auditors often waited as long as they could in order to 'buy time' and in some offices it was normal to send a draft version to many colleagues before finishing the reporting in the GSIS. This was, however, not sanctioned by managers at HQ who saw this as rather opportunistic behaviour, causing a slight rise in the time for submitting audit reports compared to the paper-based scheme, instead of reducing the time taken.

In this way, the integration of customers implied different kinds of challenges than first anticipated. Before the web-based system was introduced, managers in the GSIS project had tended to focus on improving the functionality and increasing the scope of integration. But, now, the managers were arguing for implementing more comprehensive means of user control in terms of both functionality in the GSIS and procedures that had to be followed by local auditors. Consequently, throughout 2001 and 2002, the GSIS software was updated along these lines so local users to a greater extent were forced to use the system in a particular way. This, however, was blended with a central HelpDesk that users could consult for conducting work arounds and configurations that it was not possible to do locally. In this way, loose coupling was reintroduced.

DISCUSSION: THE INHERENT RISKS OF 'PERFECTION'

Based on the examples from MCC, an alternative perspective on the aspect of integration and integrated IS in organizations can be proposed. Prevailing perspectives, widely shared both by scholars as well as practitioners, embed strong ideals of information systems as all-embracing, complete and non-redundant – ultimately, *perfect*. These ideals, technically achieved via tight or seamless integration through, for example, a Service-Oriented Architecture, which is one of the most popular at the moment (Newcomer and Lomow, 2005), are hardly new as 'integration has been the Holy Grail of MIS since the early days of computers in organizations'

(Kumar and van Hillegersberg, 2000: p. 23). This unbending, stubborn insistence of tight (that is perfect) integration in ongoing large-scale IS implementation needs to be understood as an expression of deep-seated ideals of modernity of reaching a state of completion (Beck, 1994). In this sense, the production and re-production of fragmentation is not merely an unintended consequence of poor design and management, but rather as Urry (2003: p. 14) points out, a systemic feature:

> What is intended is seen as having a range of unintended side effects that may take the system away from what seems to have been intended. However, this is a limited and often individualistic way of formulating relative failure that does not explicate just how these so-called side effects may be systemic features of the system in question.

Drawing on this, an alternative is to recognize imperfections – in the form of fragmentation, redundancies – as inherent. The inherent, as opposed to accidental, consequence of integration, with its implicated level of standardization and ordering, is also underscored in recent science studies contributions. For example, Berg and Timmermans (2000: pp. 36–7) point out the reciprocal relationship between ordering effects (like integration) and their effects:

> [T]hese orders do not emerge out of (and thereby replace) a pre-existing disorder. Rather, with the production of an order, a corresponding disorder comes into being . . . The order and its disorder, we argue, are engaged in a spiralling relationship – they need and embody each other.

It is vital to not misconstrue this aspect of inherent imperfection as merely poor design or project management. This would be to downplay the seriousness of the claim. One by one these imperfections could, in principle, be addressed and solved. But in sum, there will always be such expressions; they are systemic and inherent. They are not eliminated but rather redistributed and transformed. For example, as the GSIS project was striving to produce order in reporting in local offices by shutting down the central TSD system, the need for different software tools for maintaining the product model became acute. Without the old TSD system it became very difficult and time consuming to maintain the databases. In other words, reducing the redundancy and providing one common integrated IS, actually generated fragmentation and risks elsewhere.

Furthermore, as Law (2003) forcefully argues, the danger would be to maintain deeply normative ideals of perfection in the face of strong, empirical evidence to the contrary; large-scale, working IS of this type have (and will always have!) glitches, imperfections and overlaps.

So what's the argument here? The answer is: it's an argument about imperfection. . . . That there are always many imperfections. And to make perfection in one place (assuming such a thing was possible) would be to risk much greater imperfection in other locations . . . The argument is that entropy is chronic. . . . Some parts of the system will dissolve . . . For a manager accepting imperfection is not a failing. It is an advantage. Indeed a necessity. Perfectionism would be dangerous. (Law, 2003, p. 11)

In this respect the product model underlying the GSIS aimed for perfection in terms of integrating all relevant audit information. However, as theoretically indicated by Law, this quest to a complete and perfect solution to all kinds of information management problems in MCC, actually generated fragmentation and new risks. For example, the aims for perfection in the product model implied a highly problematic transfer of information from the old TSD system, leading to local loss of data and local solutions popping up as a substitute. Thus, aiming at perfection in this way, the MCC got into a very serious situation where it was increasingly difficult for the auditors to trace up-to-date information on ships, and reporting to customers was delayed.

IMPLICATIONS AND CONCLUDING REMARKS

Implications for the Practice of Managing Large-scale IS

Our study of MCC has potentially important practical implications for the management of implementing large-scale and integrated IS in similar contexts. In the IS literature, the problem of learning has long been recognized as an especially delicate dilemma in implementation and adaptation of IS in organizations (Argyris, 1977; Lyttinen and Robey, 1999).

Following the conceptualization of integrated IS as complex systems rather than linear systems, a practical challenge for managers and software developers is to learn from past experiences in terms of similar IS projects and versions of the technology. As recognized by Perrow (1999), while in 'linear systems we learn from our mistakes', in complex systems 'our learning curve is nearly flat' (pp. 12–14). Similarly, based on the empirical evidence from the MCC case, we see that as soon as the GSIS becomes a complex system with tight couplings between components and systems, learning from the mistakes of one version in order to improve the subsequent version becomes almost unachievable.

Due to their inherent socio-technical complexity we argue that the difficulties of learning are even more difficult confronted by integrated IS. This argument has two different sides. Drawing from Urry (2003),

Cases

we submit that integrated IS can be perceived as complex global hybrids that tend to weave together a large number of technical and non-technical components that 'through their dynamic interaction "spontaneously" develop collective properties or patterns, such as colour, that do not seem implicit, or at least not implicit in the same way, within individual components' (Urry, 2003: p. 13). Thus, since the *effects* of integrated IS cannot easily be traced back to their individual components since their behaviour emerges through their spontaneous and unpredictable interactions, learning on a very detailed level becomes nearly impossible. A particularly illuminating example of this from the MCC case is the development team's constant fight to stabilize the system by updating it with a steady stream of patches. Once a new patch that was believed to sort out the problems was installed on auditors' individual PCs worldwide, however, a slightly new problem or issue turned up as a complete surprise. Because of this, over time, the team tried to learn and reduce the number of patches, but this implied different problems for local offices that wanted to introduce other systems requiring a certain patch.

The GSIS project never learned how to handle complex integration problems. Instead they tended to deal with them as problems related to missing or malfunctioning functionality. Known problems were also transformed into new problems after the same problem had been re-produced a number of times. In this way, as pointed out by Lyttinen and Robey (1999), the team rather seemed to 'learn to fail'.

Secondly, as seen in the MCC case, when integrated IS become gradually more entangled at different levels with a corporate-wide IT infrastructure, the problems of tracing errors and failure situations become even more delicate. Infrastructures are seldom designed from scratch (Ciborra et al., 2000), and henceforth they tend to involve systems and components that were never designed to work together. The combination of a heterogeneous collection of old legacy systems integrated by a new all-inclusive system is likely to evoke unintended and complex interactions. The greater the number of different components and actors involved, the more likely it is that imperceptible and unintended interactions between them will occur. An archetypical example of this was when the implementation of a new accounting system in a local office eventually brought down the entire GSIS system. In this case it turned out that a DLL that was used in the GSIS communications architecture was substituted when the local office implemented a new Windows NT patch in order to be able to run the accounting system. This eventually made the GSIS server crash. Again, we see that the best of intentions has the potential of becoming every manager's worst nightmare. In such cases learning from past experiences became virtually impossible, since an infrastructure would change from time to time. Thus, the best thing the managers could do was to work around the problem by implementing corporate-wide policies enforcing a very conservative update frequency of the entire infrastructure. Nevertheless, this makes new potentially novel IS difficult to introduce, which again can imply a business risk for the company.

Concluding Remarks: Who 'Cares' about Integration?

Relatively little has been written about the phenomenon of integration in the IS literature. Yet, as we have seen in this chapter, the integrating character of the IS implemented greatly influenced the trajectory of the project, organizational work practices, as well as projects and customers initially *outside* its scope. Integration efforts are highly socio-technical endeavours in that they do not simply put together previously distributed and heterogeneous sources of information, but transform the meaning of information. In this sense, they can cause work arounds and unintended organizational consequences (Orlikowski, 1996). Additionally, however, focusing on the integrating character of such IS we see a different kind of unintended consequence that is both more *systemic and endemic*. Informed by Perrow (1999), we have argued that integrated IS tend to establish tight couplings and evoke complex interactions with other technologies and actors that from the outset were never meant to be linked. As an unintended side-effect of this transformation, new forms of fragmentation come to the surface. The more elements involved, the more likely is it that complex interactions are introduced, and hence new forms of fragmentation are produced. The more 'perfect' the integration, the larger the risk.

IS is not only an 'informating' technology (Zuboff, 1988), it is indeed an *integrating* technology. In this regard, 'caring' about technology implies caring about the issue of integration. On the practical side, this means a shift from the current focus on establishing perfectly aligned and all-encompassing information spaces, to being more concerned about minimizing the socio-technical complexity involved in implementing new IS. However, most techniques and methods (including prototyping and the spiral model) that are used to reduce complexity focus their attention on uncertainties regarding information – not the socio-technical complexity inherent in large-scale integration efforts. In contemporary organizations that are highly technology entangled, implementing IS is more a question of dealing with the complexity of integration than the complexity of information. Accordingly, the issue of integration should be a primary focus in future IS research.

NOTES

1. See Rolland and Monteiro (2002 and forthcoming) for a more comprehensive overview.
2. The case study of MCC is based on a longitudinal field study conducted from 1999 to 2003 comprising over 60 qualitative interviews, observations in six different local offices, as well as analysis of numerous volumes of documents related to the GSIS project. For details see Rolland and Monteiro (2002, forthcoming).
3. For example the International Association of Classification Societies (IACS) and the International Maritime Organization (IMO) are the most important regulating agencies. IMO is the United Nations' specialized agency responsible for improving maritime safety and preventing pollution from ships (www.imo.org).
4. The entire vessel is seldom investigated, only a sample, thus the experience and focus of the auditor is essential.

REFERENCES

Argyris, C. (1977), 'Organizational learning and management information systems', *Accounting, Organizations and Society*, **2**(2), 113–23.

Bartlett, C.A. and S. Ghoshal (1998), *Managing across Borders – The Transnational Solution*, London: Random House Business Books.

Beck, U. (1994), 'The reinvention of politics: towards a theory of reflexive modernization', in U. Beck, A. Giddens and S. Lash (eds), *Reflexive Modernization – Politics, Tradition and Aesthetics in the Modern Social Order*, Cambridge: Polity Press, pp. 1–55.

Berg, M. and S. Timmermanns (2000), 'Orders and their others: on the constitution of universalities in medical work', *Configurations*, **8**(1), 31–61.

Boehm, B.W. (1988), 'A spiral model of software development and enhancement', *Computer*, May, pp. 61–72.

Chari, K. and S. Seshadri (2004), 'Demystifying integration', *Communications of the ACM*, **47**(7), 59–63.

Ciborra, C., K. Braa, A. Cordella, B. Dahlbom, A. Failla, O. Hanseth, V. Hepsø, J. Ljungberg, E. Monteiro and K.A. Simon (2000), *From Control to Drift: The Dynamics of Corporate Information Infrastructures*, Oxford: Oxford University Press.

Devinney, T.M., D.F. Midgley and S. Venaik (2000), 'The optimal performance of the global firm: formalizing and extending the integration-responsiveness framework', *Organization Science*, **11**(6), 674–95.

Hanseth, O. and K. Braa (2001), 'Hunting for the treasure at the end of the rainbow: standardizing corporate IT infrastructure', *Computer Supported Cooperative Work*, **10**(3–4), 261–92.

Kallinikos, J. (2004), 'Deconstructing information packages: Organizational and behavioural implications of ERP systems', *Information Technology & People*, **17**(1), 8–30.

Kumar, K. and J. van Hillegersberg (2000), 'ERP experiences and evolution', *Communications of the ACM*, **43**(4), 23–6.

Law, J. (2003), 'Ladbroke Grove, or how to think about failing systems', www.comp.lancs.ac.uk/sociology/papers/law-ladbroke-grove-failing-systems.pdf, revised December, (last accessed December 2004).

Lyytinen, K. and D. Robey (1999), 'Learning failure in information systems development', *Information Systems Journal*, **9**, 85–101.

Newcomer, E. and G. Lomow (2005), *Understanding SOA with Web Services*, Boston, USA: Addison-Wesley.

Orlikowski, W.J. (1996), 'Improvising organizational transformation over time: a situated change perspective', *Information Systems Research*, **7**(1), 63–92.

Perrow, C. (1999), *Normal Accidents: Living With High-Risk Technologies*, New Jersey, USA: Princeton University Press.

Power, M. (1997), *The Audit Society: Rituals of verification*, Oxford: Oxford University Press.

Rolland, K.H. and E. Monteiro (2002), 'Balancing the local and the global in infrastructural information systems', *The Information Society Journal*, **18**(2), 87–100.

Rolland, K.H. and E. Monteiro (forthcoming), 'The dynamics of integrated information systems implementation: unintended consequences revisited', unpublished mansucript.

Rolland, K.H., V. Hepsø and E. Monteiro (forthcoming), '(Re)conceptualizing common information spaces across heterogeneous contexts: im-/mutable mobiles and imperfection', unpublished manuscript.

Urry, J. (2003), *Global Complexity*, Cambridge: Polity Press.

Weill, P. and M. Broadbent (1998), *Leveraging the New Infrastructure: How Market Leaders Capitalize on Information*, Boston, USA: Harvard Business School Press.

Zuboff, S. (1988), *In the Age of the Smart Machine*, New York, USA: Basic Books.

6. Reflexive integration in the development and implementation of an Electronic Patient Record system

Ole Hanseth, Edoardo Jacucci, Miria Grisot and Margunn Aanestad

1   INTRODUCTION

Hospitals are increasingly complex organizations with their different medical departments and laboratories, their medical specialities and other professions, and with the rapid growth of medical knowledge and development of more advanced instruments. Information systems are becoming very central, as collecting, distributing and processing patient information (and other data) are all critical activities. Various information systems are at work in hospitals and differ in terms of specificity to certain categories of patients, treatments, laboratory exams, patient information and so on. For instance patient administrative systems contain patient demographic information; picture archive systems store images from radiological examinations; planning systems are used for planning, for instance in the use of surgical operating theatres. Many of these systems contain clinical information which is important for decision making. Easy access to different information sources and support to data sharing are critical and system integration is seen as a key issue.

The electronic patient record (EPR) is a core information system. For decades, EPR systems – intended to be the electronic equivalent of paper-based patient records – have been a major topic in the field of Medical Informatics internationally. An EPR system can be used by individual doctors locally, or be a common shared system in a clinical department, or in an entire hospital, or even among a set of interconnected hospitals. Usually the term EPR indicates a hospital-wide system which provides a single point of entry to patient clinical information across the hospital, and which supports coordination and cooperation between departments, professions and medical specialities. The use of an EPR system is expected to reduce redundancy and inconsistency of patient information across the hospital, and to enable real time update of patient records.

However, design, development and implementation of EPR systems entail considerable complexity and challenges. First of all, the medical record is per se a complex artefact. Berg and Bowker (1997) illustrate how the medical record is one and multiple: it is an organizational infrastructure which affords the interplay and coordination of divergent worlds. The record tells and performs multiple histories which are sometimes linked but often unconnected (Mol, 2002). Second, designing an EPR entails a complex process of standardization of a multitude of data forms, and data collection and documentation practices across the hospital (Berg, 1996; Timmermans and Berg, 2003; Ellingsen and Monteiro, 2003a). Third, implementing EPR is problematic and not a short term process. Whether an implementation is successful or failed is difficult to define. Jones, for instance, reports the experience of a large UK hospital which decided to implement a new EPR with a big-bang strategy, switching the whole hospital over to the new system in one day (Jones, 2003). The initiative was neither a success nor a failure due to the complex interplay of organizational and technical factors: the big bang strategy entailed many difficulties but the switch took place and the system was running. Still divergent perspectives, different attitudes among clinicians, unintended influences on the workplace relations, and technical issues made the process cumbersome (Atkinson and Peel, 1998). Finally, it is still disputed what a 'complete' digital record is, and to what extent all the different systems typically in use in hospitals should be integrated into one hospital information system. On the one hand it is risky not to support systems integration as there are high expectations tied to integration initiatives; on the other hand integration is a risky undertaking with unexpected outcomes where for instance tight integration may lead to additional work (Ellingsen and Monteiro, 2003a).

This chapter will tell the story of an effort aimed at developing an Electronic Patient Record system. Specifically, we will report from a case study that focuses on the design and development of a specific software product (called first DocuLive, then IntEPR, then GlobEPR) by Alpha Medical Solutions[1] (the medical division of Alpha), as well as the adoption of this product via the implementation at our study site, Rikshospitalet. This is a large, specialized teaching hospital in Oslo, Norway. At the time of the study, in Norway, EPR systems had for about 20 years been widely used in general practitioners' offices and also for quite some years in small hospitals. Specialized and limited systems had also existed within single clinical departments in larger hospitals. However, developing an integrated and hospital-wide EPR system for larger and more complex hospitals had proven to be a different and cumbersome task (see Ellingsen and Monteiro, 2003b for details about EPR history in Norway).

The development of the EPR at Rikshospitalet has been a long process – started in the early 1990s and still ongoing – which has constantly run the risk of failing. The story will tell how different parallel initiatives have been undertaken to contain the complexity of the task, and how the role, scope and aim of the project itself had to be constantly redefined. Achieving an integrated EPR has turned into an ongoing process never reaching a definitive closure: complexities have hampered the attempts to achieve integration and, additionally, integration efforts themselves have led to more fragmentation. The theory chapters (3 and 4) point to the double face of integration: interconnectedness may give rise to new risks and unintended outcomes. In our case this 'double face' of integration takes on a specific form: it emerges as a reflexive process where integration initiatives aiming at increased control and less fragmentation actually lead to an opposite unintended outcome, increased fragmentation, which in turn leads to other integration initiatives, and so on. To illustrate these dynamics, we will focus on how the visions and ambitions that were driving EPR development changed and evolved over time with critical consequences for the hospital work practices.

This chapter is structured as follows: first some details about research approach and setting are provided, followed by background information on EPR projects in Norway. In section 4, we present the case articulated into four stories. Then we engage in analysis and final discussion.

2   RESEARCH APPROACH AND SETTING

The research presented in this chapter is based on a longitudinal case study over three years, from 2001 to 2004, on the EPR implementation process in its various stages. We studied both the intended and unintended consequences of this implementation with a particular emphasis on the possible side-effects of ongoing integration efforts.

The data were collected in the period 2001–2004 and derived from our previous collaborations with the IT department of the hospital since 1996. We gathered data from seven clinical departments (out of 17), as well as the archive department and the IT department. These clinical departments were chosen using the implementation stage and department size as a sampling criterion. Specifically, we sought to increase variance in these conditions and therefore gathered data from departments where the EPR system had been in use for a long time, a short time, or where it was still under implementation.

We collected data with more than 35 formal interviews with 23 different employees of the hospital including medical doctors, nurses and secretaries in clinical departments, and project leaders, heads of hospital units and senior managers in the IT department, including the former CIO of the hospital. The interviews were semi-structured and lasted from one to two hours each. Data were also collected in 18 direct observations by participating in various discussions and meetings, as well as from document analyses. The observations covered, for example, tracing a patient trajectory in or between clinical departments (and the production and use of information); use of the paper-based and electronic patient record; observation of individual- and team-work in relation to information artefacts and IT support; observation of nursing activities and use of information before and after implementation of the EPR (in the form of 'shadowing'); attendance at project meetings; attendance at EPR courses for user groups; and attendance at preliminary meetings by the IT department and clinical departments before the actual implementation.

3   CASE DESCRIPTION

3.1   Background

In the early 1990s, two of the five Norwegian regional university hospitals and a small Norwegian software company initiated a project aimed at developing an EPR system. In 1996, the project enrolled the Rikshospitalet and the other two regional university hospitals not already involved, which produced a consortium of the five largest hospitals in Norway (see Figure 6.1 to follow the timeline). This led important actors to see this project as an important opportunity to develop a common standardized EPR system on a national level – not only a specification of some of its elements. To do so, the consortium project was merged with another project of EPR development (the system was called DocuLive) which had been running for about a decade, and after being hosted by several software companies, had recently been acquired by Alpha-Norway. After the project organizations were merged, Alpha, as the largest and financially strongest company, eventually bought the EPR system from the other vendor and took over the entire product development project. This was also seen as a welcome act by the hospitals. They realized that developing the envisioned software system would be a quite complex task which required a development organization with lots of resources and competence.

In the new project, Alpha kept the DocuLive name for the product, and the deadline for the delivery of the finalized system was set for the end of

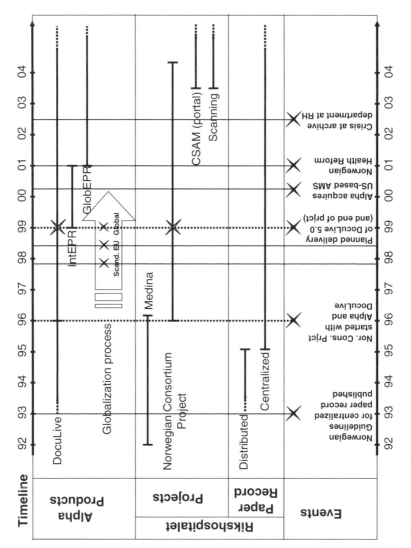

Figure 6.1 The timeline of products, projects and events for our case

122

1999. The DocuLive project started with the best intentions of involving users, acknowledging current work practices, and favouring a bottom-up development strategy. Yet, as the number of involved users grew, large-scale participatory development became unmanageable. After a few years, only a small number of user-representatives from each hospital continued to participate actively in the development. Moreover, the need to continuously find common agreements between the hospitals turned the intended bottom-up approach into a top-down one.

Overall, the strategy of the DocuLive project can be summarized as follows:

1. The EPR should be 'complete', that is, it should be one integrated patient record including all information about a patient.
2. The EPR should be realized as one shared, integrated IS for all departments.
3. The EPR should be developed to satisfy the needs of the five regional university hospitals (with the implicit plan that with the successful completion of the project, the EPR would also satisfy the needs of all other hospitals in Norway and accordingly would be adopted by them).

As we see, integration was a key issue – also in the third element of the strategy. When one system is shared by several hospitals, that system, indirectly, creates interdependencies and then in a way also integrates the work practices of those hospitals.

This joint project between the five hospitals and Alpha was terminated early in 2004 without the realization of the initial goal: the implementation of a complete EPR system. The version of DocuLive currently in use has limited functionality in comparison to the project's aims. Further development of the system, at the time of writing, is regulated by separate contracts between the vendor and the individual hospitals. At the regional level, four of the five regional health enterprises in Norway (including the one which contains Rikshospitalet) have decided to standardize on EPR systems other than DocuLive.

The focus of our study is to analyse the role of one important factor behind the failure: complexity. We have organized the empirical material into four stories. Each of them will be on one or more of the 'modes of ordering' exemplified by the strategy elements mentioned above. The purpose of each is to illustrate how efforts aimed at making order interfered with conflicting orders or order-making, ultimately producing more dis-order.[2]

3.2   The Scope of Integration

The first story focuses on the role of Alpha in relation to the shaping of the project trajectory. Alpha is a large company and its international orientation challenged the stabilization of the scope of the system.

When the project started in 1996, the project team was strongly expected to possess the economic, political, technical and medical capacity to reach its aims, both in terms of support and competence. In the end, this did not happen because the project evolved in unexpected directions. Shortly after the DocuLive project began, the IT managers of Rikshospitalet became aware that Alpha UK was also engaged in EPR development. Asking Alpha Norway for more clarification, they found out that within Alpha, several EPR development projects co-existed: at least five EPR projects were underway in Sweden, the UK, Germany, India and Norway. The IT department at Rikshospitalet realized that the Norwegian project was not at the top of Alpha's priorities since Norway represented the smallest market. Within Alpha, the DocuLive project ran the risk of being overrun by other internal projects for more profitable markets. As a consequence, the project consortium, together with Alpha Norway, decided to make the first move to internationalize the project, first to a Scandinavian level, and later to a European one. This implied that the system would have to adapt to the work practices of hospitals across all these regions.

A senior IT manager commented:

> Alpha decided and the hospital agreed to internationalize the product. At that time there were different competing systems within the Alpha company. We saw potential danger to our system and our development and requirements. We supported Alpha in bringing this up on the corporate level and getting DocuLive and the Norwegian product to become a main product for Alpha internationally. Because that would secure further development on our system. It was a strategic decision.

The strategy of the consortium was to push the project to a larger dimension in order to secure its continuity. On the other hand, this decision weakened the hospital consortium's position with respect to Alpha, since now it was not the only client with system requirements. Requirements from all other EPR projects in Alpha had to be merged and a new architecture had to be designed. Furthermore, since the original deadline for the final delivery (1999) was approaching, the project consortium agreed with Alpha to extend the time frame to include the development of the new internationalized EPR solution (called IntEPR).

At the time the IntEPR project started in 1999 (see the timeline in Figure 6.1), Alpha decided to acquire AMS (American Medical Systems), a large

US software development company. As a consequence, the scope, resources and balance of the Alpha medical division changed: the division's headquarters was moved from Europe to the US, and the project's scope became global. In this scenario, the project consortium supported Alpha to internationalize IntEPR. However, as the project became global, the IntEPR architecture was dropped in favour of a new system called GlobEPR. The basic requirements previously defined for the Norwegian customers of DocuLive were partly supported by the new architecture.

From this story we can see the meeting of two different 'worlds', each with their own mode of ordering: the one of the Norwegian project for the Norwegian hospitals, and the one of Alpha and its international scope. To Alpha, achieving economies of scale by targeting international markets is a key concern. In addition, the medical division within Alpha is large, with a traditional base within medical imaging technologies. As the imaging instruments have become digital, supplementary software systems have been built. And as the EPR development activities were increasing within Alpha, it became more and more important to align and integrate the EPR strategy and product(s) with other Alpha products and strategies. A side-effect of internationalizing the project, then, was that DocuLive became integrated with a broad range of other products.

Within this world, Norway becomes marginal, as the appetite for larger markets escalates in a self-feeding process. From the Norwegian point of view, the original interest in creating a Norwegian system had to be reinterpreted in a Scandinavian, then European, and finally global context. A side-effect of the expansion of ambitions and scope was increased complexity: the larger the market Alpha was aiming at, the more diverse the user requirements, and accordingly, the more complex the system had to be in order to satisfy them. This implied that the development costs were growing, which again implied that a larger market was required to make the whole project profitable. In other words: when the project identified risks threatening the project, it decided to increase the scope of integration. This increased complexity and generated new risks. Again an attempt was made to contain these risks by increasing the scope for integration.

This process can be described as a special case of reflexive modernization which we might call *reflexive integration*. Initially all five hospitals wanted an integrated EPR in the sense that it contained all patient record data. They knew this was a complex task which required a vendor with high competence. So they selected an international one. Unintentionally they had thereby linked their project, or integrated it to some extent, with what was going on inside this international company. When they became aware of this, they saw that there was a risk of their project being terminated by decisions made elsewhere in this vendor organization. To maintain control of their project they decide to integrate activities inside Alpha more with their own. This created a more complex overall system – and new risks. To control these risks again, the scope of integration was expanded – until the scope of integration had become so large that it more or less killed off the Norwegian part of this project.

3.3   The Complete and Integrated Patient Record

In our second and third stories we look more closely into these reflexive integration processes as they unfolded inside the hospital. The efforts aimed at replacing the fragmented paper-based record with a complete and smoothly integrated electronic one turned out to be more challenging than foreseen. In the end, the volume of paper records increased (second story) and the patient record became more fragmented (third story). This in turn increased the overall complexity and consequently slowed down the implementation processes.

Before 1995, the main problem at Rikshospitalet (as well as most other hospitals) was the fragmentation of the medical record system: each department had its own record archive. If a patient was admitted to several departments, several records would be created, each one containing locally specific information. In addition, various smaller local information systems, partially overlapping with the paper records, were in use. In this picture, a long time might be needed to retrieve critical information on patients. This could lead to situations where critical decisions were made without possessing vital information contained in all the relevant medical records.

In 1996, the same year as the DocuLive project started, Rikshospitalet centralized its paper-based patient records according to the principle: one patient, one record. This centralization process was not without problems. In particular, a major complaint was familiar: the long time needed to retrieve a patient record from the central archive. Doctors also complained that, due to the centralization, the merged patient records had become less easy to browse quickly, as a lot of the information was not relevant to their specific interests. In this situation it was widely assumed among doctors, as well as IT people at the hospital, that a complete EPR system would make information instantly available anywhere any time, as well as avoiding duplication of information and inconsistency of data.

Basically, the aim of the DocuLive project was to replicate and replace the recently centralized paper-based patient record. However, at the time when our fieldwork ended (autumn 2004), a full transition from the paper to the electronic record had not yet been accomplished. The DocuLive system mainly contained textual information, while much other information was still on paper forms (lab results, radiology reports, images and other printouts from various equipment). A manager from Rikshospitalet's IT department helped to quantify the situation: 'Currently DocuLive covers about 30–40% of information contained in an average paper-based record. Basically most of the information is text.' From an October 2002 internal report, we found an even more pessimistic estimate of DocuLive's coverage: '[It] covers 18 of a total of 66 document groups defined in the Norwegian standard for the paper patient record. In terms of volume – with a high degree of uncertainty – that accounts on average for about 10% of the total volume of a paper-based record.' (Translated from Norwegian by the authors).

Although the implementation of the EPR aimed at reducing paper and eventually replacing the paper system, the paper-based record still remained an important tool. Paradoxically, the production of paper documents increased markedly after the implementation of DocuLive. First, new laws on medical documentation required detailed records from professional groups not previously obliged to maintain a record, such as nurses, physiotherapists and social workers. Second, for legal reasons the hospital kept the paper version of the record updated. Thus, each time a clinical note was written in the EPR, a paper copy was also printed and added to the paper record. Printout efficiency was not a design principle for the current EPR, causing non-adjustable print layouts that could result in two printed pages for one electronic page form. Third, multiple printouts of preliminary documents (for example lab test results) were often stored in addition to final versions. The result was that the volume of paper documents increased. This growth created a crisis at the paper record archive department. In 2000 the hospital had moved into new facilities designed with a reduced space for the archive as it was supposed to handle electronic records only. In 2003 the archive was full and more than 300 shelf metres of records were lying on the floor. This situation also affected the time needed to find records, and often requests failed to be satisfied.

From an internal report:

> In . . . 2002 a daily average of 790 requests for paper records were received. . . . About half of the requests did not turn out as an actual delivery. There are several reasons for this. The most common are that the record has already been delivered in another department or has already been collected; that it is not possible to locate the record (due to wrong archiving); or that the archive never had the record for that patient (usually because it is a new patient). (Translated from Norwegian by the authors)

To alleviate this situation, a scanning project was started in 2003, with the aim of reducing the amount of paper documents sent to the archive.

However, even after the documents were scanned they had to be kept. One reason was that DocuLive's storage solution was not yet accredited; for that one had to wait for release and implementation of a new version of the software. Another reason was that the existing communication and coordination of work practices were based on a flow of paper documents, and DocuLive did not (yet) contain functionality that would allow the paper to be removed from the daily work practices. The result was that the benefits from the scanning activities were slow to be realized.

This story may be seen as a confrontation between what we might call 'the order of computers' and 'the order of paper'. Computers, we can argue, are best exploited if they are allowed to work the way that fits them best: where all information is stored in a shared, consistent and non-redundant database. However, the paper record is ordered according to different principles in order also to be an efficient tool for local work practices, and the assumption that all patient-related information could be ordered according to the 'computer order' has not yet been proven. At best, the transition period from paper-based to digital information will be long. During this period the electronic and the paper-based record have to coexist and 'cooperate'.

3.4   One Record (per Patient) – One (Integrated Information) System

The third story focuses on the relation between the new EPR system and the other clinical information systems in the hospital. When the implementation of DocuLive started, a few local systems containing clinical patient information already existed. Those systems often overlapped with DocuLive's (planned) functionality. The original plan as revealed by project documentation was to replace these with DocuLive so as to have the EPR as one integrated information system: '[DocuLive should] create a common platform for a multitude of customized EPR modules; [be] powerful enough to support all health-related information and legal aspects; [be] general enough to serve as a basis for a wide variety of hospital information systems . . . (Technical Overview Document, 1998, translated by the authors).

In this story, again the project's ambitious plan ended up producing the opposite outcome, which contributed to intensifying the degree of fragmentation of the medical record. The main ordering principles for achieving the integrated record were that there should be one record for each patient, containing all patient-related information, that this record should be shared among all units within the hospital, and that all patient records should be maintained by and stored in one single integrated information system. In order to achieve this, DocuLive was planned to be integrated with a few other systems: the central Patient Administrative System (PAS), and certain 'information supply' systems, notably laboratory systems that store and deliver laboratory test results, and image archives for radiological images. The idea of entirely substituting the other local EPR-like systems was slowly abandoned. Firstly, to include the functions of all these systems in the EPR would have made its development unmanageable. Secondly, users generally perceived local systems to support their work routines better and refused to give them up. For instance a doctor in paediatric cardiology stated, referring to a local system:

> If you have congenital heart defects it is very likely that you have also other congenital defects. So it is a very complex logistics of patients. These two reasons, the very detailed diagnostics, and the need of keeping track of the patient are the bases for the design of our system.

Rather than replacement, various solutions for technical integration of DocuLive with some of the local systems were considered. These intentions were realized only for a few systems, leading to a situation where users had to either perform double entries or cut and paste information between the systems. Simultaneously the number of specialized information systems was growing, based on well justified needs of the different medical specialities and departments. For example, the in-vitro fertilization clinic needed a system that allowed them to consider a couple as a unit, as well as to allow tracking of information from both semen and egg quality tests through all procedures involved, up to the birth of the child. The intensive care unit acquired a system that allowed them to harvest digital data from a vast array of medical equipment and thus eliminate the specialized paper forms previously used to document events and actions. Moreover, new digital instruments in use in many different departments include software components with medical record functionality.

Hence, the envisioned role of DocuLive has changed from being the only system to being one among a large (and increasing) number of systems (see Figure 6.2: from 'Original vision' to 'Later vision'). As the problems and the challenges with the original integration strategy emerged, the popularity of the Internet and its technology triggered the IT department at the hospital to start thinking about other potential strategies. It started tinkering with portal technology, and this led to the idea of an integrated EPR system. This would be achieved by means of a more loosely coupled infrastructure where the many clinical and laboratory systems (and DocuLive itself) were brought together under the common umbrella of a portal (see Figure 6.2: 'Current vision'). The portal was part of a larger change in strategy which went under the acronym CSAM: Clinical Systems All Merged. Thus, while visualization and access to the systems were integrated, the systems themselves did not need to be integrated with each other.

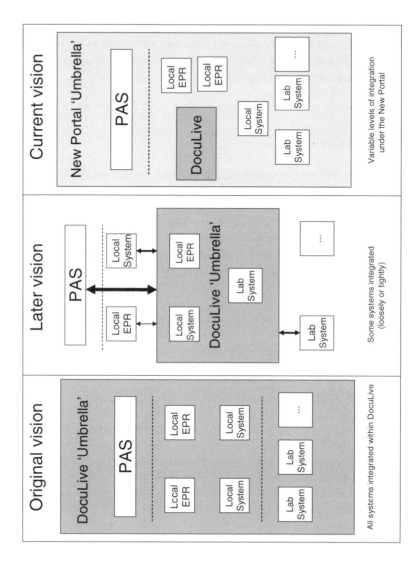

Figure 6.2   Three stages of the envisioned role of DocuLive

This story shows, again, how the world of DocuLive and its order was confronted with other worlds with different orders and ongoing ordering processes. Different medical specialities focus on different types of information (this being even truer in the case of specialized or tertiary hospitals like the one in this case). The ordering principle of 'one patient – one record' is non-problematic for many, but may interfere with and create disorders for others. As a result, the attempt to achieve a tightly coupled integration of systems (in the view of the logic of ordering of DocuLive) clashes against different logics which reflect the actual complexity and diversity of the work practices to be integrated. From this clash – this interference of orders – comes the generation of a new logic, implicit in the portal strategy CSAM.

To a certain degree, the novel portal strategy appears promising. It is a less strict and accordingly a more flexible way of integration and ordering. It seems more likely that this IS strategy can deliver a 'complete' system for accessing information. To implement such a strategy is far from trivial or without risk. It entails further development work, as adapters need to be developed between the portal software and the different applications. Moreover, the laws and regulations concerning documentation of patient information are clearly based on the envisioned all-encompassing EPR. One complete patient record is recognized to be the legal document, while the idea of keeping information in different sources as the CSAM strategy proposes is legally problematic: not all of the underlying systems are designed with adequate security of patient data in mind; therefore they do not conform to the standards of the privacy laws, either when it comes to access control solutions or long-term storage of confidential data.

3.5   The Role of the Regional University Hospitals Revisited

The fourth story describes how a health sector reform in Norway interfered with the ongoing EPR development and implementation process. When the DocuLive project started, new procedures and technologies were usually developed or first adopted by the five university hospitals, and subsequently by the other hospitals. But a major reform in the health sector, initiated in 2001, affected the process significantly.

Before the reform, the hospitals in Norway were owned by the country's 19 counties. There was a widely held view that the health system was too fragmented, did not encourage smooth collaboration and did not maintain a rational division of labour. The reform implied that the government was taking over the ownership of all hospitals by means of five regional health enterprises, which again owned the individual hospitals. The reform significantly altered the dynamics in the sector. As a health enterprise, each region had to define cost-efficient and effective strategies to realize benefits of scale. To improve collaboration and be more cost efficient to standardize on IT became a key concern, and specifically to select one standard EPR system among the three systems in use. Inevitably, this created competition among the hospitals for each to have its own EPR system prevail over the others.

At this point the DocuLive system progressed slowly due to continuously emerging new elements and demands originating from Alpha's activities and shifting strategies. In this situation, the IT department at Rikshospitalet attempted to market DocuLive as the standard system to be adopted by other hospitals, even though its development was far from complete. Moreover, Rikshospitalet sought to become the reference centre for delineating and implementing regional IT strategies. However, this strategy of promoting DocuLive was soon changed, as the IT department at Rikshospitalet acknowledged its rather weak position in the regional 'battle of systems' (Hughes, 1983). Accordingly, they made a strategic move, promoting the portal concept rather than DocuLive. This turned out to be a more flexible and robust strategy in order to enrol the other hospitals in the region in a collaborative rather than competitive standardization effort. The strategic move to promote the portal strategy also implied that DocuLive was 'buried' as 'the complete integrated EPR' (although not as product).

4   CONCLUDING DISCUSSION

The four stories presented above provide an account of the multiplicity of perspectives, intentions, constraints, challenges and agendas at work in the socio-technical network representing the escalating integration process.

Integration is about bringing together different worlds. Different orders interact with and re-organize one another: they may create dis-orders, or reinforce existing orders. While it is true that integration processes may eventually stabilize, this case suggests that, under certain circumstances, interferences between orders may also reflexively produce additional interferences with greater complexity that will ultimately destabilize the initial order.

In the first story we see how the two main actors, Alpha and the Norwegian EPR project, mutually and iteratively redefined their aims, strategy and design of the system as the project gradually escalated to a global level. The overall result of this dance of orders and redefinition of interests was that the Norwegian project, as initially conceived, did not succeed. The integration process turned reflexive and self-destructive. The second story highlights conflicts between (the order of) the electronic patient record and (the order of) the paper-based record. As a result, the

strategy for creating an integrated record created, as an unintended consequence, a more fragmented one. The third story illustrates how the ordering principle of 'one record (for each patient) – one integrated Information
System' created dis-orders in terms of making it more difficult for workers
to have easy access to the specific information they needed. The final story
illustrates how a new order enforced by the government interfered with the
ordering principles of the project.

The failure of DocuLive, at least as a standardization story, can be seen
as a failure in attempting to control complexity. Arguably, the main mistake
was to follow a 'traditional' integration and standardization approach –
typical for (first) modernity, that is, overemphasizing criteria of universality, uniformity and centralization of control to achieve alignment, stabilization and closure. In line with our theoretical framework, our case data
suggest that the complexity defines standardization as the emergence of
multiplicities, inconsistencies, ambivalence and ambiguities (Law, 2003;
Law and Mol, 2002). Ironically, what happened became the opposite of the
initial aims. When actors tried to stabilize the standard by enrolling more
actors, this made it less stable. Attempts to improve fragmented records by
means of one integrated EPR made the records more fragmented. The
complexity of DocuLive turned out to be one where the ordering efforts
created dis-orders. The side-effects triggered new ones, which again were
reflected back on the origin – the standardization process turned out to be
reflexive and self-destructive. The dynamics of reflexive processes at work
are summarized in Figure 6.3.

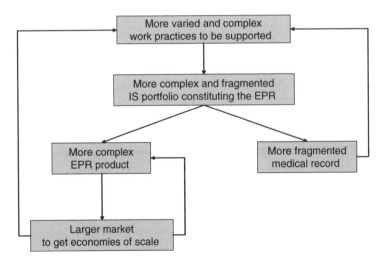

Figure 6.3   The reflexive integration process

The concept of reflexivity thus offers an interpretation of the dynamics of the case. The theory of 'high' modernity helps to observe how the logics of the 'first' industrial modernity find their limits (Beck et al., 1994). The intensified interconnectedness of social practices with technical artefacts on the one hand, and the need to align geographically dispersed actors on the other hand, effectively undermines the reductionist approach to control complexity. The weakness of such an approach becomes visible when the control itself reflexively reproduced the complexity – thus creating the immanent paradox of modernity.

ACKNOWLEDGEMENTS

We would like to thank the IT department of Rikshospitalet, Oslo, Norway. We owe special thanks particularly to Ivar Berge and Arve Kaaresen for setting up the research project and for the long-lasting research relationship. We thank Eric Monteiro, Marc Berg, Geoff Walsham, Judith Gregory, Sundeep Sahay and Ola Henfridsson for valuable discussions around our case study.

NOTES

1. The company name has been disguised.
2. The reader should refer to the timeline in Figure 6.1 to better follow the unfolding of the four stories.

REFERENCES

Atkinson, C.J. and V.J. Peel (1998), 'Transforming a hospital through growing, not building, an Electronic Patient Record system', *Methods of Information in Medicine*, **37**, 285–93.
Beck, U., A. Giddens and S. Lash (1994), *Reflexive Modernization: Politics, Tradition and Aesthetics in the Modern Social Order*, Cambridge, UK: Polity Press.
Berg, M. (1996), *Rationalizing Medical Work*, London: MIT Press.
Berg, M. and G. Bowker (1997), 'The multiple bodies of the medical record: toward a sociology of an artifact', *The Sociological Quarterly*, **38**(3), 513–37.
Ellingsen, G. (2002), *Global Reach, Local Use: Design and Use of Electronic Patient Record Systems in Large Hospitals*, PhD Thesis, NTNU, Trondheim.
Ellingsen, G. and E. Monteiro (2003a), 'A patchwork planet. Integration and cooperation in hospitals', *Computer Supported Cooperative Work*, **12**(1), 71–95.
Ellingsen, G. and E. Monteiro (2003b), 'Big is beautiful. Electronic Patient Records in Norway 1980–2000', *Methods of Information in Medicine*, **42**, 366–70.

Hughes, T.P. (1983), *Networks of Power: Electrification in Western Society, 1880–1930*, Baltimore, MD: Johns Hopkins University Press.

Jones, M.R. (2003), 'Computers can land people on Mars, why can't they get them to work in a hospital? Implementation of an Electronic Patient Record System in a UK Hospital', *Methods of Information in Medicine*, **42**, 410–15.

Law, J. (2003), 'Traduction/Trahison: Notes on ANT', Manuscript, www.comp.lancs.ac.uk/sociology/papers/law-traduction-trahison.pdf, (last accessed November 2004), November.

Law, J. and A. Mol (2002), *Complexities. Social Studies of Knowledge Practices*, Durham, NC and London: Duke University Press.

Mol, A. (2002), *The Body Multiple: Ontology in Medical Practice*, Durham, NC and London: Duke University Press.

Timmermans, S. and M. Berg (2003), *The Gold Standard: The Challenge of Evidence-Based Medicine and Standardization in Health Care*, Philadelphia, PA: Temple University Press.

7. From risk management to 'organized irresponsibility'? Risks and risk management in the mobile telecom sector

Jennifer Blechar and Ole Hanseth

1 INTRODUCTION

Telecommunications, particularly mobile telecommunications is a rapidly advancing area, presenting a constantly changing landscape for mobile telecommunications organizations. In order to remain competitive in such an environment, these organizations must stay abreast of technological advances including a constant revision of their product and service offerings. Such changes in the design and structure of products and services often require significant systems implementation efforts. These efforts, which can include major revisions in the underlying technological infrastructure, such as those required with the shift from GSM to the third generation of mobile systems, can present an extremely complex and inherently risky undertaking. While these organizations will naturally embrace various risk-control techniques, these efforts to control risk may not always succeed, and, in some cases, may indeed result in an increase in lack of control.

This chapter will present such a case, where Telco,[1] a leading mobile telecommunications operator, initiated a major systems implementation effort in attempt to remain the market leader in the dawn of 3G services. This effort consisted of a project aimed to upgrade Telco's billing system. Billing systems are major office systems often deeply integrated with other systems within the entire organizational infrastructure, thus making them extremely complex. For telecommunications organizations, billing systems are also key systems residing in the critical path from the design of new products and services to their deployment in the market. Failure in these systems can mean failure of specific products and services and in some cases, failure of the entire organization.[2]

For Telco, this project, referred to as ProjectBilling, was viewed as necessary in order to remain successful in the next phase of mobile telephony.

However, ProjectBilling was also faced with various risks stemming from a variety of sources, many of which emerged as side-effects of actions taken within the project. This project did not aim at integration in itself, but at a major change of a 'hub' in a very complex socio-technical system. This complex 'system' was the result of a long term growth and integration process covering rapid growth of customers, services, call plans, telecom-munication infrastructure, personnel, supporting information systems, and so on. At the same time, the overall 'system' was also changing rapidly in parallel with the efforts aiming at replacing the billing system. The risks involved, their growth and evolution within the project, including a discus-sion of the methods used by Telco to combat these risks, will be the focus of this chapter. Through the exploration of the billing system project in Telco, this case will illustrate the manner in which the complexity of the billing system was disclosed to the project members and how many of the risks faced by the project propagated through the network and emerged as side-effects or unintended consequences resulting from the very actions meant to control these risks.

2   METHODOLOGY

Data was collected for our case through two primary methods, namely through narratives and interviews, and included other secondary methods such as document analysis. Narratives are a method often applied in ethno-graphically inspired research (for example Ellis and Bochner, 2000) and consist of the researcher developing a descriptive 'story' or manuscript of the case after their involvement in it. In the case presented in this chapter, one of the authors was involved in the project discussed as a consultant from 2000 to 2002. After this time, a narrative was developed documenting the progression of the events in the case and the details involved. Development of this narrative involved a self-reflecting process whereby the researcher reviewed and consulted several personal notes, archived email transmissions, project presentations, meeting memos and other docu-ments to provide details of the case and inform the contents of the narra-tive. This narrative was written as descriptively as possible with limited or no analysis or interpretation of the events in the case other than the inher-ent processes of sense-making (Weick, 1995). Several themes were then elicited from the narrative, which were further pursued through interviews conducted with several other participants in the case. Interviews were all tape recorded and partially transcribed.

While the use of narratives and autoethnography in general is a debated topic, especially related to the 'accuracy' and validity of these types of methods (Holt, 2003; Walford, 2004), the use of this method in this chapter was as a basis to guide further research and thus other sources of data were used to confirm and further explore some of the topics identified through the narrative. In this sense, use of this method was extremely beneficial as it allowed us to identify concepts and themes that could otherwise have been difficult to recognize without full immersion in the case, offered by the authors' direct experiences.

3 TELCO'S HISTORY

We will now turn to introduce our case involving the telecommunications operator, Telco. Telco has its origin in a national telecommunication monopoly. Its mobile phone operations started in the 1970s and it was established as a separate organization in 1990 when the local government opened the mobile telephony market to competition by awarding two non-governmental organizations licences to the GSM mobile market. These two organizations, including Telco, were the sole providers of mobile telecommunications until approximately 1998, when the local telecommunications market was deregulated resulting in the introduction of several new service providers. In the beginning of the 1990s, when Telco and its competitor began to offer GSM services, a new network infrastructure had to be built. Thus, these two organizations battled to provide the most sound technical infrastructure to allow for GSM coverage. As the technical infrastructure became fairly solid, the competition between the two organizations shifted to providing mobile phone handsets. This eventually stabilized and the competition shifted to providing lower calling costs, which eventually stabilized resulting in the competitive shift to where we are today, which is focused on providing newer and improved mobile products and services.

In the case of Telco, as its competitive focus altered and evolved into the arena in which it is today, so too did its information infrastructure (that is its collection of Information Systems supporting the business). Specifically, this information infrastructure grew and was adapted both to the growth of the organization as well as the specific missions of the organization at various points in time. Included in this information infrastructure is the billing system, which was also growing and changing in unpredictable ways as the traffic increased, the underlying technology changed, and Telco itself altered its competitive focus. While each of the specific growth points experienced by Telco are of interest, the focus of this chapter is on the final organizational evolution to the goal of providing improved mobile products and services. Specifically, during the late 1990s, 2.5 and 3rd generation mobile systems were beginning to be planned, and with these came many new infrastructure requirements, not only in the technical requirements to enable these types of systems to be functional, but also in the functional requirements of the office systems needed to support the new products and services these types of systems would offer. Included in this was the billing system within Telco, which needed to be modified to be able to rate and bill calls (and other services) made from these new systems.

With 2nd generation products and services on the GSM network, calls by customers were generally rated and billed depending on the length of call, destination number and calling plan of the customer. However, with 2.5 and 3rd generation systems, calls also needed to be able to be rated and billed by content and amount of data transferred, not just call length and calling number. In addition, with these 3rd generation systems, organizations such as Telco were beginning to explore the concept of billing customers according to the value of the content accessed, not just the amount of data downloaded. So, for example, although accessing stock quote information would result in relatively small amounts of data accessed by the customer, the value to the customer for having this service may be higher than for example downloading a weather map, which although it would require large amounts of data to be accessed, may provide a relatively small value to the customer. This type of billing concept presented the challenge of determining the content actually accessed by the customer, not just measuring the amount of data downloaded. Thus, the entire foundation of the rating and billing structures needed to be revisited to provide more flexibility, allowing organizations such as Telco to explore new methods of billing customers based on the products and services anticipated to be available with these next generation telecommunications systems. For Telco, this meant that changes needed to be made in this infrastructure by the time these systems would technically become available, originally planned for January 2001.

4 PROJECTBILLING

In order to address the perceived changes in its information infrastructure needed to support the new mission of the firm in terms of growth, innovation and flexibility with 2.5 and 3rd generation mobile systems, Telco decided to initiate a project. This project, referred to here as ProjectBilling, began during 2000 and was given the goal of evaluating the current information infrastructure and implementing necessary changes to allow the infrastructure to be more flexible and thus more easily adapted to these newer types of products and services. The date set for the project completion was January 2001, when the technical infrastructure was to be readily available in the market. Thus, ProjectBilling was required to analyse and implement changes in Telco's billing system to allow the system to rate and bill calls using products and services on the new generation of mobile systems. This meant a substantial technical change in the manner in which calls were rated and billed.

During the beginning of the assignment, Telco staffed the project primarily with personnel from inside Telco, supplemented by a few consultants including those from a major consulting firm, ConsultCo, with which they had a long-standing relationship. The focus at the start of the project was to analyse the existing billing system and determine how the system could be modified to be more flexible to allow for the new types of rating and billing structures coming in the future. The decision was soon made that a new rating and billing system was needed to replace the old system, which up to that point had already had so many modifications due to the rapid organizational growth and the changes in the existing products and services as well as the number of new services introduced, that it was believed to be too complex, dispersed and expensive to support continued modifications. With the decision to implement a new billing system, the decision was also made to make use of a packaged application rather than to build a custom application. The search then began to analyse available package applications, and shortly thereafter, a contract was awarded to a packaged application called Billex made by Billex Corp., which was deemed to require the least modifications to suit the needs of Telco. Towards the end of 2000, Telco and ConsultCo project members were sent for training on Billex, and Billex Corp. consultants joined the ProjectBilling.

Billex Corp. and ConsultCo consultants worked together with Telco to determine which aspects of the packaged application to keep, which to discard and which to modify. However, it soon became clear that the release of the new billing system in Telco would not be delivered by January 2001 as had originally been planned and a new release date was set for March 2001. In addition, due to the project delay and other mitigating circumstances, the existing project manager was terminated from ProjectBilling and another external independent consultant was hired for the role. After some months of work, a disagreement emerged between the Billex Corp. consultants and Telco regarding the actual billing system requirements. Specifically, Billex Corp. argued that they were unable to work properly without having a detailed set of requirements from Telco on their new billing system. Yet Telco, at that point in time, was not able to actually document in detail what they needed the billing system to do, especially with regard to the functionality between Billex and the other office systems in Telco. Billex Corp. consultants were then terminated from ProjectBilling until the project could properly document the system requirements.

However, due to this unforeseen issue, the release date was again shifted into later in 2001.

Focus was then placed on determining the requirements for the new billing system. The new project manager hired several teams of consultants from a consulting firm with which he had past working relationships, and placed them in charge of defining the requirements of the new billing system. Throughout these changes in ProjectBilling from 2000 until approximately mid-2001, Telco itself also underwent significant organizational changes. Some of these were major, including restructuring of the entire organization into new business units. However, some of the changes were smaller scale in nature yet directly impacted ProjectBilling. One specific change that impacted ProjectBilling was that Telco no longer wished to be dependent on any one supplier of consulting services. This meant that ProjectBilling was to expand and no longer use personnel only from ConsultCo, but also other consulting firms. The initiative by the project manager to begin using consultants from his own consulting experiences was also influenced by this decision by Telco to expand their consulting relationships. The project then continued for a few months with consultants from ConsultCo, the new consulting firm, and Telco working to determine the system requirements.

The new consultants in charge of determining the system requirements used several different methods in an attempt to elicit and document the requirements; however, each of these attempts was met with resistance and uncertainty and eventually failed. In addition, the time the consultants estimated in order to document the requirements properly was much longer than the existing release schedule allowed. At that point in time, ProjectBilling underwent a significant change in organizational structure. The project up to that point had been organized in 'silos', where a team was placed responsible for each functional area. However, because of the difficulty in determining and documenting the requirements, as well as other perceived issues within the project such as the project delays, a matrix organizational structure was introduced. This structure, in addition to the functional teams on the x-axis had project teams on the y-axis. For example, functional teams such as products or billing had corresponding project teams such as analysis, design and testing. However, with this change in organizational structure, additional personnel were needed on the project. Following Telco's wishes regarding not being dependent on any one consulting firm, people were hired from several different consulting firms. One large team was hired from a firm that was a direct competitor to ConsultCo and other teams were hired from various local firms. The result for ProjectBilling was a team of over 100 personnel from more than six different firms.

The new organizational structure of ProjectBilling and the new personnel and teams brought onto the project meant Telco had to settle for a new
release date set for February 2002. The new ProjectBilling moved forward,
with typically one consulting firm responsible for a specific team. The
requirements effort which began in mid-2001 still had not completed,
however most teams had some list of requirements to begin working with
while the requirements effort continued. Throughout 2001, the complexity
of the existing and future billing system was beginning to be understood.
As the teams each worked as best as possible, the timeline slipped and the
scope of the release set for February 2002 was systematically reduced.
Ultimately, the February release went from being *the* release of the billing
system with a migration of all of Telco's customers to the new system, to
being a pilot release with the migration of only one customer (the project
manager) to the new system. In addition, the new billing system at that
point in time was still only attempting to recreate the existing billing system
and had not yet even concerned itself with the implementation of new
rating and billing structures, for which ProjectBilling was originally initiated. Due to the complexity of the existing information infrastructure, the
project also changed from having the intention of entirely replacing the
existing Telco billing system, to only supplementing the existing billing
system with Billex (a decision which was later recalled). This allowed the
existing system to continue to rate and bill customers with existing products and services, while Billex was to be used to rate and bill all new customers with new products and services.

As the February 2002 pilot release of one customer was becoming a
reality, the remainder of ProjectBilling was planned, with supplemental
releases scheduled throughout 2002 and a final release scheduled for
February 2003. The supplemental releases were intended to allow
ProjectBilling to update the original February 2002 release with additional
functionality as well as changes and errors identified through testing, which
was to occur throughout 2002. The final release scheduled for 2003 was
intended to be the last release and allow for the migration of all customers.
However, during 2002 market and external conditions changed and Telco
began to make internal organizational changes. These included a cost
cutting effort that resulted in the majority of the consultants from
ProjectBilling being terminated. Although one release had been completed
and one customer had been migrated, much work was still left to be completed on ProjectBilling, including most of the testing, correction of all
errors and changes identified, as well as the further development needed for
the final release scheduled for 2003. With the termination of the majority
of the consultants, some personnel were taken from within Telco to replace
the consultants, however the overall size of the project was drastically

reduced and progress slowed. ProjectBilling then continued for several months; however the one customer that was migrated to the new system in February 2002 was again migrated back to the original billing system due to the maintenance cost of running two different billing systems in parallel. In addition, the February 2003 release date was not met and the final release of ProjectBilling was not completed until April 2004.

5 THE PROPAGATION OF RISKS

During ProjectBilling, as with any other systems implementation project, there were of course many risks which developed and were managed within and by the project. However, in many of these instances, the very efforts to reduce the project's risks seemed to produce the opposite effect of generating new risks, which in turn resulted in additional efforts to control the risks, which again resulted in new risks, and so on. There are, of course, many elements involved in these processes, and important aspects of the processes may be highlighted drawing upon many perspectives and theoretical approaches: decision making under uncertainty, organizational politics, IS strategy, and software engineering methodologies, just to mention a few. We have, however, decided to focus on the complexity of the information system and its social and organizational context from which it cannot be separated. We do so because we believe such socio-technical complexity is indeed a key factor in the risks discussed in this case. Further, the (socio-technical) complexity of information systems is rapidly growing due to their expansion and integration, and, accordingly, so also are the implications of this complexity and the need for research into the issues it raises.

The complexity that ProjectBilling intervened in fits very well with the definition of complexity presented in the introduction chapter, that is seeing complexity as the combined result of the number of types of components linked together, the number of types of links between them and the speed of change. Taking the last of these first, speed of change, the speed of change was indeed a major source of the complexities in our case. Change was taking place in terms of a rapidly growing customer base. And as the customer base was growing, so too was its heterogeneity regarding the way the users used the phones and the kind of services they preferred. The telecom infrastructure was also rapidly growing in order to increase the area covered by mobile phone services and to allow for an increase in traffic. As more mobile phone operators were emerging around the world, roaming agreements were signed and the telecom infrastructures and billing systems were adapted to support this. New generations of mobile phone technologies were coming along (NMT 450, NMT 900, GSM 900, GSM 1800, GPRS,

UMTS, and so on) and their infrastructures were adding to the existing ones. New services and call plans were introduced, partly to get the benefits out of new generations of technologies, partly to be competitive regarding various user groups and their changing preferences or demands. Indeed this was the very reason for the introduction of ProjectBilling in the first place: it was viewed as a solution to the need for increased flexibility in the rating and billing infrastructure due to advances in the next generation of mobile technology. All this growth and change affected the billing system which accordingly was changing and growing at the same speed. And the expansion also required a vast range of other IT systems to support the operations of the organization, as well as an increase in the number of employees, all of which again added to the growth in complexity.

Some measures were taken to address this growing complexity and reduce some of the risks. For instance, for some tasks they hired consultants rather than recruit permanent staff, and the operations of some systems were outsourced. Among these were actually the billing system and the 'printing house' (the latter is responsible for printing and sending the bills to the customers). However, in the case of ProjectBilling, many of the actions and decisions meant to reduce the overall complexity interacted and triggered side-effects and unintended consequences, which again led to further actions and further side-effects, and so on (see Figure 7.1 for a chain of these events). Thus, many of the actions meant to control and reduce the risks in the project also contributed to their increase. We will now look at how the complexity of the billing system was disclosed to those involved by looking at the complexity of the requirements for the new billing system, the complexity of the information infrastructure of which the billing system was a vital and tightly integrated part, and the complexity of the organizational structure; side-effects that were triggered by interventions into these complexities and how they propagated; and finally issues of reflexivity, that is, how interventions aiming at reducing and managing the complexity actually increased it and how these interventions enforced the problems they were intended to solve.

5.1 The Complexity of the Requirements

With the start of ProjectBilling, Telco understood that at a general level the new system would need to allow for the rating and billing of 2.5 and 3G products and services, yet, because those products and services were still in the future and not yet developed, the exact requirements related to the rating and billing of those products were not yet known. In addition, it was clear that because the new system was intended to replace the old system, all functionalities currently handled by the old system would need to be

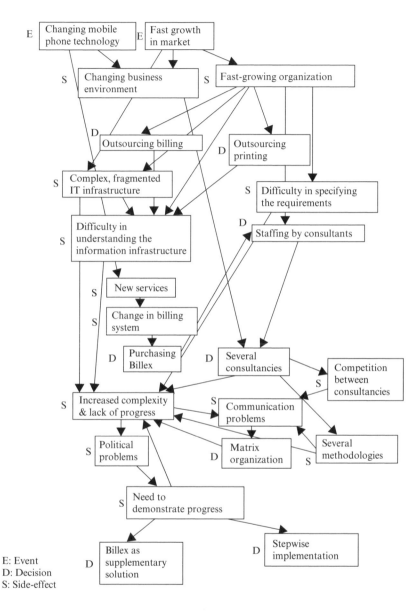

Figure 7.1   Events, decisions and side-effects

transferred to the new system. However, because the existing system had evolved for more than two decades with many patches, maintenance releases, and so on, and the organization was structured in such a way as to allow for various autonomous units and employees, the knowledge of the specific items handled by the existing billing system was extremely dispersed. Thus, no one group of people within Telco had a complete and clear view of the entire billing system. Instead, many different personnel had in-depth knowledge about very specific aspects of the billing system and surrounding applications.

All this contributed to a very vague set of requirements with general wording, for example, requirements such as 'The new system must rate and bill all existing products and services'. Specifics of how exactly current products and services were rated and billed and how the existing system processed those products and services, were not readily available as the personnel having the detailed knowledge of the various areas were not yet identified nor involved in the requirements process. In addition, because Telco had outsourced the existing billing system years earlier, information regarding the existing functionality became even more difficult to obtain. ProjectBilling then spent much time and effort in an attempt to identify and enrol the various expert users and specify the requirements. However, each effort to determine the requirements eventually failed.

This difficulty in determining and documenting the specific requirements for the new billing system had a very real impact on the implementation of the Billex package. In one sense, because there was no clear and complete understanding of the requirements at the onset of the project, Telco made the assumption that their billing-related requirements should be similar to other organizations' billing requirements, thus leading them to purchase a packaged solution with the hope that this could be quickly implemented within their environment. However, once ProjectBilling began, the reality was that the requirements were not very easy to document and now an entire project staffed with consultants waited, re-worked and searched for personnel with the needed knowledge as the requirements effort continued. As the difficulties of specifying the requirements emerged, more consultants were hired. This increased the complexity of the project, slowed the progress of ProjectBilling and eventually increased the political pressures forcing the project to demonstrate success.

5.2   The Complexity of the Information Infrastructure

The changes and growth in the market faced by Telco also contributed to an increasingly complex and fragmented information infrastructure (of which the billing system was one component). As Telco expanded, continuous fixes and tinkering with the infrastructure led to an infrastructure which supported the organization, but was very fragmented and extremely difficult to comprehend. Specifically, the information infrastructure within Telco was dispersed with many integrated applications. This meant that the existing billing system had many complex interfaces with other infrastructure components. For example, interfaces with Customer Service applications, Internet applications, and so on, the interfaces with accounting/financials and the interfaces with the printing house. These interfaces needed to be re-created with the new Billex package; however, as with the requirements, Telco did not have a clear and collected indication of the existing information infrastructure.

Just as the distribution of knowledge within Telco affected the requirements effort, it also affected the effort to understand and document the information infrastructure. Specifically, when ProjectBilling was unable to locate documentation regarding the existing systems, it turned to the various employees within the organization for this information. However, because the employees all had very specialized information regarding select technical areas, the project had difficulty identifying and enrolling the necessary personnel. In addition, as the printing house and existing billing system had been outsourced, ProjectBilling was faced with even more uncertainty regarding the existing systems. And just as in the case of the requirements specifications, as the difficulties of uncovering the interfaces to other systems emerged, more consultants were brought in, and with the same effects: the complexity of the project's organization increased and the progress of ProjectBilling was further slowed down, eventually contributing to increasing the political pressures experienced by the project.

5.3 The Complexity of the Organizational Structure

The growth in number of consultants involved also increased the complexity of the organizational structure of the project which again triggered more side-effects which had further repercussions on the overall complexity of the project and its performance. Initially a limited number of consultants from ConsultCo were hired to the project. When the complexity of the requirements started to emerge, the project leader hired some consultants from a company he had previously worked with. When the timeline continued to slip, the project leader decided to try to overcome the problems with the communication and schedule by implementing a matrix organization. This implied that more documents had to be produced and read and more meetings had to be held, which again implied that more personnel were required. Due to the decision by Telco to not be reliant on any one consulting firm, this led to consultants from various different firms being hired onto the project, and as even more consultants were brought in, the complexity increased.

With a project as large as ProjectBilling, which at many points in time exceeded 100 personnel, communication was naturally a real issue. Even if all personnel had been from the same firm, communication with that many actors would in itself have been difficult. However, adding the fact that many different consulting firms were used, each with their own method-ology and terminology, made just daily communication a challenge. In addition to this, the eventual project structure within ProjectBilling further escalated the communication issues in the project. As ProjectBilling changed from a one-dimensional organization to a matrix organization, each team was generally staffed with personnel from one consulting firm. This meant that each team began to work as an independent and isolated organization, creating an uncooperative and competitive environment. Thus, Telco's decision to expand their consulting relationships combined with the organizational structure of ProjectBilling resulted in a side-effect that further contributed to an increase in the cost and effort of the project.

For example, one consulting firm was placed in charge of the project team 'analysis', however, a different consulting firm was placed in charge of the functional team, 'billing'. Therefore, when the analysis team attempted to work and gather information from the billing team, a conflict arose. Providing information to the analysis team took time away from tasks the billing team was working on and helped the analysis team appear success-ful, both of which provided little reason for the billing team to support the efforts of the analysis team. Similar issues with the lack of sharing of information existed between most teams on the ProjectBilling and arose primarily because competing consulting firms were placed in leadership positions and were asked to work together. The end result was a project that lacked communication and had an overall competitive atmosphere, all of which negatively impacted the overall project.

Both the decisions to change the project structure to increase communi-cation as well as the decision to use consultants from several different con-sulting firms were based on very real issues and concerns. ProjectBilling did lack communication and the intent to change the organizational structure was a valid effort to remedy the situation, as was the decision by Telco to use consultants from different consulting firms in an attempt to avoid being reliant on any one consulting firm. However, each of these decisions had its own side-effects as well as combined ramifications, contributing to the overall turbulent and complex environment shaping the implementation of the new billing system. Because the development of IT in organizations is inherently political (Bloomfield and Danieli, 1995), and the political pressure to deliver results increased following repeated delays, adding competing consulting firms to the mix only escalated the already stormy environment. Crossing this with an organizational structure where each consulting firm was primarily responsible for one team, the outcome was a project that no longer had sight of the ultimate goal of replacing the old billing system with the new Billex package. Rather than focusing on what needed to be done collectively in order to implement Billex, teams instead focused on outdoing the competition. Thus, the decisions intended to increase communication and improve Telco's IT possibilities instead prolonged the implementation of Billex and increased the complexity of the overall effort.

6 RISK MANAGEMENT

It is evident from the above that ProjectBilling was faced with many risks. However, the project also used various risk management techniques such as the use of risk matrices and other risk documenting and reporting methods. These will be introduced in this section.

At the onset of the project, risk matrices were used. These were one of the most prevalent methods for documenting and reporting risks and consisted of a graphical listing and ranking of top risk factors categorized according to probability of occurring (on the y-axis) and possible impact if occurred (x-axis). Typically, these matrices were completed by the lead supervisor in each of the teams and were reported upwards to the project manager to be compiled into one risk matrix for the entire project. The matrices were updated on a regular basis at the request of project management and were meant to bring attention to the most important risks for each team. Risk matrices such as this were also a common approach used by some of the consulting firms when discussing the project internally within the consulting organization.

As the project progressed and the risks increased, several additional forms of documenting and reporting risks were used. Specifically, a risk table was included in all formal team deliverables. This table listed the risk, description, mitigation tactic, impact (high/low) and probability (high/low). This method of documentation closely resembled the risk matrices described above, although with potentially less visual impact as risks were displayed in a table format versus graph. By being included in each formal team deliverable, however, this assured that all teams were aware of the risks in all of the other teams as these deliverables required a formal sign-off by all lead supervisors in each team. In addition, a similar risk table was added to the weekly status reports delivered by each team to the project manager. The intent, as with the risk matrix, was to allow the project manager to consolidate and combine all team risks into one overall risk document for the project as well as to ensure that all lead members in the project were aware of the most important challenges facing each team.

Once the project approached the revised release date, a third approach for documenting and reporting risks was used, namely the listing and categorizing of risks according to the image of a traffic light. Green was used for risks which were under control or were being mitigated, yellow for risks which had the potential to develop out of control and red for risks which were not being controlled and could potentially impact the success of the release. This image was used by all teams and was reported in the weekly status reports as well as status meetings. These status meetings typically occurred weekly, however as the project approached the release date, status meetings were held more often, sometimes on a daily basis.

While the project did use several methods for reporting risks, the management of these risks did not seem to be handled as coherently. Namely, there were issues related to the sheer number of risks as well as the manner in which these risks were addressed by project management. Related to the number of risks, on a project the size of ProjectBilling, it could be argued that there simply were too many risks to be handled and thus that the project failed to address all risks properly. Therefore, while the project may have been successful in identifying and documenting the risks, it was perhaps less successful in actually mitigating and managing the risks identified. It could be argued, then, that the whole project should have been considered of too high a risk and that it should have been stopped. At that time, however, being able to provide (and bill) 3G services 'immediately' was considered crucial – otherwise one would run the risk of soon being out of the entire mobile phone business. Compared to this, continuing the project was considered a lesser risk.

As the project increased in size and competing consulting firms began to enter the same project meetings intended to discuss risks, another phenomenon occurred. Some consultants used the opportunity to essentially document risks in a manner in which to avoid being held responsible for potential future issues or failures. For example, risk items for teams responsible for development of various functional areas would include risks such as 'unclear requirements' with 'high probability' and 'high impact'. This essentially allowed the teams to state officially that the requirements were not complete, thus theoretically alleviating their responsibility if the system did not meet user needs, and so on. In addition, because of the severe competition between consulting firms on the project, many teams did not want necessarily to present their 'true' risks because of the concern that they might be replaced with a different consulting firm if their team was not reporting success.

These two issues of the transferring of the responsibility of risks and lack of reporting of all actual risks seemed also to impact project management in many instances. Namely, as the project became more complex and the number and scope of issues continued to increase, the project management in one sense needed to illustrate the ability to control the project and thus, although management was responsible for aggregating all risks reported in the various risk management documents, a detailed list of the actual risks did not necessarily exist nor get reported upwards. In addition, major risk items that were passed onwards from the project were often quite vague such as 'unclear requirements' or 'lack of support from the existing organization', making it difficult for these risks to be addressed.

It is evident that ProjectBilling faced many challenges related to the reporting and management of project risks. While the risk reporting at the onset of the project was fairly successful, as the number of consultants on the project increased along with the complexity and uncertainty in the project, several other issues began to surface. Namely, risks were not necessarily being reported accurately and those that were, were not necessarily reported further due to fear of illustrating failure. In addition, the project suffered from a consistent transferring of responsibility of risks from the teams to the project management and onwards. Much like the passing of a 'hot potato', no one on the project wanted to be left holding the risk items at the end of the day, and thus mitigation and resolution of the risks suffered.

7 CONCLUDING DISCUSSION

We have in this chapter described the complexity of the billing system – the 'hub' in a larger and more complex system – of a mobile telecom operator. The complexity of this system was substantial and the result of long and rapid growth, change and integration processes. The first, and perhaps most striking element in this story is that the telecom operator initially considered its billing system and the integration of it with the rest of the socio-technical system of the organization, as being rather simple, simple enough that it could be replaced with an off-the-shelf product within a few months. Reality was different and the project took four years. How could an organization underestimate its own complexity such as this? We cannot give bullet-proof answers to this question, but two of its elements are, first, the nature of complexity – we see only a small part of it – and second, 'myths-in-use' (Lyytinen and Robey, 1999) within both the IS and management fields that say by default everything is in principle simple and can be dealt with by traditional IS development and management approaches.

The complexity of the billing system was disclosed gradually as the project got further and further into it. And as project management's aware-ness of the complexity increased, measures were taken to address it. But the measures taken were largely unsuccessful. They addressed the problem and risks that were discovered, but as a side-effect, others emerged. When the complexities of the requirements and existing information infrastructure of which the billing system was an integrated part were discovered, more people were put on the project, without being able to specify the require-ments, and as a side-effect the complexity and communication problems increased within the project. When the awareness of the risk of being dependent on only one consultancy emerged, people from competing con-sultancies were hired, which as a side-effect increased the complexity of the project organization, introduced different methodologies and documenta-tion practices and a competition oriented atmosphere which again further increased the communication problems. A general pattern here is a reflexive process where awareness of increased complexity triggers actions to address the complexity, but the actions taken all contribute to increasing the complexity they were supposed to help overcome, that is increasing the problems rather then solving them.

The project applied what must be considered state-of-the-art risk man-agement strategies. But all proved to be of modest help. One reason for this was that the risks in themselves constituted an unmanageably complex system. The complexity of this system of risks was to a large extent gener-ated by the political character of the project as competing consultancies became involved and the project management felt pressurized as the project became more and more delayed.

The way risks were addressed in this case illustrates Ulrick Beck's (1999) catch-phrase characterizing the contrasts between first and second moder-nity as a change of focus from the distribution of goods (wealth, resources, and so on) to the distribution of 'bads' (that is, risks). The risks that were discovered were not controlled, they were just shuffled around: when project management tried to address them, for instance by adding more resources, hiring consultants from other companies, and so on, the risks were not resolved, they were just transformed. And when applying risk management methods, rather than addressing the risks directly, the actors just tried to direct the risks elsewhere. This again can be seen as an illus-tration of what Beck (1999, p. 6) calls 'organized irresponsibility'. He uses this concept when discussing the Asian financial crises in the late 1990s and the global financial markets. The global financial market has substantial effects on most of us; it is a complex system and its outcomes are the result of interactions among a huge number of actors, but no actor has any responsibility for the market's aggregated effects. Are the increased complexities of ICT solutions and the organization of the actors involved in developing and maintaining them about to reach a level where risks are related to the overall complexity in such a way that no actors may be able to address them properly, and accordingly cannot realistically be held accountable or responsible?

NOTES

1. All names of organizations and products in this chapter have been changed.
2. See Avison et al. (2003) for a case where the complexity of an Australian telecom operator's billing system and the organization's inability to modify it led to bankruptcy of the entire organization.

REFERENCES

Avison, D., D. Wilson and S. Hunt (2003), 'An IT failure and a company failure: a case study in telecommunications', in *Proceedings from the 8th AIM Conference*, 21–23 May, Grenoble, France.
Beck, U. (1999), *Risk Society: Towards Another Modernity*, London, UK: Routledge.
Bloomfield, B. and A. Danieli (1995), 'The role of management consultants in the development of information technology: the indissoluble nature of socio-political and technical skills', *Journal of Management Studies*, **32**, 23–46.
Ellis, C. and A. Bochner (2000), 'Autoethnography, personal narrative, reflexivity', in N.K. Denzin and Y.S. Lincoln (eds), *Handbook of Qualitative Research* (Second edn), Thousand Oaks: Sage.
Holt, N. (2003), 'Representation, legitimation, and autoethnography: an autoethnographic writing story', *International Journal of Qualitative Methods*, **2**(1).
Lyytinen, K. and D. Robey (1999), 'Learning failure in information systems development', *Information Systems Journal*, **9**, 85–101.
Walford, G. (2004), 'Finding the limits: autoethnography and being an Oxford University proctor', *Qualitative Research*, **4**(3), 403–17.
Weick, K.E. (1995), *Sensemaking in Organisations*, London: Sage Publications.

8. The duality of risk and the evolution of danger in global ICT integration

Daniel Osei-Joehene and Claudio Ciborra

1 INTRODUCTION

In this chapter we undertake an examination of the changing characteristics of risk and danger in the process of ICT integration within the context of global information infrastructure (II) development. Evidence is drawn from an ethnographic study of email infrastructure development in a large financial, multinational corporation. We adopt a framework of risk based on concepts and ideas presented in the theory chapters to reveal details behind the unfolding narrative of risk and danger in the process of ICT integration against the background of reflexive modernization. For the purpose of the current study, we also wish to focus on Luhmann's distinction between risk and danger:

> we will give the concept of risk another form with the help of the distinction of risk and danger. The distinction presupposes (thus differing from other distinctions) that uncertainty exists in relation to future loss. There are then two possibilities. The potential loss is either regarded as a consequence of the decision, that is to say, it is attributed to the decision. We then speak of risk to be more exact of the risk of decision. Or the possible loss is considered to have been caused externally, that is to say, it is attributed to the environment. In this case we speak of danger. (Luhmann, 1993: p. 21)

The findings from this research point to a widening discrepancy between the concept of risk that guides conventional managerial approaches and the reality of threatening dangers which they aim to address. Our analysis finds that despite radical changes in the characteristics of dangers through ICT integration, tools for the management of risk within this process remain firmly rooted in an outdated concept of risk. Hence, rather than managing risks, contemporary organizations are finding themselves engaged in the multiplication of risks through the naïve application of outdated and inappropriate tools to real threatening dangers. The case presented in this chapter shows how the adoption of a top-down managerial approach to the integration of ICT, as a process of reflexive modernization and a consequence of the risk society, leads to drift and the emergence of newer, more threatening dangers.

The next section presents the research strategy and ethnographic data gathering techniques adopted in the research. This leads us into the narrative of ICT integration, which forms the focus of this chapter. Analysis of the case is presented not only after this presentation of the case material, but also in the key areas of the case narrative. Here, we draw on sociological concepts of risk to illuminate the dynamic of risk and danger emerging for the case. In concluding we summarize the key findings from the study.

2   ETHNOGRAPHIC RESEARCH

Our primary research strategy can be described as an overt ethnographic study conducted over a three-year period between 1999 and 2002.[1] Before this period, a member of the research team worked for several years in the European IT infrastructure team of GCWB Financial Markets. The experience of the research during this period before we commenced the study was drawn upon as a valid source of information. Data collection techniques employed for this case fall within the domain of autoethnography (Holt, 2003). The bulk of research data was collected through participant observation in which the main criterion was to observe activities of the IT infrastructure development team within a multinational financial corporation. From these initial observations and the previous experience working in the company, we selected issues for further research through interview and direct observation wherever possible.

The technique of participant observation represented an effective approach for gathering evidence of danger within the IT infrastructure through the realization of risks. One of the main cases of danger discussed in this research occurred during one of our visits to the research site. We therefore had the privilege of observing at first hand, the implications and details of this failure on the IT infrastructure. During interviews with technicians involved in this case of danger, which we conducted several months after the failure, we sensed a tone of reluctance on the part of the technicians to discuss the details of this event. The responses that we received to fairly open-ended questions about this incidence of failure tended to appear in the form of explanations to justify the actions of technicians or the actions of their colleagues. This finding suggested to us that many more instances of dangers of the type reported in this research remain buried within the histories of organizations.

Interview techniques ranged between semi-structured and unstructured interviews held on the site of research. Interviews were conducted in the style of ethnographic interviews. Focus was placed on asking open questions in the initial stages of the interview, then focusing on specific issues following on from the interviewee's response. The technique of asking informants to comment on specific events during the research interview, as discussed by Whyte (1984), was found to be useful.

Data collection was mostly conducted in the London Office of the European division of the GCWB over several years of participant observation. Data was also gathered from the company's head office in North America, where more than 30 interviews were conducted with senior directors, middle managers and technicians within the IT infrastructure support team. In addition, the research team observed weekly conference calls, held between members of the IT infrastructure team based in offices in Singapore, London, Toronto and New York. These conference calls, which were mostly conducted on a weekly basis, were observed between August 2001 and January 2003.

Analysis of the research data began with an iterative process of reflection during the period of data collection. This was conducted in parallel with a review of the literature on risk and IT infrastructure development. Key issues were identified through discussions with senior members of the research team, some of whom visited the research site and participated in interviews.

3   CASE BACKGROUND

The Global Canadian Wiz Bank (GCWB) has been providing financial services for over 100 years. The Bank has over 42 000 employees distributed throughout its global offices. Most of these employees are based in North America where the bank remains one of the key players in the financial sector. The annual report (2001) identifies four key business lines that form GCWB: Electronic Commerce, Retails and Small Business Banking, Wealth Management, and GCWB Financial Markets. These business lines were characterized by an IT director based in the Toronto office: 'GCWB can be best described as a coalition of business units. This applies equally to the Financial Markets investment banking group as well as the other groups like the retail bank.'

3.1   GCWB Financial Markets

The IT infrastructures of three of the four key businesses are managed by outsourcing contracts. The exception is the GCWB Financial Markets group, which remains the focus of our research. GCWB Financial Markets (FM) is an investment banking corporation specializing in securities, brokerage and asset management services. The Financial Markets group was formed in the late 1980s under the name of GCWB Wood Gundy when GCWB acquired the investment trading business of Wood Gundy (a trading house founded by an English immigrant to Canada). In 1999 GCWB abandoned the Wood Gundy name and adopted the name of GCWB Financial Markets for its worldwide investment banking businesses. Over the past decade, the company has grown through a series of acquisitions.

About 13 000 of GCWB's total workforce work within the Financial Markets group, which has offices in over 63 cities in 14 countries, including all the major financial centres: New York, London, Tokyo, Toronto and Singapore. Most of the Financial Markets employees are based in North America, in either of the two central offices in New York (about 6000) and Toronto (about 3000). In the London office, where much of our research was conducted, the company has around 600 employees.

Financial Products (FP) trading division

One strategy used by GCWB to grow its business has been the establishment of new business groups. This process, which mostly reflects the state of the financial markets and whichever financial products happen to be in vogue, has had a major impact on the development of the IT infrastructure. One of the largest business groups established in Financial Markets was the Financial Products (FP) business unit. The FP division was created in the mid-1990s as a response to the boom in derivatives products. According to an IT Director in the Toronto office: 'FP was created by recruiting some senior traders from Lemon Brothers and some of the top people in derivatives in the industry. They were given a clean sheet and the authority to build a global business from scratch.'

Prior to the formation of FP, all the business units of Financial Markets were supported by one technology division called Global Technology (GT). As the title suggests, the Global Technology (GT) division was responsible for providing technology services throughout all Financial Markets business units unchallenged. Consequently, the entire IT infrastructure in all the global divisions is fully operated and owned by GT. Much of Financial Markets' services were structured around the Fixed Inform trading group. The IT infrastructure provided by the GT at the time was in a fairly basic form in investment banking terms, as explained here, by a former director in FP.

> [When FP was first set up] the existing IT support group [GT] here could absolutely no way support derivatives traders . . . Because the demands of fixed

income traders are a spreadsheet, Bloomberg and 'I'm happy' . . . Reboot their
PC three times a day and you know they're happy. But the complexity of what
they're trying to do in Financial Products [FP], you need development support,
you need applications to be built . . . for you cannot get off-the-shelf applications. Where as you can get away with a spreadsheet and a Bloomberg terminal
for fixed income, to trade and risk manage complex derivatives; you pretty much
need to grow your own software to do that . . . to give you the edge. . . . To risk
manage these products requires intense computer power . . .

The business managers of FP chose not to use the bank's standard of GT
for its IT services. Instead FP formed its own IT services group named FP
Tech. The strategy and structure of FP Tech was very different from the GT
division. Whereas FP Tech was closely aligned to the FP business users and
quick to respond to its needs, GT was more structured and slow in respond-
ing to the needs of its many business users in comparison. Hence the formation of FP Tech led to the creation of two very different IT departments
providing IT support within GCWB Financial Markets: GT, with a generic
services and ailing technologies; versus FP, offering customized solutions
on the latest technology platform.

3.2 Cost-cutting through Restructuring

In 1998, GCWB underwent one of the most extensive restructuring projects in its history. This project was driven by a new strategy within the
senior management team to reduce spending within the group and cut the
overall costs of the bank's operations. The root cause of this strategy was
the heavy financial losses incurred by the Financial Markets group as a
result of the 1998 Asian financial crisis. A senior executive of GCWB
described the immediate impact of this strategy on the company's earnings:
'GCWB earnings in 1999 were reduced by a restructuring charge that will
enable us to substantially reduce our cost base in the coming year.'

One of the projects to emerge from the original restructuring programme
was an effort to reorganize the structure of the Financial Markets group.
Previous to this reorganization project, the structure of GCWB Financial
Markets was decentralized. Business units within the group (such as Equity
Trading, Treasury, and Foreign Exchange) were all locally managed. The
effect of the reorganization project was to merge the local business units into
single globally accountable business groups. The bank reduced its trading
activities in both Europe and Asia to concentrate on the North American
markets. The former IT director explained the situation as follows:

Before the 1999 restructuring program the strategy of the bank was to build a
wide menu of financial services and products for our clients. As a result, a great

deal of autonomy was given to local business groups in the European offices to create new financial products. There was a big push into the European and Asian Markets at the time. After the restructuring program, GCWB pulled out of these markets to focus on the US and Canadian clients. . . . Within Europe itself our new strategy [in 2000] is to focus on servicing these clients. . . . Generally our aim now is to grow a North American Franchise with a global reach.

IT services integration

The impact that the reorganization had on the IT service departments was to assimilate them all into one department, under the structure of the Global Technology (GT) department. Rather than support various different systems the strategy changed to one global technology division with one standardized profile of technologies. The restructuring programme resulted in the initiation of several global projects aimed at centralizing the management of the organization's key IT infrastructure components. Amongst these were various outsourcing contracts to integrate the email infrastructure through an outsourcing contract.

3.3 History of Electronic Messaging at GCWB

Traditionally each business group within the bank was responsible for maintaining its own email systems. As GCWB grew and expanded, over time several diverse electronic mail systems emerged, which included Lotus CC:Mail, Lotus Notes, Office Vision (DISOSS), and Novell Group Wise. This decentralized approach resulted in major inconsistencies in email parameters (message retention, message size, mailbox size, and so on) across the various mail systems. At the turn of the century there were approximately 42 000 internal email users, 10 external gateways, 250 post offices, 100 internal gateways and multiple Internet access points with multiple DNS domains.

At the time of FP's initiation, email was not recognized as a business-critical system within GCWB. In the European division, GT had standardized around Lotus CC:Mail. Here again, FP chose a different email system to the CC:Mail standard supported by GT. The strategy behind this selection was explained by a former email administrator of FP:

> you've got to understand the time line of all of this, from day one it was CC:Mail throughout the whole bank. Now I don't remember exactly why we chose to go to HP Open Mail, but probably because . . . HP Open Mail is like a server end replacement and because it's running on a Unix platform it's much . . . much more reliable . . . because CC:Mail was never a client server architecture, for CC:Mail to work you had to have a drive mapped from the user's PC to the CC:Mail server. It was very unreliable . . .

Diverse email management practices

The management policy for the two email systems was also very different for the two departments. FP users had direct access to the email administrator for immediate recovery of any email issues. Most importantly, FP users had unlimited mailbox sizes. Some of the users' mailboxes grew to about 1Gb in size. This was a very important requirement for FP users who became heavy users of email. As a maintenance procedure the email administrator would send an email to FP users asking them to help maintain the upkeep of the system by regularly deleting unnecessary emails. Whenever this strategy proved ineffective, the mail administrator would generate a report identifying heavy email users, which he would then visit to help identify and remove unwanted emails.

On the other side of the fence, GT maintained a strict regime on email usage. Mailbox size for all GT users was set to 20MB for all users. Emails would be deleted automatically from users' mailboxes after a set period of time. GT users had no direct access to the email administrator and were required to go through a central help desk system. An interesting observation at the time is that both groups of technologists considered their practices and approach to email administration superior to the other. Although the email management practices of GT appear highly structured and rigid when compared to those of FP, this was not the case when compared with other areas of the bank. For instance, in the retail banking business, which was the largest business group in the company, with over 30 000 users based in North America, the email service was mostly based on old mainframe systems with very strict limitation on its usage.

3.4 Risks in Early Messaging Infrastructure

During this early period in the mid to late 1990s, the email infrastructure throughout the entire bank was considered unstable. Email users were constantly faced with the risk of technical breakdowns in the messaging infrastructure. These risks appeared in many forms with the common denominator that they were localized in both origin and impact. Hence the operational impacts of early dangers remained and were confined (in most part) to their special location of instigation.

Risk of mismanagement practices

Much of the dangers posed to the organization in the early email infrastructure can be attributed to poor management practices or professional misconduct on the part of the technical support personnel. In one case the email infrastructure manager in North America reported how she found the email system in a dishevelled state when she joined the organization.

This, she claimed was the outcome of poor systems management leading to a host of technical problems with the system. She explained this situation as follows:

> In the first three or four months when I was here so many problems . . . the backup was not running, the maintenance on the database was not running . . . It was totally not reliable . . . you could barely communicate with the bank [Retail banking]. So when the upgrade path came through I redesigned it with the people reporting to me.

Risk of virus attacks
Email systems managers have over the years become more and more concerned with systems failure through computer virus attacks. Due to the architecture of early messaging systems, emails would be downloaded from the server, and onto the client PC. As such, the problem of viruses were mostly confined to the individual user PC. Email viruses were therefore mostly a problem for users and their PC support technicians and not the email administrators, who would only be required to send out a message informing mail users of a new virus. These early viruses rarely posed any threat to the business operations within GCWB.

Risk of network failure
Another source of risk in the old messaging infrastructure was from the network infrastructure. However, such problems were seldom experienced in the cases we examined. This may have been due to the fact that email messages were very small in size. Moreover, most of the people in GCWB that needed to communicate electronically did so using electronic trading systems like Bloomberg, Reuters and Telerate. This does not mean that network problems did not occur, but rather, that they occurred very seldom, and their impact on email would be limited to the short time frame in which such problems were often resolved.

Risk of sabotage
Another form of risk to appear from our investigation was the risk of deliberate acts by technical staff, with the aim of causing damage to the operation of the email system. In one instance, the CC:Mail administrator in the European division after being made redundant took it upon himself to change some settings and passwords in the email system before leaving the premises. To overcome this problem, management recruited the technical services of Lotus (the manufacturer of CC:Mail) and a senior member of the North American CC:Mail team in the organization. This problem had minimal impact because the company was quick to identify it and respond. Direct impact was restricted to London because of the localized

architecture of the email systems. This decentralized loosely connected architecture was necessary because of limitations in bandwidth over the corporation's wide area network, a consequence of limitations in telecommunications technologies at the time.

Risks of mail transportation error

Also connected to risk of network failure is the risk of failure in the transportation of email messages. Such risk could result from any number of sources, ranging from problems with routing tables to problems with the messaging gateways as explained by the technical administrator of the OpenMail messaging system used in the European FP (Financial Products) division.

> The system [OpenMail] was rock solid. The only thing that ever went wrong was the mail gateway, which was based in Toronto, would go down. It was this 'crappy' old gateway that just kept on falling over, which meant there would be a backlog of email being sent over to CC:Mail.

Another important observation to note here is the casual acceptance of the problems with the gateway causing breakdowns in mail delivery and other technical problems with the email system. This can be attributed to the organization's partial dependence on email at the time. Because of the low status of email at the time, these breakdowns did not impact critically on business operations.

3.5   Consequence of Risks in Early Messaging Infrastructure

A key feature of the early email infrastructure was that the above identified errors occurred frequently. In each of the organization's main offices, there would always be a number of users with virus-infected emails on their PC, as explained by a former GT email administrator. Additionally, minor technical problems occurred regularly to the email mail servers in local regions. As described by a former CC:Mail administrator in the London office:

> Whenever the CC:Mail server went down (which happened often), all we did most of the time was reboot the machine. Sometimes you had to clear temporary files to make some space before rebooting, but it was never more than that.

Mostly all technical problems were addressed by the local IT support team. With the exception of the central mail gateway based in Toronto the threat of dangers within the email system was mostly confined to local email users in a particular region. For example, if the CC:Mail server in London (back in 1998) was to fail, the global impact would be that email users from other regions (such as New York, Singapore, Tokyo, Toronto and so on) could not send or receive emails from CC:Mail users in the London office. The impact of such a problem directly affected about 600 users in the London office using the GT CC:Mail system. Indirectly, however, all members of the organization (and those external to the organization) trying to communicate with users in London through email were also affected. However, because email was not such a business-critical service at the time, this impact was muted.

Risk localization

Following from this simple observation, a key nature of risks in the earlier (less integrated) email infrastructure is the localized feature of their impact. Furthermore, technical resolutions were in most cases localized within the regional IT support team. This was true in all examples of email failure in the early email infrastructure that we encountered, except in the case of sabotage. However, even in this exceptional case the damage was not global because it only affected the management of the London CC:Mail system. Its successful resolution required cooperation between the London and Toronto IT staff because of the lack of technical expertise within the London IT team for the Lotus CC:Mail system. This, however, should not be interpreted as a direct technical impact on the Toronto email infrastructure.

4   TOP-DOWN MANAGEMENT STRATEGY OF ICT INTEGRATION

As part of the 1998 restructuring project aimed at cutting costs, senior management took the decision to implement a strategy to integrate all GCWB disparate email systems into one coherent, global messaging infrastructure through an outsourcing contract. The aim of this integrated email strategy was to align the various decentralized email systems throughout GCWB into a standardized global email system with a central point of management and administration. The integrated email solution was intended to bring about many benefits, one of which was to fix the burgeoning cost of email services throughout the entire enterprise. This strategy would also help to reduce the many technical faults and administrative problems that were now common throughout much of the locally managed email systems. To achieve this objective of a globally integrated email infrastructure senior management recruited the services of an outsourcing company called Integra Consulting Associates (ICA). The following statement, by a senior IT director of the European division, points to the problem of redundancy as a key factor behind the new integrated email strategy.

> The outsourcing of our email system represents a crucial opportunity for us to
> resolve problems of duplication of efforts caused by the many email systems that
> we maintain. It helps us to bring costs under control. You'll be surprised, just
> how much it costs maintaining these different messaging systems.

In the first quarter of 2000, ICA (Integra Consulting Associates) presented
the bank's management team with a proposal to replace GCWB's email
infrastructure with a more reliable messaging service. In addition to basic
electronic mailing, the proposed messaging service would enable greater
collaboration between email users, which was achieved through the newly
released MS Exchange 5.5 integrated email solution. For GCWB the integrated MS Exchange solution was an important part of the proposed solution. 'The MS Exchange solution that ICA put forward presented an
opportunity to move the Bank's email infrastructure into a single manageable platform. This solution would provide, not just emailing functions, but
also file storage and information management . . .'

After winning the contract to manage all the bank's email services, ICA
proceeded with the development of the integrated global email infrastructure, as agreed with the bank's senior management team. In the following
narrative, we examine in detail the implementation of this strategy. The
story that follows illustrates the unfolding dynamics of risk and danger in
the integration of global ICT and the drifting of top-down strategy implementation, against the background of reflexive modernization.

4.1 FP Tech MS Exchange Solution, Y2k Bug and GT CC:Mail

In order to illustrate the dynamics of risk within this case, we must study
closely the actions of local actors in the email development. To do this, we
must first turn our attention to some of the local activities within the
European IT division prior to and during the implementation of the integrated messaging strategy.

Towards the end of 1998, the FP technology team within Europe had
made the decision to upgrade their now ailing HP OpenMail system. There
were several reasons behind this decision. First there was the concern over
the Year 2000 computer bug (Y2k) since the version of software used with
FP was no longer supported by the manufacturer. Another, less obvious,
motivation was the desire within the FP technology support team to gain
experience with the latest enterprise emailing solution. As we mentioned
earlier, the FP division was furnished with the latest computer technologies.
The members of FP Tech maintained the importance of working with
cutting edge technologies as a way to maintain their high value within the
IT job market. This requirement of working with the latest technologies
occupied a fairly high priority amongst the members of FP Tech, who often

mocked their counterparts in GT for working with older technologies. Consequently when the problems with the Y2k compatibility of OpenMail appeared, the London FP Tech team took this as an opportunity to upgrade to the latest advanced email solution.

The alternative option open to the London email development team was to integrate its email system into the GT email infrastructure by migrating its email users from their current OpenMail system to CC:Mail. However, this option would result in the transfer of control of their email system to GT. As explained by a former member of FP Tech, this was not an option which the London FP team wanted to consider.

> The GT standard of CC:Mail locks us into the structure of GT support. This would mean we would lose control locally because administration is controlled centrally from GT's headquarters in Toronto. They would determine the mailbox sizes and everything. Anytime we want to add a new FP user to the email system a request would have to be sent to Canada. With the OpenMail system, you have to do the administration locally, here. This is much better for our users because we can customise the properties of each mailbox on a user-by-user basis.

Therefore, rather than hand over control of the email system to GT, FP Tech took the decision to replace the OpenMail system with MS Exchange. This decision was taken in the first few months of 1999, after several weeks of testing MS Exchange.

The decision to migrate to MS Exchange in 1999 by FP Technology clashed head on with the organization's Year 2000 project (Y2k), which at the time remained the highest of the organization's operations priorities. The Year 2000 (Y2k) project team of the investment bank took the decision to standardize all email services around Lotus CC:Mail, which was Y2k compliant. The IT management team of FP put forward a proposal to replace OpenMail with MS Exchange early in 1999, which was rejected by senior management. This proposal coincided with the impact of the cost-cutting restructuring programme in the Financial Markets group. As a result of this restructuring the FP group was dissolved into the newly established globally aligned business units within the Financial Markets group. Technology services for all these new business units would be provided by the largest IT department within Financial Markets, which was the GT (Global Technology) division. Consequently, the FP Tech team was brought under the direct management of GT.

Once the FP Tech group was brought under their control, the senior management of GT from the Toronto head office insisted on the abandonment of efforts within FP Tech to migrate to MS Exchange from OpenMail. Instead, they insisted on the migration of all email users on the FP OpenMail to the GT CC:Mail system. By this time the MS Exchange solution that FP Tech staff had been testing had been developed into a small information sharing system supporting several of the FP users in the London office. Many of these users had Personal Information Managers (PIM) like the Psion and Palm personal organizers, which they used to maintain details of business contacts and diary entries. These pocket computers were designed to integrate fully with the MS Outlook desktop organizer, which was the email client for the MS Exchange system. With MS Outlook on their desktops users could synchronize the information held on their PIM with the MS Outlook and work with the information on their PCs.

Migration of FP email users to CC:Mail

Following the integration of FP Tech into GT and the subsequent decision by GT to migrate all FP email users from OpenMail to GT's CC:Mail, the FP technicians continued supporting their small MS Exchange service. Furthermore, following the amalgamation of FT Tech into GT, the members of FP Tech soon combined their efforts with their GT counterparts in the London office in order to continue the development of their MS Exchange email solution.

Although this small MS Exchange solution did not meet the exact specifications of the original FP MS Exchange proposal, it allowed the former members of FP Tech to maintain the high-level, customized email support for users of the OpenMail email system, whose email services they now supported on MS Exchange. As was the case with the OpenMail system, they maintained support for unlimited email accounts for the users now on MS Exchange. They continued to customize this system through a process of learning as they became aware of the many features of the system and the needs of their users.

4.2   Global Email Integration

After winning the contract, ICA proceeded with the planned strategy of email integration throughout GCWB. The integration project began with the rollout of MS Exchange to the retail banking and other non-investment trading divisions. The integration of email by ICA was conducted in two parts. The first part was the non-trading business groups. The deployment of MS Exchange within these areas was reported to have proceeded relatively smoothly. In this section we focus our attention on the project within the investment banking group, where much of our research was conducted.

Unlike the rollout of MS Exchange within the non-trading sector, ICA's efforts to bring the email infrastructure under their direct control proved far more difficult. By the time ICA won the contract to integrate email services throughout the entire bank, the restructuring project had already brought FP Tech under the structure of GT. In the London office of the European group, the email technicians had migrated users from the old FP OpenMail system over to the MS Exchange server. The technicians used a CC:Mail connector to link this small London MS Exchange server to the CC:Mail email infrastructure of GT within the Financial Markets business group. At the time ICA began the integration project within the investment trading group, the small London MS Exchange solution had been customized expensively to meet the needs of about 200 email users.

The project to integrate email services and manage them centrally by ICA was seen as a threat, not just by the local email support team, but also by other IT staff and business users, some of whom were receiving very customized email services. A member of the newly integrated technology team explained their reaction towards the ICA's proposal.

> The outsourcing contract with HP threatened a lot of jobs in the technology group. You must understand the structure of MS Exchange. It's not just a simple email application like CC:Mail or Openmail, it's more like an information management system that stores all data, very similar to Lotus Notes with features that integrate well with the internet. Although MS Exchange was being proposed as an email solution, we knew it could do more . . .

The first major problems encountered by ICA in taking control of email management within the Financial Markets group occurred when ICA submitted its proposal to the Financial Markets managers. The manager of the CC:Mail team in Toronto explained their reaction to this proposal.

> When ICA presented their proposal for mailbox standards to our senior managers it seemed like a good deal, but after we looked at the detail, it became clear that it would cost us a lot of money in the long term and we felt we could provide the same thing much cheaper in-house. I mean when we did the maths, the package was going to cost a lot more to give us the sort of service our users in Financial Markets needed.

Although ICA had been awarded the contract to manage the email infrastructure of all the business units in GCWB, they were unable to proceed with the integration of the Financial Markets email infrastructure because of the complaint of the Financial Markets technicians regarding the generic standardized email service which ICA was proposing.

One of the biggest stumbling blocks was ICA's agreed response times. Because the local IT support team in GT were situated on-site with business users the general response times which they could offer were much shorter than ICA, who proposed to provide technical support from their off-site data centre.

Other problems encountered by ICA concerned their proposed training plan. Because the majority of users in the Financial Markets group were not familiar with the MS Outlook email client at the time most of them required training. ICA proposed to provide these Financial Markets users with a self-training CD ROM package, a strategy that had proven successful with users in the retail bank. In this way the investment traders and other World Market users could develop their skills on the MS Outlook application. A former member of FP Tech and now of GT Europe contemplated the likely consequences of this training strategy within Financial Markets.

> Well you can imagine what would happen if you armed those traders (Financial Markets email users) with CDs. I could just see them playing Frisbee all day – just chucking the CDs across the trading floor at each other. It became obvious to us that ICA really didn't appreciate the nature of the trading environment. You really have to customise the service you provide to meet the needs of the users on a per user basis. Sure, you may find one or two users who would go for the CD method, but most of them just haven't got the time. They want someone from tech support to show them through every step of the way. Just look at how Bloomberg and Reuters do it. Whenever a new trader joins they send a personal trainer to sit with them and show them how to use the service. And this is the sort of thing we have to do whenever we want them to take on any new software.

Opposition from the internal IT team to ICA's integration efforts quickly developed throughout all the global divisions of Financial Markets. Realizing the problems with ICA's generic solution, members of the local email support team within GT organized themselves into a team consisting of key technicians from the main regional centres such as Toronto, New York, London and Singapore. Based on the work done by the MS Exchange support team in the European division, the team of global email technicians presented a counter proposal to that of ICA. The motivation behind this effort was described by a technician in London.

> We also knew that we had the skills locally within London to run this project [MS Exchange email integration] internally. ICA submitted a very generic proposal to install MS Exchange, which only included the most basic email features in Exchange. Most of the features that we had in our local set-up weren't even mentioned in their report. When we queried this, it became clear that the bank would face more charges in the future to have these features added on.

The team of local email technicians were able to use the Exchange email solution in the London office as a working example of how MS Exchange could be configured throughout Financial Markets. They were able to call on support from the email users on this small MS Exchange system based in the European division, who had been privileged to have a relatively customized email service.

Since the time MS Exchange was first installed in the London office by the former members of FP Tech, these technicians had gained extensive experience with the system, customizing it to meet the needs of their small user base. When confronted with this system, ICA refused to customize a proposed solution to match this London MS Exchange solution. A member of the ICA project team is said to have made the following comment, when presented with the local MS Exchange solution developed in London. 'Honestly, I don't think we could replicate this set-up if we wanted to. . . . It would take too much time and effort; it's just not worth it.'

After several months of delay, GCWB's senior management and ICA both accepted the proposal from the team of local email technicians in GT to manage the implementation and subsequent administration of MS Exchange within the Financial Markets business group. As in the case of the original proposed integrated global email solution, there would only be one MS Exchange email structure within GCWB. All previous email systems would be dissolved and accommodated under this one integrated email hierarchy. The compromise was that rather than one centralized management hierarchy for this integrated solution, the technology group in the World Market business unit would be allowed to manage its own set of MS Exchange servers within the integrated email hierarchy. This compromise meant that the goal of an integrated global email infrastructure serving all the different business groups of GCWB could be achieved, but not under the single, centralized management control of ICA, as originally envisaged. Instead, management of this compromised solution would be shared between ICA and the various email support teams across the global divisions of Financial Markets.

According to this compromise, control of the new email hierarchy would be maintained by ICA; however a sub-unit within the email structure would be controlled and maintained by the Financial Markets group on behalf of their users. Each of the regional divisions of Financial Markets would have their own sub-tree under the structure of the globally integrated MS Exchange structure.

Local customization within a global standard

Upon reaching the compromise, the team of local Financial Markets email technicians proceeded with the rollout of MS Exchange within their business units. The strategy they chose was to allow each region in Financial Markets to decide locally what standard they would use for mailbox sizes and other email administration procedures. This loosely organized email management standard followed the general practice of technology management between the regional divisions of Financial Markets. This strategy of open standards was necessary to allow the different regions the flexibility necessary to customize the integrated MS Exchange solution to meet the needs of local email users.

In the North American division of New York, with the largest portion of World Market users, the local team of technologists chose to set fixed mailbox sizes for users of the new MS Exchange email solution. This was consistent with their previous CC:Mail administration practices. The Asian offices (Singapore, Tokyo and Sydney) and the Canadian division of GT (in Toronto) followed a similar policy. This practice of fixed mailbox sizes was followed throughout most of the Financial Markets group as was originally proposed by ICA. This was possible because the local mail administrators had maintained similar strict limitations on the size of user mailboxes.

The exception was the European division of London, where there were two separate practices; the one of unlimited mailbox sizes inherited from the former FP email technicians, and fixed mailbox sizes maintained by GT to the majority of London users on CC:Mail. Rather than following the practices of the majority, the email technicians in London chose to extend the practice of unlimited mailbox sizes to all their 600 users.

The limitation on user mailbox sizes is a generally accepted email administration procedure. It serves as protection against inflation of the email *message store* (the aggregate of all user mail boxes on a mail server or post-office) beyond the limit of the maximum capacity of the email system. By setting a maximum limit for all mailboxes, the email administrator is assured that the email systems will not permit this limit to be breached. This procedure therefore protects against possible damage that may occur to the email systems in the event that (manufacturers' recommended) maximum size for total messages stored on the email server is breached.

The decision by the London technicians can be explained in many ways, but the most obvious to emerge from our analysis is that the working practices of the former FP technicians had been passed on to the GT email team following the restructuring project and the integration of FP Tech and GT. Prior to restructuring, only FP users on the HP Open Mail solution in the London division had unlimited storage capacity for the email service. When the FP division was dismantled, the CEO of FP in the European Financial Markets division was appointed as head of the entire European business group. As a former member of the FP division, the CEO of the European group was accustomed to unlimited size restrictions on email. In fact, this CEO was one of the heaviest users of email, possessing the largest mailbox in the London office. With this powerful actor supporting them, the former technicians of FP, who were firmly committed to customizing technology to meet the needs of their business users, became influential actors, not just within the European email infrastructure but also within the wider IT infrastructure of World Market. It was these technicians who had pioneered the initial local MS Exchange 5.5 system in the European division. These influential technicians insisted that, if the London email service was to be standardized, then it should be to the standard of the FP email service. The consequence of this was that unlimited mailbox sizes would be extended to every European email user on MS Exchange.

This requirement won the support of the European business users, many of whom had been frustrated by strict mailbox size restrictions imposed on the GT CC:Mail service. The London email support team were able to scale their unlimited email service from the current 200 former FP business users to encompass all the users within the European group because of the small user base, which remained less than 1000 in total. This was not the case for the Toronto and New York divisions of World Markets, each of which supported more than 3000 email users.

The first region of GT to deploy MS Exchange within the technical hierarchy of ICA proposed structure was the European division. They successfully completed the rollout within six weeks of initiation with a small team of four technicians. The successful completion of the London MS Exchange rollout was shortly followed by the rollout of MS Exchange throughout all other divisions of the Financial Markets business group. During the period of implementation there was close cooperation, not just between the regional IT support teams of Financial Markets, but also between the regional support teams and ICA.

4.3 Technology Drift: The Consequence of Top-down Strategy Implementation

The outcome of the implementation of the integrated email strategy following the deployment of MS Exchange in the Financial Markets group was a single, globally integrated MS Exchange email infrastructure. This tightly coupled email solution was organized as a globally structured hierarchy under the single technology architecture of MS Exchange. This outcome was in most part coherent with ICA's original proposal, with only one major exception. The exception was the World Market investment banking segment of global MS Exchange infrastructure. This portion of the integrated email infrastructure was technically integrated as part of the new global MS Exchange infrastructure. However, unlike other parts of this infrastructure, the Financial Markets portion was managed and administered, not centrally by ICA, as originally planned, but locally by the email technicians based in Financial Markets.

This deviation from the original strategy provides a useful demonstration of technology drift in that the actual outcome of technology implementation represents a shifting, or deviation, from the original strategy. This shifting away from planned objectives has been found to be a common feature in cases of top-down IS strategy implementation (Ciborra et al., 2000).

5   POST-INTEGRATION RISKS AND THE CONSEQUENCE OF DANGER

Following integration, various instances of danger have occurred within the global MS email service. In this section we focus on one significant narrative of danger that occurred within the email infrastructure since integration. We have singled this one particular case for attention for various reasons. First we believe it demonstrates the changing characteristics of risk and danger that occur though ICT integration. Secondly, the researcher was present within the main field of research during much of this event and was therefore privileged with firsthand observation of the event. Finally, by focusing on one case we are able to provide a richer, more detailed description of the event, which may allow for a more in-depth understanding of such events.

5.1   The London Easter Bank Holiday Email Disaster

The Easter bank holiday email disaster occurred in the London office, within the European division of Financial Markets, during the Easter bank holiday, almost one year after completion of the project to implement the integrated MS Exchange solution in London. Following a standard shutdown, the email server crashed, failing to start. The system was eventually recovered to normality after several days, resulting in major disruptions not only to the London email service but throughout the wider, globally integrated email infrastructure.

Every Easter bank holiday the building managers in the London office carry out a test on the power generator by turning off power to the building. During the bank holiday, all critical computer servers throughout the building are shut down at the beginning of the weekend and brought back up by the last day of the bank holiday. However, at the end of this bank holiday, the London email technicians were unable to start their main MS Exchange email server after several attempts. The server needed to be fully functional for any part of the London email service to work. Appreciating the seriousness of this fault, senior technicians in the London email team worked through the evening to resolve this problem without success.

By the next day, as business users arrived in the London office to commence work, one of the first tasks on their mind would have been to log onto the network to check their emails following the long weekend. However, they were prevented from doing so because the London email technicians, despite their overnight efforts, had not been able to recover the failed email server.

The atmosphere within the London office gradually became unusually tense as the response of the business users moved from one of general concern to anxiety and panic as they began to realize the full implication of the failed email server. A member of the email support team described the situation.

Well . . . I've never been in a situation where people have been using their Hotmail accounts. People that didn't appreciate the importance of email were basically dragged firmly into the 21st century . . . without a shadow of doubt! People [business users] where screaming. We set a temporary server up and we created new accounts for people temporarily, because there were certain people who couldn't do without it . . .

The unintended consequence of unlimited mailbox size

The email server failed to start up properly because of a fault with the information store database service that ran on the MS Exchange server computer. The information store database is used by the MS Exchange service to store email records. This database had grown to about 70Gb in size, which exceeded the manufacturer's recommended maximum size of around 35Gb. The manufacturer's documentation warned of unpredictable consequences, should the size of the information store grow beyond 50Gb. For the European email server, the consequences were that this database became too large for MS exchange application to read and manage, resulting in the subsequent email failure.

The large information store database size resulted from the practice of providing unlimited mailbox storage capacity to all email clients in the European division. A member of the London email team, who had been responsible for maintaining the GT CC:Mail system in the London office prior to integration, identified issues that he believed contributed to the bank holiday email disaster.

We [the local email team in London] had done the MS Exchange rollout incredibly cheaply. We used existing [CC:Mail] servers, we bought a bigger hard disk and some memory for it, and that was it. We had taken an existing box with absolute minimal spend, we got the Exchange system in London, and we weren't allowed to spend any money on it. So it had grown from being this 5½Gb system, and it had grown and grown and grown.

The other thing is, on the CC:Mail we used to run very strict maintenance, which is the other thing me and [the former FP Tech email technicians] still argue about . . . on Exchange we don't run it. [On] CC:Mail we used to have maintenance so that would run . . . if there was a message over 100k, it would delete it after five days . . . Any message in the entire system over 180 days was automatically deleted. Anything in the Inbox was deleted after 90 days . . . On Exchange we don't have anything. In London we have no restrictions: we have no restrictions on the size of the mail you can send and we have no restrictions on the size of the mail you can receive, even via the Internet. Although you can't send anything beyond 4m internally outside London, because of the mail restrictions [imposed by the email team in the other global regions GCWB Financial Markets]. The problem was that our system just grew [. . . until the Easter bank holiday when] we had the power down and the systems wouldn't come back up.

Negative global consequences of local disaster recovery

Returning to the incident of the email disaster, after diagnosing the cause of the problem, the local email technicians decided to undertake a set of steps that would at least guarantee the partial recovery of all email services. They decided to swap the failed email server with a back-up email server from their off-site business recovery centre (BRC). The email server at the BRC site was updated only three weeks before the bank holiday. Therefore all email service would be recovered, except for emails generated within three weeks prior to the crash. Once this temporary back-up solution was put in place, the local email team could then turn their attention to recovering the missing emails from the failed email server. This idea was supported by the ICA email administrators (based in Toronto) as the best option.

The manufacturer's recommendation was to wait for restoration of the information store database to be completed. However, because of the large size to which the information store had grown, there was no way to determine when this restore would be completed, and whether it would work properly once completed. The local email technicians decided instead to replace the failed server with the back-up server as a temporary solution.

They then transferred the back-up email server from the BRC site to the main office and proceeded to configure it in preparation for the switch with the failed server. To complete this procedure the local email technicians ran a software utility which configures the coded identification, and permissions for the new server to allow it to operate in the same way as the old email server. To run this utility, access was required to the entire global MS exchange directory structure. These permissions (in the form of usernames and passwords) were provided by the ICA consultants who have control over the entire global MS Exchange directory.

Until this stage of the recovery process the problems and activities of the London email technicians had been limited to the London site. However, the utility used by the London technicians to change the coded identification of the replacement server (in order that it matches the failed email server) affected the email configuration of other regions within the global MS Exchange hierarchy.

When the local email team ran the software utility it resulted in the replacement server being registered with the MS Exchange infrastructure as intended. This meant that email users in the London division could now use email. Globally, however, the consequence of this recovery procedure was less positive. This negative outcome was that the public folders service within the global MS Exchange infrastructure became corrupted. Next to the information store, the public folder component is the other data storage area within MS Exchange. The public folder facilitates group work and collaboration between users of MS Exchange and is shared throughout the entire email infrastructure. The head of the email support team in Toronto recalled this situation as follows:

> I can't recall exactly what the incident was but what happened was that, let's say for instance you are in Telephone Banking [which is one of GCWB's non-trading business groups in Canada] and you own a public folder called My Phones [. . . the software utility used to restore the email server] changed the ownership of that public folder to EU01 [the ID of the European email server]. So it's telling Telephone Banking, 'you have no rights to this, you can't get in this folder'. So [to get over this problem], you have to wait and let every message inside that folder replicate, and then change the permission on your side access to a public folder [EU01] to say 'hey, it's not my folder' and allow somebody else to take ownership. . . . And that's what the thing was that replication had to happen over the WAN . . . it had to go over, come back fully (and there are 8000 items) so that they could be reassigned. There was a utility I think that he [the London email administrator] ran, and he actually ran it on the full [global MS Exchange] database including the public folders and that's what changed the permissions.

The subsequent problem with the public folder resulted in the London email site owning all the public folders within the global MS Exchange hierarchy, which impacted on all other business organizations within GCWB now sharing the integrated global messaging platform. From an operational perspective, this situation posed major risk to the integrity of GCWB's global business operations. This situation required immediate resolution. A member of the London email team explained how they responded to this global disaster.

> Me and another email technician looked through a whole lot of TechNet papers and sussed out a way to re-home the [public] folders . . . By this time Guernsey had Exchange as well. We had been out to Guernsey and put Exchange in, and the problem affected them as well . . . And we tested it with them, and it went back perfectly and there were no errors. And the next day we had a conference

call with ICA and the [Financial Markets] Canada mail administrators and the New York mail administrators.

Side-effects of unintended consequences

Following the agreement between all the main global email support teams on the conference call, the London team proceeded to re-home all the public folders over which they had incorrectly taken control. However, this procedure also had a negative side-effect, which was to slow down the speed of message transmission throughout the global messaging infrastructure. This situation was explained by a member of the GT email team in Toronto.

> The [email] system was dying a slow death because it was replicating so much information and . . . It's basically snails pace message flow . . . It slowed down all of London and our communication to London, so when we were trying to get to London, to send messages, it was taking for ever.

Eventually, after methodically reassigning the correct permissions to the public folders and patiently waiting for replication to occur throughout all the sites in the global messaging infrastructure, the operation of the email system was settled. The final procedure in the resolution of the European email failure was the restoration of all emails created within three weeks before the server crashed. These emails were still held in the information store database of the server, based in the London office, which originally failed. After recovering this server, the London technicians imported the missing emails from the failed server and transferred them into the active Exchange server. One week after the bank holiday email crash, the MS Exchange email service was restored to full working order throughout all divisions of GCWB.

Review of London email management procedures

Immediately after recovering from the bank holiday email disaster, the team of email technicians in the London office began working on a solution to address the problem of the large information store.

Eventually, they decided on a product called the Exchange Archiving solution. This application, when configured on the MS Exchange server, compresses the size of email messages below their original size. This reduces the overall size of the information store database used by the MS Exchange server to store and retrieve email messages. A member of the European email team who researched and implemented this solution made the following comments on this work and the additional motivation behind the effort.

> Me and Jackie had to work very hard to put in the Exchange Archive Solution. Even the company we bought it from was surprised how fast we managed to roll

it out. We were working to about 10, 11pm every weekday for about two months. Then going home and logging in through terminal server at around 1 or 2am to check that everything was running ok, only to be back in the office at 10am the next day . . . The thing that kept us going is that we knew after the Easter crash, we couldn't risk another problem like that. As long as we had users on unlimited mailbox sizes, there was always a risk of that happening again. That is until we fully rolled out EAS to all our users, which cut down the size of the Exchange information store by more than half to just over 30Gb.

Using the Exchange archiving solution allowed the London email team to continue supporting unlimited mailbox sizes for all their users whilst maintaining the Exchange information store within Microsoft's recommended limit. In addition the London technology group undertook an extensive review of their business recovery procedures with the aim of protecting their local IT infrastructure against further risks.

6 LOOSE VS TIGHT COUPLING: OLD VS NEW EMAIL INFRASTRUCTURE

Normal Accident Theory (NAT) asserts that a system that is loosely coupled 'allows certain parts of the system to express themselves according to their own logic or interest. Tight coupling restricts this' (Perrow, 1984: p. 92). In both the old and the new email infrastructure, the team of local email technicians are free to determine the management and administrative procedures for the email system within their local region. Hence both systems can be identified as loosely coupled in some way. However, a key difference between these two systems exists in that the new email infrastructure is based on one single technology platform throughout. This is very different from the old email infrastructure, which was made up of multiple technologies. For example, in the London office, email users were mostly divided between the FP OpenMail system and the GT CC:Mail email system. Whilst the GT CC:Mail system was more hierarchically structured, the Open Mail system in FP was more decentralized. The different email technologies that formed the old email infrastructure were independent systems in that their operations were not in any way interdependent, unlike the new MS Exchange infrastructure. This meant that technicians responsible for the CC:Mail system did not have any direct access to, or influence over the administration of FP's OpenMail, or other email technologies within the CII. Connectivity between the different email solutions in the old email infrastructure was facilitated by mail gateways, which translated messages from one email technology for transmission over another.

In the new, integrated email infrastructure, based around MS Exchange, these gateways and the translation service they provide are not required because all the different email services in the different regions are organized around MS Exchange 5.5 as the sole email technology. In various ways, the old email infrastructure is more heterogeneous than the new integrated email infrastructure. Compared to this older email infrastructure, the new email infrastructure based on MS Exchange 5.5 is a far more tightly coupled system.

Other than the consolidation of the different email technologies into one technology architecture, the new email infrastructure can be seen as more integrated for other reasons, the most obvious of which being the hierarchical structure of the new global MS Exchange system. Here, not only have the different email technologies been replaced by a single platform, moreover, the email systems of the different regions have been organized into a single global MS Exchange hierarchy. In this hierarchy, the technology team of the outsourcing contractor occupies the highest position, with all the email sites (MS Exchange email services in each regional division) organized under it. A number of the regional divisions may have smaller sites under them in turn. Hence the highest position in this global MS Exchange email hierarchy is controlled by the outsourcing contractor.

7   EASTER BANK HOLIDAY EMAIL DISASTER: ANALYSIS

The concept of the system remains pertinent to any analysis using Normal Accident Theory (NAT). For the purpose of this analysis the globally integrated MS Exchange 5.5 email infrastructure represents the system as the highest, *fourth level* of the *system*. We may consider a group of (MS Exchange) email servers in a single regional office as a *subsystem*. The *second level* components of our system, referred to as the *parts*, include non-critical servers such as the back-up server, and the Information Store database held on the main email server. The client applications and hardware used by users to access the MS Exchange email service (such as the PC, and MS Outlook email client) represent the first, lowest level of this system, referred to as the *unit*. Having established the parameters and subcomponents that form the system for our analysis, we now turn our attention towards the characteristics of our system, in order to develop our analysis of danger in the email infrastructure. To do this, we draw on the concepts of complexity and coupling from NAT.

7.1   Initial Information Store Corruption

The bank holiday email disaster commenced with the corruption of the information store database file; this corruption prevented the London MS Exchange server from completing the initiation process, following the shutdown.

The escalation of the initial damage from the information store, at the second-level of the email system, into a third-level (subsystem) disaster, with the failure of the London Exchange server, can be attributed to tight coupling between the information store database and the email server computer.

The information store did not have to reside on the main London MS Exchange server. Due to the importance of the Information store database to the operation of the MS Exchange server, Microsoft even recommends the information store should be distributed between two or more MS Exchange servers. This recommendation was meant to facilitate fault tolerance in the event of a disaster. However, because the London division only possessed one MS Exchange server computer other than the back-up server, the entire information store database was held on this server.

During the first day of the bank holiday email disaster, the impact was confined to the London office because failure of the technical components and services were confined to the London email service. Other offices in the global Financial Markets business were affected in that they could not send or receive emails from users in London. Hence, with the exception of the London office, the global MS Exchange email service was fully operational in all other areas of the world.

The first major step that the London technicians took to try and resolve the fault was to try and recover the failed database file through the standard recovery process designed into the MS Exchange software. However, for a combination of reasons, including the capacity of the computer's random access memory (RAM), the processor speed, and the large size of the corrupted information store database, this recovery procedure progressed at a very slow rate. Consequently, the London technicians decided to abandon this process for the more controversial, but faster recovery procedure.

The complexity associated with these different recovery procedures, which translates to the entire MS Exchange email system, is illustrated by the uncertainty that accompanies their use. In the case of the former, standard recovery process, the technicians decided to abandon this procedure not only because of the slow rate of progress, but because Microsoft's technical support specialists, who were assisting the London email technicians to resolve the fault, could not determine how long this process would take to complete. The problem here was that within the customized context of the London CII, with its unique portfolio of interconnected technologies, it was not possible to predict the behaviour (and hence outcome) of the standard recovery procedure.

7.2   Disaster Escalation: The Public Folders Crisis

Similar to the standard information store recovery process, the alternative recovery procedure was to further reveal complexity in the integrated email service and consequences that the London technicians had failed to anticipate. These uncertainties, however, when played out in the disaster recovery process of the bank holiday email disaster, resulted in the escalation of the email disaster from the *third-level* subsystem of the London MS Exchange server, to the *fourth-level* of disaster, affecting the public folders service of the global MS Exchange email system. In their haste to address their local needs by resolving the corrupted information store database, the London email technicians did not consider fully the impact that their chosen strategy had on other divisions in the global email infrastructure.

The team of local technicians failed to anticipate the connection between the alternative DS/IS recovery process and the global public folders service on the MS Exchange infrastructure. The corruption of the public folders, following the activation of the DS/IS recovery process, further illustrates the complexity of interactions, and the consequence of tight coupling, brought about through the integration of ICT. As Perrow points out: 'in a large [complex] system some parts are so remote from each other that the chances of their interacting in unexpected ways can be disregarded [. . .] Complex interactions may be unintended ones, or intended, but unfamiliar ones' (Perrow, 1984: p. 76).

7.3   Disaster Escalation Over WAN

In addition to the corruption of the global public folders, other problems occurred in the email infrastructure as a result of the DS/IS recovery process. The most serious of these affected the corporation's Wide Area Network (WAN) used for transmitting data between the different global divisions of the organization. The speed of data transmission was reduced to the extent that email messages were being lost in the system. This problem was triggered by a dramatic increase in replication traffic throughout the global MS Exchange email infrastructure following the initiation of the alternative disaster recovery procedure.

Here, we argue that this replication service, amongst other things, produces tighter coupling in the new email infrastructure, which did not exist in the older, more loosely coupled corporate email infrastructure of

GCWB. This tightness of coupling resulted in the automatic generation of replication traffic throughout the global email infrastructure, which in turn caused problems in the transmission of email data over the corporation's wide area network.

7.4 Normal Accident of MS Exchange CII

Overall, the London bank holiday email disaster illustrates the occurrence of a danger in a subsystem and its escalation to a fourth-level danger affecting the entire system as a consequence of efforts to resolve the initial danger. In NAT terms, this disaster can be considered as a *normal accident* (or *system accident*). We attribute this *normal accident* to the complexity inherent in the MS Exchange email infrastructure. The level of complexity within this new email infrastructure is far greater than that of the complexity in the previous email infrastructure. Moreover, the loosely coupled configuration of the older email infrastructure served as protection against the proliferation of local dangers into global disasters, within the system of the CII and beyond.

The escalation of the initial danger from the London email system to the entire global email infrastructure, could not have occurred in the same manner within the older, less complex email infrastructure because of its loosely coupled design.

On the basis of this analysis we attribute this escalation of the initial local fault into a fourth level global disaster to the tightness in coupling which characterizes the new globally integrated MS Exchange email infrastructure as a complex system.

8 CONCLUSION

This chapter has presented the case of ICT integration through the development of a global email infrastructure. Using concepts from the theory chapter we have attempted to examine changes in the characteristics of risk and danger within this process of ICT integration. In concluding we will summarize the main findings from our analysis of this case. This finding is based on the distinction between risk and danger (Luhmann, 1993).

Conventional IS management strategies, which provide the ideological foundations for ICT integration and corporate II development projects, have been shown to be rooted in the techno-scientific concept of risk based on the probability calculus. Although suited to the risk management of organizations in the industrial epoch, the techno-scientific concept of risk and the management approaches it supports have been found to be unsuitable for risk management of advanced industrial processes such as the integration of ICT.

The case of email integration at GCWB demonstrates the adoption of a conventional IS management approach to the integration of ICT, an approach underpinned by a techno-scientific concept of risk. The case shows the unfolding of technology drift as an outcome of the implementation of top-down IS strategy within the context of a global risk society. Finally, the case showed the changing characteristics of danger from that of locally situated hazards into globally impacting normal accidents.

Another, less obvious finding from this case is that despite changes in the characteristics of dangers from the locally impacting dangers of the industrial age to globally impacting dangers, the notion of risk and the approach to risk management remains firmly rooted in the previous industrial era. Consequently, organizational managers are being presented with situations of danger which their outdated armoury of techno-scientific based concepts of risk serve only to multiply.

NOTE

1. The case presented in this chapter is derived from the PhD research of Daniel Osei-Joehene in the Information Systems Department of the London School of Economics and Political Science.

REFERENCES

Ciborra, C., K. Braa, A. Cordella, B. Dahlbom, A. Failla, O. Hanseth, V. Hepsø, J. Ljungberg, E. Monteiro and K.A. Simon (2000), *From Control to Drift. The Dynamics of Corporate Information Infrastructures*, Oxford: Oxford University Press.

Holt, N.L. (2003), 'Representation, legitimation, and autoethnography: An autoethnographic writing story', *International Journal of Qualitative Methods*, **2**(1), March, 1–22.

Luhmann, N. (1993), *The Sociology of Risk*, Berlin: de Gruyter.

Perrow, C. (1984), *Normal Accidents: Living with High Risk Technologies*, New York: Basic Books.

Whyte, W.F. (1984), *Learning from the Field*, California: Sage Publications.

9. When is an Intranet? The topsy-turvy[1] unfolding of a web-based information system

Claudio Ciborra

1 INTRODUCTION

This chapter is third in a series of reports on the unfolding of a web-based information system, today in the form of an Intranet, that taken together represent an exceptional, longitudinal case study spanning over almost 20 years in a major pharmaceutical (henceforth, pharma) company, Hoffmann-La Roche (in the following, simply Roche).[2] The pharmaceutical industry is becoming a network of joint ventures, alliances, partnerships, licensing and outsourcing arrangements. During the last 20 years, Roche has followed the industry trends, trying to become an efficient giant able to develop and deliver blockbuster drugs. It has so far avoided a megamerger that would dilute its identity; instead it has been active in alliances, acquisitions (in diagnostics and genomics), licensing, and tapping into R&D boutiques. Roche spends between 5 and 6 per cent of its turnover in ICT, and has one of the highest investment percentages in R&D activities in the pharma industry. In Roche, Intranets are being deployed across all the departments with the aim of sharing knowledge and encouraging collaboration. In general, web technologies allow documents to be stored, retrieved and published. The thus streamlined processes improve the efficiency and speed of web publication. Also, contents can be tagged for rapid search and retrieval, and better displayed on a variety of media, hence improvements from better documentation handling to effective knowledge management and to enhanced collaboration.

A long time span and wide access have to date characterized the empirical study of the deployment of a variety of information systems, many of those of an Intranet type or functionally equivalent, in a number of related functional areas within and across the boundaries of this knowledge-intensive multinational, specifically in its major division: pharmaceuticals. But if the reader expects that the empirical material collected through more than 60 interviews will provide enough evidence to support the current theories (or recipes) of web-based Intranet development, or to establish new ones, he or she is going to be deeply frustrated. Over the period considered, if this series of case studies shows anything, it is that the only theory is that there is no theory, at least within the ontologies in good currency in the information system discipline. Rather, one can discern a series of 'events', and a few 'big bangs' of a varying socio-technical nature, accompanied by scattered initiatives and innovations possessing different momenta, but each lacking so far an overall impact. These events seem to endorse Star and Ruhleder's (1996) suggestion that there are no genuine universals in the deployment of large-scale ICT platforms and give evidence to their paradoxical idea that the right question to put forward in studying infrastructures is not, what is an infrastructure in a particular context, or how has it been developed, but 'when is an infrastructure?' An infrastructure emerges *in situ* out of practices, activities and structures, and can be understood only in relation to these. And specifically, for the web-based information systems here considered, the 'when?' needs to be repeated several times, across many areas of practice and organizational context. Attending to and reporting on the unfolding of an Intranet in a complex business cannot result in anything other than a fragmented, kaleidoscopic picture of systems and use practices, impacts and side-effects, especially if one sticks to the current IS ontologies. In other words, and to address the puzzlement of the reader head on, first, stage theories envisioning an Intranet evolutionary path towards more structuring appear at best Danish fairy tales. Here, an Intranet-like proprietary network starts top down, centralized and structured, and fails. The subsequent switch to an Intranet made of hundreds of separate initiatives is sanctioned by the top. Attempts at structuring restart from some of the departmental initiatives as a reaction to the chaos started from the top. Indeed, chaos theory finds applications in limited, but momentous episodes. For example, there are situations where local initiatives seem to trigger system-wide consequences, like the adoption of a new standard. But these episodes dwell next to other instances where anarchy is established by decree.

Even ignoring, for the sake of simplicity, the business strategy re-orientations of Roche, its active policy of acquisitions, the micro-management of sourcing, joint venturing and limited alliances that obviously affect and put strains on the unfolding of the internal and external (web-based, or functionally equivalent) information systems, and just focusing on governance and standards, one cannot come up with a picture that makes any straightforward, unitary sense. Governance sometimes is centralized and keeps a close eye on the networks and applications development, sometimes intentionally castrates itself, sometimes exerts a weak, distant influence. A CIO role at times is there, but sometimes it is the top management of an entire functional area who takes over, and for some periods there is plainly nobody accountable in sight. After 20 years there is still no common portal for the entire Pharma Division, nor is there any Intranet tsar to date. Do not even dare to ask the question about role and steering impact of corporate IT. They always have been around, but the developments that are the object of this study have consistently and intentionally by-passed them. A more powerful actor has been, for sure, the infrastructure technical standards: at least in a couple of key episodes they seem to have triggered or occasioned some of the 'when?' of the infrastructure. To the influence of standards one should add the social dynamics of aligning, transcribing, but also tinkering and negotiating the infrastructure within the departments and functions. In this study the list of questions that should remain taboo (or that just sound plain silly) is long and varied: from the role of cost–benefit analysis up to the concerns for data security. These issues have always been present, discussed, negotiated, or sometimes addressed as a ritual of face saving, but the Intranet infrastructure has been substantially unfolding, evolving and diffusing, no matter what.

To be sure, such a case cannot represent the universe of Intranet experiences in the business world. Still its uniqueness defies most of the current theories of information systems development and the safe harbour of their consummate ontologies. In particular, if there is one theoretical contribution of this case, it is to unveil the 'zombie-like'[3] nature of current IS categories. On the one hand, these provide order and a simplified insight into complex ICT infrastructures, their design and development: in the Roche case they are valid, or (half) alive, usually for organizationally and temporally limited settings. On the other hand, other settings and instances disconfirm the very same theories, frameworks and categories, hence they appear to have little or no validity: they are half-dead.

Finally, it should not come as a surprise in the context of these developments (characterized even by industry experts as 'a tower of Babel', see Lerer and Piper, 2003, p. 193) that risks connected to ICT implementation are very diluted and dispersed. The Intranet initiatives going on simultaneously offer such a fragmented, tectonic platform, that the risk of failures, and side-effects, travel in all directions, and may affect all sorts of business processes and technical systems. However, at the same time they seem to have a short-lived span, and disappear as often as they emerge: the risk of making mistakes is multiplied; the actual hazards appear to be limited.

It is hard to provide a full description of such unfolding web-based information systems, their dynamics and risks. Only a series of probes in various directions can hope to capture the happening of the multiple 'when?' The empirical material for the chapter is somewhat arbitrarily organized as follows. First, there is a short review of the few leading theories about corporate Intranets. These are based on various case studies and provide a background on which to place the current case. Second, the previous episodes of the Intranet in Roche are briefly summarized, drawing from early publications. Next, what has been happening in 2000–2003 is discussed, focusing on the area of Pharma Development (PD) function. Different applications are followed up in areas such as decision-making, publishing, communication and knowledge management. What happens in other functions and in one affiliate is briefly mentioned in order to illustrate the coexistence of different styles of developing an Intranet. Focus is on current projects, initiatives, new developments, but also on their intrinsic risks and challenges. Somewhat frustrated concluding remarks follow.

2   CURRENT THEORIES ABOUT THE INTRANET

Taking a recent definition, an Intranet can be identified as 'a distributed hypermedia system within an organization that has the capability to enable people to access information, communicate with each other, collaborate in a geographically distributed manner, share knowledge, and learn from each other' (Jacko et al., 2003, p. 98). Intranets have at their core www technologies and protocols. Web browsers serve as the software to access, retrieve, share and display content, knowledge and information. After the initial spreading of Intranets in a variety of organizations, (circa mid-1990s) research and reflection have begun to characterize Intranets as web-based information systems, that is systems for which management need to deal, next to the purely technical ones, with issues of governance (planning and development), use, impacts on productivity and organizational forms, pattern of use, cost–benefit analysis, and, last but not least, interdependence with other parts of the corporate infrastructure (Isakowitz et al., 1998; Lai, 2001). Continuity and change seem to characterize the ways such issues are tackled when moving from traditional client server or mainframe information systems to the web-based ones. For sure, continuity inspires the concerns at the core of the management agenda on how to steer the new segment of the corporate infrastructure enabled by the TCP/IP protocol: integration, standardization, streamlining of content, cost–benefit evaluations, alignment with the business, re-engineering of the organization. On the other hand, the emerging empirical evidence testifies that the web information systems are rather recalcitrant to the extant portfolio of management initiatives. One can distinguish two different classes of interpretations of why this is the case. The first invokes a variety of evolutionary explanations. The second states that it is useless to expect Intranets to adhere to the management agenda. It is not a matter of reaching maturity: it is more likely that the IS management agenda simply does not apply to web-based systems. The two schools of thought illustrate the debate about the development and management of Intranets in the corporate context, debate that the present case study cannot eschew.

According to the evolutionary explanations, Intranets should be the object today of a well-planned integration effort (Carlson, 2000). If this does not seem to happen in most organizations, it may be the result of a lack of maturity in Intranet development and governance. This conclusion is reached on the basis of a limited number of case studies. Thus, for example, Duane and Finnegan (2000) have traced the evolution of Intranet adoption in the Irish unit of Hewlett Packard. They are able to identify six stages of growth, ranging from introduction, where applications are explored and diffused, up to institutional absorption, when the Intranet becomes part of the 'fabric' of the organization. It is a process of learning through which, once the maturity stage has been reached, the company is able to reduce costs, improve communication, and find new levels of integration and coordination of development of common applications.

In the same vein, Damsgaard and Scheepers (2000), though claiming that Intranet technology differs from traditional information systems and hence requires 'a fresh new approach' (p. 147), venture with a speculative paper, into applying one of the oldest conceptual tools in the IS field, Nolan's stage theory (1973), to the case of the Intranet and the interpretation of conflicting evidence coming from empirical business situations they looked at. Their approach aims to meet the recurrent need to find a normative theory for the management and use of computers in organizations, especially when dealing with confusing developments of the corporate ICT infrastructure. The authors look at Intranet implementation as going through four stages: initiation, contagion, control and integration, characterized by three 'existential crises' that require management intervention. The latter are: how to get the resources for Intranet diffusion; how to achieve a critical mass of content and users for effective 'contagion'; how to implement the planning, procedures and structures needed for the Intranet to stay up-to-date and useful. Each of the crises, if not addressed adequately, may determine the failure of the Intranet. The evolutionary model is supposed to offer guidelines to address the relevant managerial challenges at each stage. Contagion and control stages are seen as unstable, intermediate stages. The theory predicts that Intranets cannot remain indefinitely in these stages: they will either progress or implode.

In a parallel study with colleagues, the same authors have a more open-ended view of web-based information systems (Bansler et al., 2000). They contrast two different styles of Intranet deployment, listing their pros and cons. One style, found in an international toy manufacturer, is characterized by top-down development, consistency and streamlining of content and looks; carefully designed governance structure (including the definition of organizational roles such as web coordinator, developers and content providers in each business unit) and 'planned change'. The approach is accompanied by a relative scarcity of content: what emerges is a sort of traditional, top-down information system. The other (found in a pharma company, hence of closer relevance here) is chaotic, 'improvisational' and basically unmanaged. Contentwise that Intranet is much richer, but tends to grow out of control, with a lot of outdated information and broken links. Reflecting upon the two cases, the authors put forward the suspicion that there may not be any dominant optimal design strategy for Intranet implementation.

This is very much the core idea of the second school of thought, represented by the empirical studies and new theories submitted by Lamb and Kling (2003), and Lamb and Davidson (2005). The authors' intent is to get at what is really new with Intranets, and more in general with web-based information services, actively confronting the need to try out alternative theoretical frameworks. By looking at about 60 firms located in the Midwest of the US, Lamb concludes that in a typical corporation there is no such thing as 'the' Intranet. 'Instead there are many loosely connected "intranet islands" that offer opportunities for integration across organizational boundaries where integration must be flexibly negotiated' (Lamb, 2003, p. 9). Models that want to address the complexity of organizational integration opportunities and challenges faced by an Intranet should avoid the bias that a single, integrated information system does or should exist. There are continuities with the past: Lamb and Davidson (2005) suggest that the Intranet phenomenon follows the same track of End User Computing (EUC) in the 1980s, and hence one can learn by analogy from the trajectory of institutionalization of EUC. But relevant differences ought not to be swept away: there is now a common network standard, where before there were isolated PCs; there are many computer-savvy end-users where before there were only few; internal IS departments play a limited role, whereas before they were the main promoters of EUC. A truly fresh approach should be able to host notions such as pluralism of Intranets, negotiated integration, and arrangements that are multiple and changeable. Integration opportunities, if and when they present themselves, turn out to be distinctively different from those valid for traditional information systems: they do not rely on structure or encompassing transactions of a supply chain type. Instead, they are negotiated and largely project-based. Lamb (2003, p. 29) advises: 'take pre-integration intranet boundaries more seriously. The boundaries of grass-roots intranets, in particular, can provide important clues about how and what to integrate.'

Here the normative management agenda and guidelines, instead of pointing to a unilateral evolution towards growing integration, standardization and control, feature different action items, such as the unpacking of integrated systems, reverse integration or possibly disintegration, fostering autonomy, and design for ready deconstruction. These items are particularly relevant when Intranets are involved at the boundaries in complex, and temporary, interorganizational arrangements (see also the case study presented in this chapter). One needs also to consider in a critical manner the various attempts at integration that may create the illusion of stage development, from chaos to unity. Often what starts out as an archipelago of Intranet islands does not become an integrated platform for knowledge management just because the pages have a standard format and portals guarantee predictable navigation (Lamb, 2003, p. 12). What matters is instead how the Intranet gets appropriated by the local practices, becomes part of the organization identity, and how integration can emerge out of the project interactions and negotiations between the different unit identities. In other words, precisely because Intranets penetrate and are intertwined with activities and practices throughout the organization, trying to address issues of Intranet governance by relying on the elements of the formal organization (roles, departments, hierarchy), or on abstractions such as business processes, is bound to fail. What gets overlooked are the practices, the informal communities, the de facto project arrangements that actually use the Intranet *in situ*. Hence the attempt by Lamb and Kling (2003) to introduce new categories of agency, such as the notion of 'social actor', borrowed from Touraine (2000). While the literature that wants to understand the phenomenon of Intranet applying the same categories of the MIS, talks about roles like champions, sponsors and technology agents (Scheepers, 1999), the social actor construct aims at capturing the multiple influences that the institutional context (such as the regulatory environment or the industry) has on the shaping of the Intranet even from outside the company walls; the affiliations users have within formal and informal networks of practice; the interactions in which they are embedded, both prescribed and informal; their identities as they unfold interacting with the technology. In the same way that technology is no longer a tool, but an environment (Lamb, 2003, p. 14), or an 'enframing' Gestell (Heidegger, 1993 [1977]; Ciborra and Hanseth, 1998), there needs to be a notion of agency that is as diffuse, open-ended, and with an identity very much dependent on its practice with the technology (or 'islands of practice' as defined by Lamb and Davidson (2005)). The present case study broadly supports the second school of thought, providing further empirical evidence.

3   NETWORKED INFRASTRUCTURES: PREVIOUS EPISODES AT ROCHE

3.1   A Precursor: MedNet

According to industry observers, pharmaceuticals, despite being heavy users of digital technologies, have been relatively slow to embrace the Internet, since they did not perceive it as a threat if they were not to be in the e-business, and remained cautious and conservative in trying it out as a factor of competitive advantage (Lerer and Piper, 2003). However, net-worked information services began at Roche, at least in spirit, even before the Web entered the pharmaceutical world in a significant manner. In the mid-1980s a newly created function, the one of Strategic Marketing, for-mulated the vision of a corporate network supporting a variety of global services for marketing: it was an Intranet-like environment, before the Intranet technology was available. The corporate network built to imple-ment that vision was called MedNet. Its demise, which occurred eight years later, was caused largely by the Internet protocol and the failure in attract-ing a critical mass of users, especially in the affiliates.

MedNet was thought of as a strategic information system enabling mar-keting information to be shared from the headquarters to the affiliates throughout the world (Ciborra, 1996). Subsequently, information was to be funnelled to medical advisers and sales reps, ideally reaching the physicians and their patients, the final customers. MedNet was also supposed to invest other functions in pharma, for example development, by providing a plan-ning instrument for clinical trials and a publication outlet for their results. Medical marketing would be able to identify key trials, simplify clinical pro-tocol work, select trials for medical symposia and integrate them directly into marketing programmes. Other functionalities provided by MedNet included literature retrieval, product information publication, handling of drug safety data and an integrated office application environment. MedNet was piloted during 1987–90, and launched during 1991–93. At the end of that period there were 600 registered users in 34 countries. Heavy internal marketing campaigns to spread the use of MedNet, coupled with various trials and letting the organizational units such as the affiliates pay for its services, failed to attract a critical mass of active users. Around 1997 MedNet (in the meantime nicknamed MedNot (used)) was discontinued by Strategic Marketing.

MedNet constituted an *ante litteram* 'Internet plus Office' environment, built at very high cost before the Internet protocol and the Windows office environment were available on PCs. It was a revolutionary infrastructure for Roche in many respects. First, it had a distributed architecture, which was at odds with the pre-existing mainframe-based systems. It was a user-driven development, led by Strategic Marketing rather than corporate IT services. It was conceived as a strategic infrastructure aligning a business vision (defined in 1992) of a more centralized and global marketing with a network technology. On the other hand, MedNet suffered a series of drawbacks. Its being too avant-garde, user sponsored (and staying outside corporate IT services) led to the development of a proprietary environment that soon was out of sync. with the emerging de facto standards of Office Windows and TCP/IP. The very high costs of a proprietary solution were not matched by an adequate number of users willing to pay for its services. Unexpectedly, also, affiliates showed strong resistance to the penetration of MedNet, perceived as 'yet another application' coming from the headquarters in Basel. Technical problems plagued its use: connections were often slow and unreliable at the periphery. Marketing managers avoided using it, delegating its use to medical data library assistants. Design was also affected by the typical problems of an IT-led effort: cursory needs analysis, training that was too technical, too much effort required to fix local computing and networking environments to make them MedNet ready. All this slowed down the diffusion of MedNet dramatically, right at the time when local and central departments and affiliates were appreciating the new MS Office applications and Internet was knocking at the doors via its creeping use by the scientific personnel throughout Roche.

3.2 An Internet/Intranet Revolution in Strategic Marketing

Strategic Marketing can intervene to influence the local marketing activities of the affiliate by providing the background knowledge for carrying out marketing in each country, including training materials, information from clinical tests, prescription strategies, drug safety data and so on. MedNet was the paramount tool to push such knowledge 'templates', that could be adapted, modified or enriched locally. Though revolutionary in its conception and development, MedNet still carried the stigma of a headquarters-based vision, a centralizing bureaucracy wanting to harness the IT infrastructure to standardize local organizations and control them. All this was resented by the affiliates. Very high costs and competing emerging infrastructures obliged top management to discontinue MedNet in 1997–98. The void was filled naturally by the Internet and its new formative context (Ciborra, 2000): decentralization, autonomy and loose coupling. Putting aside the previous top-down alignment strategy, top management adopted the no plan/no strategy approach. Just let the thousand flowers bloom. This led to the blossoming of a variety of initiatives, mostly articulated through the Therapeutic Units (TU) within the Strategic

Marketing function. Each unit could now develop its own website for its main products, choosing the look and feel, the degree of interactivity, the contents, the access and especially the supplier (usually an outside agency, since the TU lacked the development personnel needed to set up and manage a website). Thus the Intranet emerged (next to the Roche Internet) as an internal tool for downloading presentations, reading hot internal news, accessing training materials, and, why not, sharing party pictures at office unit level. Increasingly, a vast amount of preformatted knowledge or loose information began to accumulate and be accessible on the Intranet. Developments were chaotic. There were no standards in look and feel except the logo on the right-hand corner (but whether or not the logo is active (hides a link to . . .), depends on local, improvisational design choices!). There were duplications: for example, affiliates could develop their own sites on the same product but adapted to local circumstances and language. The richness of a site and the pattern of access and interactivity vary, but seem to depend upon the knowledge intensity and complexity of the drug (Ciborra, 2000). Data security could be enforced only *ex post*. With no preventive 'censorship', often sensitive content might end up on the web by mistake; once someone noticed it, the content was pulled back or stored in a secure way. Also, the fact that it was, and still is, outside advertising agencies that create and manage the websites, may put at risk the handling of sensitive information. The number of users has increased dramatically, but actual use depends upon the local circumstances. For example, in an affiliate this can depend upon the support role of the local IT department, the presence of local champions, the users' level of competency, and so on. The resulting picture is of a relatively fragmented organization and development, with hugely varying levels of adoption in the affiliates. At headquarters level the adoption of TCP/IP and the release of control has spurred local development, increased the number of users, and decreased costs. There is no need for internal marketing for the network: diffusion happens by imitation and by putting hot (uncensored!) content on the net. The process that has replaced the enforced, top-down alignment is thus centrifugal and self-reinforcing, but lacks coherence.

4 ROCHE INTRANET TODAY (2003): A SELECTION OF DEVELOPMENTS

4.1 Organization and Intranet since 2000

In 2003 Roche has about 70 000 employees worldwide and sales of about 30 billion Swiss francs (15 per cent more than the previous year), while profitability of the core business has grown to 20 per cent. It has had major approvals for and launched a number of new drugs for AIDS (Fuzeon) and in the oncology and osteoporosis (Boniva) areas, and is consolidating its collaboration with the fully owned Chugai in Japan; developing a SARS test; and identifying new risk factors for osteoporosis with deCODE Genetics. Research and development investments have increased 27 per cent reaching 2.2 billion Swiss francs in the first half of the year. The overall economics of healthcare is pushing the industry (and Roche) to improve service and especially cut costs (Lerer and Piper, 2003). The ICT infrastructure presents itself as a varied and ramified platform. It is embedded in all activities, locations, processes and organizational units. This is typical of a knowledge-intensive company, where expenditures in ICT have reached almost 6 per cent of annual sales, slightly above the industry average. Data held in systems grows each year at a rate of 30–40 per cent. The growth of network capacity requirements currently reaches 80 per cent per year.

In the period considered in this study two strategic trends characterize the ICT milieu at large. The first is the recent business policy of 'managing for value' that focuses the company activities along the whole supply chain to manage every activity so as to maximize value. This implies, among various forms of local restructuring, a host of decisions related to the outsourcing or insourcing of certain activities, establishing alliances, mergers and joint ventures, engaging in various forms of licensing and collaborations. These forms of new governance at the boundaries of the various segments of the supply chain aimed at maximizing value indicate that the old model of unified internal governance of the whole chain is gone for good. Focus is on where Roche can add value and how to re-organize in order to get the value. In general, this means that ICT needs to be more flexible, that is to be able to reach out to new activities, but also to dispose of others, and to be more open to outside environments while retaining the concerns for security and confidentiality typical of a pharma company. These new and often conflicting requirements might actually increase, rather than decrease, the risks of fragmentation of the infrastructure broadly considered. The second trend characterizes the ICT infrastructure itself and it is influenced by the other side of the business policy: reducing costs of ICT operations, possibly decreasing the overall ICT budget so that it attains 5 per cent of sales. Here the focus is on making information even more pervasive throughout the supply chain, with a more mature ('grown up') infrastructure and services, with a special emphasis on information and knowledge management (KM). Alas, benefits in these areas remain vague, hard to assess and difficult to manage. Who can assess information? Who owns knowledge? These turn out to be difficult questions especially when the boundaries of the company are more porous and dynamic, and segments of the supply chain change ownership frequently. Risks in the governance of intangible assets are bound to increase: the infrastructure contributes both to their becoming more severe and to offering possible solutions.

Today, the Intranet within Roche penetrates all the major areas such as Development, Research, or Discovery, Global Informatics, Sales & Marketing, Strategic Marketing, Human Resources. There are about 500 websites. In 2001 there has been a call for action in Global Informatics (or PG) that has led to the hiring of a CIO, who now sits on the management board of Pharma with the task of reshaping the whole informatics organization and strategy. Within PG there are two main subfunctions, IT infrastructures (ISO) and Information Management (IM). The latter is split by functional specializations, such as Research, Lifecycle and Licensing, and Affiliates. Within Lifecycle and Licensing there is a further split of the IM subfunction into Pharma Business (PB), Pharma Development (PD), and Pharma Licensing. Each one with a different number of users, the largest being PD.

The Roche Intranet possesses at least three main dimensions. First, by function (Research, Development, Marketing). Here the main purpose of the Intranet is to publish information belonging to the respective functional area. Second, by project team. Project teams are mostly cross-functional. Here the Intranet supports project management tools and is a repository for information belonging to a team. Typically, some so-called life cycle teams use the Intranet as work environments (see below); they share content through a specific KM tool, Shareweb, for the Intranet and Extranet. Finally, there is a site dimension: a plant or an affiliate can have a site where it publishes news for the local employees. Ideally, all these dimensions should work together and be mutually supportive. In general, there are duplications, redundancies and broken links: in some areas the growth of disk space utilization reaches 20–30 per cent a year. This is creating an urge to govern content and interface design.

What follows constitutes a series of probes into the rich and varied world of the Intranet in Roche, taking into account mainly the Development function, and in much less detail Sales & Marketing, Strategic Marketing and Research, all at headquarters level and one affiliate in the UK.

4.2   Design: An Emerging New Standard in Development

In Pharma Development, the functional area in charge of the drug development phase, downstream from Discovery and before the Marketing phases, a new approach to intranet design has started in 2000 centred around the standard XML. Following the unfolding of this new approach one can get a better idea of the more recent developments in the Intranet, where they come from, their direction and their current status of maturity. In a nutshell, such an approach has the ambition to become by 2007 the new standard throughout Roche of a globally managed Pharma Intranet. It promises to shift the effort from building web pages to manage content more effectively. It started from local tinkering, and so far has reached most of Development, but not all the affiliates, and has been expanded to some of the other functional areas. It is still, however, the initiative of one Information Management (IM) group. The other groups belonging to different functions do not necessarily conform to the new standard and still seem willing to retain their independent approaches. Corporate IT does not seem to interfere or have a say on the initiative.

4.2.1 Brief history
During the wild phase of Intranet diffusion within Roche, everybody was building web pages through Frontpage. The function Development was no exception. This offered total freedom of development, but left content very hard to maintain: one could not manage content separately from the web pages in a neat way. Updating content was cumbersome on a not so user-friendly interface. This led to the accumulation of old, unused content on all the websites and the practical impossibility to clean up the sites, if not for the initiative of single web masters. Also, the actual insertion of new content was the task of many assistants, or secretarial staff, to whom managers de facto delegated the maintenance of the more than 500 sites. Only a few functionalities of the web programmes were actually used, so that the quality of the pages varied greatly and in general was not impressive.

Reacting to this unsatisfactory situation, and to improve the overall quality of the Intranet, the PD IM group launched in 2000 a project named PD World based on a new (XML) standard, aimed especially at supporting the communications of 5000 PD users. The technical goal is to obtain a separation between the content and the logic, that is the layout and the presentation, so that the two can be managed and maintained separately. In the existing Oracle environment with Frontpage, this is not possible. Also, the new standard should improve the overall consistency of the pages. Unfortunately, the launch of the project coincided with a significant budget cut within IT. The cut did not allow the purchase of proprietary software for the XML implementation. But this did not stop the developers, who decided to get the software from the open source environment (the Cocoon platform). The documents (the content) were instead put on a proprietary Document Management System, browser-based, called Shareweb/ Livelink. The XML standard, through its metadata hierarchical structure, would allow easy manipulation and transfer of documents, much better than using HTML on Frontpage. XML also allows easy exchange of data between systems and applications. In general, the new standard fosters integration between systems, better interface design, more effective data mining, and a better integration with legacy systems and applications. The new platform proved to be very quick to set up, with a lot of reusable components. It provided various interfaces to Outlook, calendar and data. Most of the functionalities were of a read-only type for the users. Some confidential areas were ring-fenced, such as those related to NDA (New Drug Application) documents. Content would be managed by newly appointed content managers. This implies a reallocation of responsibilities and a change of job for the staff previously dedicated to the handling of Frontpage (see below the case of the UK affiliate).

The PD World environment is now integrated with the KM environment (Shareweb): one can publish a document in one system and transfer it to the other (see below).

The new platform is gradually expanding into IT Operations (with eight new sites) and the Regulatory Department (where there are now three XML content managers). To be sure, diffusion is difficult because there is a lack of standard operating procedures throughout the business: hence, the diffusion and adoption phase by a new standard for information processing and presentation is not straightforward. On the other hand, pressure is coming from external forces, such as regulation by the FDA, which requires a large amount of detailed documentation to monitor any stage of the process of development, to make the entire process more transparent and accountable. The consequence is the adoption of a consistent system for documenting the entire workflow in the critical areas, especially Development and Operations (but again this pressure may be different for different parts of the business, for example manufacturing vs. marketing).

The new technical platform is already undergoing change, however. Cocoon has worked out fine, but a few drawbacks have been noticed, such as the parser and the interpreter using too much memory. Also, the open source environment requires designers to constantly keep up with the technology. These have been the reasons to move now to a proprietary platform by BAE. This would keep the same philosophy, but would mean dealing with a commercial product, maintained by outside specialists (especially for the updates).

A number of technical challenges are currently being addressed by the IM group within PD. These include the establishment of an appropriate security model (sometimes this is made complicated by the joint distribution initiatives with competitors – see below); and specifying the syntax of the XML schema. Also, it is envisaged that the new platform could be one that delivers integrated 'web services', and not just an Intranet.

PD World is expanding smoothly and the designers appreciate the cleaner architecture of the intranet so obtained: it allows for local management of content, thus respecting the needs of the original location of the content creators or providers. However, the expansion to other areas does not seem to be automatic. In areas like Pharma Business (previously Strategic Marketing), the Intranet is still based on autonomous groups (the Therapy Units – see above) and use of external agencies. Another hurdle is the mismatch between an increasing push towards cross-functional Intranet work and the budget which tends to be articulated by function only. This difficulty affects, for example, the development of licensing-related applications (see below). Last but not least, note that Informatics has its own Intranet services and tools, tailored for its own internal use.

PD World now has an editorial board, a sort of governance body that takes care of the framework, schemas, structure and taxonomy. Still, there is a trade-off to be met between uniformity of PD World solutions and the need for personalization. PD World increases the ease of implementation, provides uniform interfaces and helps define standards in the technical environment (other portals within Roche do not yet have a metadata structure). And it is very quick for building websites. The challenge is for content management: there are already many users, but will the new technical standard impact their practices, improving them significantly, matching the needs of the Development organization?

The question is to what extent is PD World only a browser, with content managed somewhat hierarchically, in order to push news, memos and announcements to the PD global organization? Can something born out of moonlighting around a cheap open source software solution, and on the back of a document management system, become 'the' new Roche Pharma standard? Is PD World a 'castle' in Roche's Intranet reflecting the old monopoly mindset of Development stemming from the clinical trials data processing? Can it reach the affiliates or does it just push down content from the headquarters?

4.2.2 Knowledge management applications

As already pointed out, the web publishing functionalities of the Intranet are linked to the KM environment within Roche. Here is a glimpse of what this environment looks like especially in the Development area. In the last decades the need for integrated forms of collaboration has been constantly on the increase. By collaboration is meant both synchronous and asynchronous joint work. In general, such an increase is justified by the reduction of travel across the main research labs (in the USA, UK, Switzerland and Asia). The main platform for KM is a commercial software, Lifelink, internally baptized as Shareweb. This collaborative environment today has

about 7000 users. It is a collaborative tool, a content management software
and an application development platform. It is a Mega file system, handling a common repository of documents. The division of labour between
the platforms is as follows: the Intranet manages the portals (PD World),
while Shareweb is aimed at supporting KM and learning organization
processes. Uses range from interdisciplinary and cross-functional team-
work to access to scientific literature. It requires adequate training for
effective use. The original idea involved using the Internet in Development
not just as an email tool, but as a unified platform for knowledge sharing.
A steering group formed by members of the various development areas in
different countries came up with the idea and design of a KM organization. This was based on an analysis of the requirements of the international teams working on new product development. This led to a new
platform called Pathfinder. The platform was supported by different business champions, such as life cycle team leaders, and even by some promo-
tion initiatives such as a cybercafe! Pathfinder was a portal containing an
information taxonomy. But it proved somewhat cumbersome. This implied
an effort to re-engineer the whole application, distinguishing a content
layer, an information organization layer and an architecture shadowing the Pharma organization (j2e framework). Further progress in the
KM environments points to the need for identifying and defining organizational processes and linking them to information and metadata
taxonomies.

The use of Shareweb, however, is not ubiquitous. Not all the life cycle
teams, for example, use it. Around 40 per cent of the users are to be considered marginal, while a good 20 per cent can be regarded as superusers.
The level of use also varies according to the drug development phase: the
closer to Research (RD teams), the higher the percentage of good users
(60–70 per cent); the closer to Strategic Marketing, the less enthusiasm
one encounters. Life cycle teams are in the middle. One reason is that
there are alternatives: such as transferring files with Outlook or even
exchanging sheer paper copies for confidentiality reasons. Lack of comprehensive, not purely technical training, has been put forward as one of
the possible reasons for not using the KM system properly. Recall, on the
other hand, that the use of Shareweb is going to be affected by the fact
that its scope touches activities that are, or are going to be, highly regulated by the FDA.

4.2.3 How the Intranet is used by Life Cycle Teams

The role of the Intranet and KM tools in Development is best appreciated
if one looks at the patterns of usage of a key organizational unity: the Life
Cycle Team (LCT). There are about 65 such teams ongoing at any time in

the area of Research, comprising 20–40 people. The LCTs in the subsequent drug development phases can have a larger size (up to 100). Around 3400 are the team users of the ICT infrastructure. Intranet and Shareweb constitute the ubiquitous workspace for communication, data conferencing (net meetings), document consultation and sharing (document repositories). Given the increasing variety of means available, recently a new approach has been implemented to improve access and especially the use of the various components of the Intranet and KM. Thus, every time a team is set up, members receive a start-up kit that introduces them to the various tools available. A team information manager is also identified, who can help the members use the various tools at their disposal. Web pages are created, links with portals are established, browsers for the most interesting sites, and so on. It is possible to consult the project workspace, goals, milestones, people, links to other sites, and so on. The actual level of use varies, though. Most of the tools available play a marginal role. Key applications seem to be email and Shareweb. The new XML platforms also allow a smooth transition from Shareweb to publishing websites. A bridge exists between applications such as PD World on the one hand and the team collaboration zone on the other. This should enhance the opportunities for collaboration once publishing is done: but whether these two environments are used as one or not, is unclear, though the vision is for this to happen. The team leader is responsible for making decisions about the level of access, especially towards the external business partners. This is particularly important in the licensing environment: decisions should be made strictly on business grounds (see below). The evolution is towards more sharing: from the single team collaborative workspace to the rest of the company, the affiliates and up to the general public. But this process is not going to be smooth: there are different platforms, for one thing, and the regulatory environments for different countries are not homogeneous.

4.2.4 A spin-off: Intranet for top decision making

The Intranet constitutes a platform supporting a variety of business applications, too. It is an environment open for new designs. PD World has enabled a set of competencies to be perfected internally in XML, which can be applied to develop applications to support specific business activities. One of particular importance has been targeted in the last couple of years and it regards the decision making process by the top management group involved in the advance of the development of a new drug. This process goes through a number of phases, each steered by committees: the RPC (Research Portfolio), RDC (Research and Development) and LCC (Life Cycle). The committees deliberate on the basis of large sets of documents and produce new documents (basically the committee meeting minutes) that feature the main decisions taken and their rationale. The development of a drug from its initial stages until it reaches the market is accompanied internally by an evolving documentation that results, at the strategic level, from the workings of these committees. Decisions basically may cut development or authorize its continuation.

Key points for improving the process using IT tools are: how to deliver documents to the participants in an organized way. How to constitute an intelligent memory of the deliberations, for future use and reference. Namely, many decisions at various points must take into account rationales of past decisions made at previous meetings. No systems exist to date to help the managers involved: only their recollections and lots of Word documentation and archives. Actual deliberations can be not only complex, but also frantic. Schematically, each drug developing team must submit to the relevant top management committee documents coming from various sources, dependent upon the specific stage of development. The documentation must be prepared for the committee to assess and to enter into the agenda for a scheduled meeting. The agenda with the attachments is sent to the members one week before the meeting. In theory, teams flag the documents by putting them on Shareweb. There is considerable secretarial work required to assemble and prepare the documents for the top managers. In practice this happens in a way that leaves very little time for a thorough consultation of the attachments. Hence, there is scope for a system that fetches documents from Shareweb, organizes them historically, and traces their evolution longitudinally along the sequence of meetings dealing with a given compound or drug.

XML tagged data would allow documents, minutes and memory to be managed intelligently, to have also a dynamic project memory, easy to access and retrieve: a sort of information flow repository. All this would start from automating the agenda of the meetings and the attachments for the participants. Queries would be possible by way of documents, dossiers, or date.

The implementation of the system is in progress and there are various orders of difficulty. First, not all the phases pose the same challenges. For some committees the problem is more clear-cut, the decision is usually final and a system managed by an effective secretary can greatly improve the management of information (RPC and RDC). In other phases (LCC) there are many more factors to take into account of a different nature (issues of marketing and clinical data at the same time, although having different weight and impact), so issues are more complicated and blurred, as there are many threads and paths a decision can take. For example, one component can end up in multiple phases, drugs, or marketing strategies simultaneously, thus the decision to stop development in one area cannot be taken in isolation from other areas or phases where the same component is present. Issues and documents may be intertwined. There are various versions of a document. How are the different versions connected to an issue or to a component in the database? Can the system sort them out? Also, the number of participants grows for the later committees.

Another difficulty is that the larger and more cross-functional the committees are, the less clear it is who is going to be the funding unit for the IT system itself. The early committees are in the R&D areas only, to which the new application developers belong. This is not the case when Sales & Marketing intervene in the later committees.

The new application is of course linked to the existing platform for knowledge management, Shareweb (Livelink). As usual, when implementing the new system, designers have to establish bridges across different platforms. For example in Development, KM takes place through Shareweb. In research this is not the case: members use share drives, 'C', or web pages as permanent or temporary repositories. Patterns of actual use suggest that the 14 members of the RDC are learning to use the new tool to which they are not accustomed. Lots of functionalities are neglected: for example, top managers do not consult the project history but tend to focus on the decisions and documents at hand. The system speeds up the preparation of the documents and gives more time for consultation. Still, it seems that attachments actually get consulted only at the last minute. New teams, on the other hand, seem to be able to adopt it straight away. This leaves open the case of older, 'legacy' teams being rather cold to appropriating the new tool. There is then a non-uniform level of entry of documents and in general discipline, even at the feeding of the system, which may undermine its overall utility.

What is not clear for the future adoption of the new application, once it is fully operational, is the actual amount of discipline required of its users, the members of the top management teams, to feed in all the documentation, for example, by sending files as attachments to email messages, thus bypassing the system. The presence of a project leader/champion is considered to be essential for the success of the project. The secretary of the RDC team has so far played this role and this has greatly helped the continuation of the project.

The question mark looming over the new application again regards the level of actual use by the members in using the new sophisticated system. If already in the relatively protected environment of the RDC committee, use is not fully consummate, what is going to happen when the system is introduced in the other committees where the size, the level of complexity and the diversity of platforms are all higher?

5   OTHER AREAS

5.1   Sales & Marketing

There is a huge potential for Internet/Intranet applications within Sales & Marketing. Currently, sales reps use email, printed material and lots of reports and printouts coming out of various corporate systems. For the rest, sales reps (who in general are Roche employees) also value direct contact. There are some experiments going on, for example in Latin America, to send sales information over the Internet. Or, Personal Digital Assistants (PDAs) are being used in some affiliates. But many S&M relations concern outside customers, wholesalers, pharmacies, and other businesses and institutions. There is a project to establish a common Internet framework, to set up an internal competence centre, and develop content synergies and so on. The function is near to Strategic Marketing, which has a different approach, that is outsourcing to external agencies (see Ciborra, 2000). Technical issues concern control over development, standardization and cost reduction. Portals may need to be set up focusing on specialized areas. It is envisaged that in the future the Intranet and Internet will also have to be geared for launches of the same product all over the globe. The same approach everywhere.

5.2   Research

The Intranet within the Research function, called internally Discovery, is fragmented. Each organization possesses its own. Discovery is divided by theory areas, disease areas, and scientific subareas, such as vascular metabolics. Historically, the Intranet has also grown by country sites, around the large research centres. Accountability for development and use lies within the single department. There is no policing, nor tsars. Research Informatics is trying to bring in a higher degree of commonality, for example through screen layout standardization. Second, it ensures that industry standards are used for the applications domain (such as Weblogic). The authoring tools vary too, however. Content is considered rather relying on static information. Future developments regard the implementation of a more sophisticated search engine. Browser compatibility is an issue (Explorer vs. Netscape) both internally and for outside collaborations. KM platforms like Shareweb are much less used in Discovery than in Development. A further development towards commonality is the definition of a role-based environment for different classes of users. A user will be able to find on his or her screen the typical set of applications, together with the relevant project portfolio, in a way that is updated automatically along the life of the project and for the changing role of the user.

5.3   An Affiliate

A test of the reach of the new systems and applications in a company like Roche is given by what happens in the affiliates (see Ciborra, 1996 and 2000). The most important ones enjoy a high degree of autonomy, and one way of assessing the penetration of the Intranet is to see how concepts, methods and contents coming from the headquarters are appropriated at the periphery. In what follows, developments in the UK affiliate are sketchily reported, in particular those related to Development and Licensing and the diffusion of the XML standard of PD World.

In this affiliate there is a Web Strategy Team that gives general guidance to the various applications and a Technical team that takes care of standards related to content, guidelines, support and new tools. The current situation sees a migration from a highly distributed use of Frontpage, with 'wild' authoring and content management to the standard of PD World. People used to go to web design courses and started building websites. Neither the look nor the content were policed, only the positioning of the corporate logo in the top right-hand corner. For example, the telephone book could be found in 20 different sites. Content was copied from one site to another. Sites had pictures of office parties with cake throwing accessible directly from the main 'business' page. Generally, the old sites are outdated and there is no stringent content review (content is old and smells 'like rotten eggs').

The aim of the new approach is to introduce new ways to keep the content updated through the XML protocol. Before, emphasis was on the 'look' of the sites rather than the content. It is hoped that training times and updating will be carried out faster, once the new systems are in place. Also, an environment like PD World, configured as a portal, is supposed to actually provide a service, structuring and organizing content, using standards and guidelines, adding value through these. The site will be linked directly to Shareweb, thus providing immediate access to the KM tools. From now on, the plan is to police content, design and technical platform. The transition is, however, complicated by some human resource issues. Adopting and using Frontpage has created lots of Intranet 'experts' in each Department, that is individuals like secretaries or managers who took upon themselves the task of creating/managing their website. For example in Sales & Marketing there were 40 content/web managers! This activity has been included over the years in their job descriptions. With the new standard most of these individuals will be stripped of their web-related tasks, possibly having an impact on their salaries. Hence, there will be a subtle resistance to the new standard until this HR issue is solved. The idea is to have a better use of resources: IT skills are supposed to be in IT-related units, and not in the line business units.

Also a governance structure is going to be put in place. While before responsibilities and accountabilities were diffused, the new framework envisages the creation of an Editorial Board, content managers reporting to the board and content contributors. The aim is to be able to put on the web only 'sharp' information for effective communication. The Editorial Board members should act as the filters necessary to elicit only the key information. There will also be clearer content ownership. Here, the governance structure set up in Basel's headquarters is being replicated in the affiliate (but not always in PD!) An Intranet team is implementing the changes in the affiliate, starting January 2003. Roll-out of a first phase took place in April 2003, covering PD and other functions like Finance, but there are delays in rolling out the next phases because of the need to migrate from Frontpage and the somewhat different approach in other functions like Sales & Marketing. First experiences are positive, though Shareweb is perceived as not straightforward or a bit cumbersome to handle. Usage has been confined within projects which were not time critical. Also, the application handling drafts is complicated, while for releasing a final version of a document it proves to be more solid. Finally, there is the issue concerning personalization of the sites: to what extent should the various departments in the affiliate be similar or on the contrary have a different look and feel?

6   MULTIPLE AND DYNAMIC BOUNDARIES

Another feature of the Intranet is the porosity and constant change of its boundaries and the problems this sets for its designers. In Roche typical complex cases have been those of de-mergers and licensing. In the former instance, the need arises to maintain links and access to the sites of a company fully owned but with a separate legal status. But part of the new company Chugai, was the previous Roche affiliate in Japan. Now what was shared on the Intranet with the affiliate needs to be kept separate. Licensing poses the opposite problem: some of the internal contents need to be shared . . . sometimes with a competitor, or with an unknown partner until the deal is signed, and usually for a limited period of time. Hence, a temporary Intranet for an interorganizational collaboration zone needs to be created, and soon dismantled (typically after four weeks). In all these cases there is no standard procedure, and a trial and error resolution strategy (tactics, actually) is used. Temporary boundaries then need to be set up. Buffers are implemented. Temporary e-rooms are created, the 'collaboration zones', where the two separate companies can exchange shareable material. Security mechanisms get deployed on an ad hoc basis, too. A more effective governance is invoked at different levels, so that one would know what can be published and by whom; which are the confidentiality levels; security; access from the inside and from the outside. A style of governance with a more granular influence. At the same time all this seems to be missing, because there is no authority that can enforce it. The structure, boundary and temporality of the Intranet are thus heavily determined by the structure and temporality of the project (the 'when'!). Despite the complexity of the forcibly makeshift arrangements, the Intranet enables many activities and makes them faster and more agile.

Licensing is another area where legal and security concerns plague the use of the Intranet. Again a trial and error attitude seems to prevail. An interesting case is Boniva, a new drug against osteoporosis, on the verge of being launched jointly by Roche and GSK. The drug is owned by Roche, GSK has the marketing expertise, and it was developed by a third party. Preparatory work relies heavily on Intranet use. Work is affected by issues of confidentiality and trust. The emerging collaborative framework is purely tentative at this stage.

Initially, the means used were CDs so that there was no connectivity between the corporate applications. Subsequently, connectivity was created to facilitate collaboration and enhance speed. GSK users (about 70) can now access, through various firewalls, the applications, the servers of Shareweb and various zones including the review cycle (a Netscape application called Rapid to view virtual documents during the review and approval cycles for the NDA). Connectivity has delivered the reduction of 'weeks' in the NDA submission time (recall that in the pharmaceutical business one day saved is equivalent to $1 million in sales).

Currently there are 15 licensing agreements and around eight collaborations with external partners for which similar problems, risks and opportunities may present themselves. The role of Roche in setting up a collaborative infrastructure varies. With small biotech firms, Roche offers an Intranet complete environment. With larger partners such as GSK one tries to agree on a common standard platform. In the specific case, unfortunately, GSK had an Explorer-based internal standard, while Roche relies on Netscape.

An even more ephemeral way of collaborating is the sharing of documents in a sort of 'grey zone' with a partner that is not actually known (for business sensitive reasons), before the actual licensing agreement is signed. The key point here is how to grant access to the grey zone through registration of the users. The goal is to reduce the (electronic) red tape during the certification process: and once again time is crucial. For the licensing people the speed of the deal can be a matter of hours. But how can one be sure to register all the possible users during the entire collaboration? Professional culture issues also get in the way: licensing people are typically sharply business oriented, while the researchers are rather open. Some companies in the partnership, like the recently disenfranchised Japanese company, depend upon Roche products, so though being separate legal entities from the point of view of their knowledge supply, they need a level of access to Shareweb as if they were an internal unit. Ideally, then, every piece of information should be valued as critical or not, as shareable or not. At the same time, creativity in the process cannot be stifled. And development needs to take place as fast as possible. All these processes are managed sensibly, but inevitably on an ad hoc basis: there seems to be no standard approach. Still, wild moves may happen in the grey-grey zones, such as setting up a clinical data portal over the *Inter*net, immediately pulled down . . .. In particular, functions that interact with the outside world, typically Pharma Business, are exposed to practices that may temporarily and unexpectedly expose or leak information.

7   DISCUSSION

Describing the evolution of an Intranet in a knowledge-intensive context such as a pharmaceutical company is a complex task, because of the multiple dimensions involved. Developments and changes, applications and platforms 'happen' by functional area, by product, by location (affiliates, headquarters, research centres), by stage of the drug development process, by technical platforms (archives; protocols; standards); by organizational unit (cross-functional project teams vs. functions), by closeness to the boundaries (alliances, joint ventures, licensing) or to the centre of the firm; and last but not least, by type of application and use (KM, communication, project tool, and so on).

   An Intranet strategy is beginning to emerge and it encompasses ideas on a technology framework based on portals, XML and j2ee; a content framework and a governance model. The latter is formed by an Intranet Board including representatives from each main department, the development teams and from the management team. The Board should plan for the future development of the Intranet and guide the different content managers. Also a security framework is being defined specifying who is allowed to access or see what. This turns out to be an issue that is not so easy to solve given the contradictory and shifting requirements of the business, especially at the Intranet boundaries. To date this governance organization is being applied successfully to the Development function. The Board members seem to be satisfied with the new environment, its improved cost effectiveness, especially for the application development tasks, through re-usable software, reduction of development time, the consistency of the look and feel of the user interfaces, the global information repositories, and the definition of clearer responsibilities as far as content managers are concerned. Still, the open question is whether this organization, and its reference platform, can be transferred/adopted by other areas such as PB, and in the affiliates. First attempts at bridging out are being carried out, for example in the oncology therapeutic area, and in the UK affiliate. But also within Development there are new areas to conquer, for example the clinical studies activities: they presently use a lot of Excel spreadsheets.

Note, next, that the Intranet, in supporting and adapting to the various businesses and activities, is influenced in its design and use by the different temporalities of the business. For example, PL has 'life cycles' of a couple of months: thus archives, accesses, uses start and end within a quite limited period of time characterized by intensive, high peak use. In PB business the typical life of a project spans over a year and a half. In PD it can last between three and five years. Also the reach is different. PD needs to communicate a lot within itself, on a fairly homogeneous basis. PB has to deal mostly with the affiliates, which are extremely different from one another and still pretty autonomous. The various cross-functional teams, temporary or long-lasting, are different for composition, existence, culture and location. As a result, PD is a truly global organization in five different sites adopting uniform procedures. PB, or Strategic Marketing, deals with 35 different affiliates, as quasi-autonomous organizations. Can the Intranet be the same thing to both worlds?

In terms of technical platforms, PD World is joined up with Shareweb, given the intense KM uses in development in general. But this is not the case in PB, where reliance is mostly on external and not internal resources and systems, such as the external agencies that set up conferences and advertising campaigns.

As for PB, PL poses another challenge to the expansion of PD World and possibly marks another set of contrasts. PL, in setting up its collaboration zones, relies on Global Informatics for infrastructure. Note, also, that a Pharma division portal does not exist yet (it is underway), nor is a Pharma Intranet tsar in sight: pluralism still prevails over divisional branding and identity.

Overall, then, the Intranet may still be appreciated as a nice thing to have. Environments such as PD World should be able to exercise a stronger pull, instead of just pushing content (from the centre to the periphery). Despite the multiple team arrangements, still crossing the departmental silos remains a challenge.

And from a risk perspective, fragmentation, redundancies and pluralism mean a complex and varied infrastructure that minimizes risk, that is it can swallow any technical or managerial hazard rather quickly with no major impacts, as it routinely does with the problems posed by data security.

The 'dark side' of PD World is to appear the expression of a large, independent self-sufficient organization. Does the new style still retain some of the old clothes of a legacy monopoly data processing environment? Is PD World condemned to be a new standard in a close, albeit large, functional island within Pharma? Is the new reproducing the old, albeit in XML? Is 'structuring the Intranet' the new, more mature behaviour of just one (big) chunk of Roche's still fragmented Intranet?

8   CONCLUDING REMARKS

What are the main features of a topsy-turvy unfolding of web-based information systems? The case investigated so far shows a dynamic and complex world of computing, communicating and knowledge exchange over the net, full of shadows and light. It is a world where monopolies have boundaries; where communication environments may have enclosures towards the inside while being porous on the outside; where KM is essential but the kits for its use are still in part marginal in face of the frantic pace of work; where standards emerge from tinkering; where autonomy and distribution are initiated from the top; where the learning curve starts from centralized systems and dissolves into fragmentation; where structuring the net means further balkanizing it; where corporate IT services stay away from it all; where the vision is of a royal palace at the headquarters and the reality is a network of decentralized feudal castles; where clicking on the company logo on the top right-hand corner of every Intranet screen triggers an unpredictable navigation path, depending upon the context. Where all this is far from being the result of bad bricolage coupled with incompetence, rather the very outcome of business necessity, planning and extremely high levels of competence and expertise. Not surprisingly, industry observers like Lerer and Piper (2003) conclude that even if standards such as XML ensure that in the pharmaceutical industry data can be better formatted, stored and distributed, the main barriers to better management of knowledge and collaboration remain institutional rather than technological. If a true, all-encompassing infrastructure obtains when the tension between local and global gets resolved (Star and Ruhleder, 1996), Roche's infrastructure is still 'happening', since these tensions have not been solved;

if anything they seem to multiply in constantly new guises. Hence, the questioning about its 'when' is bound to remain open, and any framework able to capture it inadequate. We trust Latour (2004) when he states that where frameworks do not apply or do not turn out to be that useful, we may be close to having something relevant to say about a phenomenon.

NOTES

1. For want of a better term. Chaotic would be an alternative, but it would be misleading: even chaos theory does not seem to apply here as shown in the main text. The interpretation of the case lies solely with the author. Hoffman-La Roche has generously supported the logistic of the fieldwork and has granted access and time of very busy professionals and managers. It is with a slight sense of embarrassment that the author is not able to deliver a more constructive case to the company who might have hoped after 20 years of having the Intranet for a more 'structured' account.
2. The first case study published in Ciborra (1996), reports on developments in 1993–1994 and reconstructs previous work on the corporate networks and applications which started in 1986 within the Strategic Marketing function. The second case study published in Ciborra (2000), reports on developments between 1996–1999 again in Strategic Marketing and the corporation at large. The present update captures new developments especially in the area of the drug development function during 2001–2003.

   Each field study is based on about 20 interviews, both in the headquarters and in a couple of affiliates. Interviewees have been line and ICT top managers, Information Management specialists (between five and twelve) and users (between two and ten). The percentages have varied for each case study depending upon circumstances of the fieldwork. For the present study, many more designers have been interviewed than users. A limited number of informants have remained the same for the three studies.
3. Term borrowed from a lecture given by Ulrick Beck at the LSE in February 2004.

REFERENCES

Bansler, J., J. Damsgaard, R. Scheepers, E. Havn and J. Thommesen (2000), 'Corporate intranet implementation: managing emergent technologies and organizational practices', *Journal of the Association for Information Systems*, 1(10), 1–39.

Carlson, P.A. (2000), 'Information technology and the emergence of a worker centered organization', *ACM Journal of Computer Documentation*, **24**, 204–12.

Ciborra, C. (1996), 'Mission critical: challenges for groupware in a pharmaceutical company', in C. Ciborra (ed.), *Groupware and Teamwork*, Chichester: Wiley, pp. 91–120.

Ciborra, C. (2000), 'From alignment to loose coupling: from MedNet to www.roche.com', in C. Ciborra, K. Braa, A. Cordella, B. Dahlbom, A. Failla, O. Hanseth, V. Hepsø, J. Ljungberg, E. Monteiro and K.A. Simon, *From Control to Drift*, Oxford: Oxford University Press, pp. 193–211.

Ciborra, C. and O. Hanseth (1998), 'From tool to Gestell: Agendas for managing the information infrastructure', *Information Technology and People*, **11**(4), 305–27.

Damsgaard, J. and R. Scheepers (2000), 'Managing the crises in intranet implementation: a stage model', *Information Systems Journal*, **10**, 131–49.

Duane, A. and P. Finnegan (2000), 'Managing intranet technology in an organizational context: Toward a "stages of growth" model for balancing empowerment and control', Proceedings of the 21st International Conference of Information Systems, pp. 242–58.

Heidegger, M. (1993 [1977]), 'The question concerning technology', in M. Heidegger, *Basic Writings*, edited by David Farrell Krell, second edition, revised and expanded edition, San Francisco: HarperSanFrancisco, pp. 307–43.

Isakowitz, T., M. Bieber and F. Vitali (1998), 'Web information systems – introduction', *Commun. ACM*, **41**(7), 78–80.

Jacko, J.A. et al. (2003), 'Intranets and organizational learning: A research and development agenda', *International Journal of Human–Computer Interaction*, **14**(1), 93–130.

Lai, V. (2001), 'Interorganizational communication with intranets', *Communications of the ACM*, **44**(7), 95–100.

Lamb, R. (2003), 'Intranet boundaries as guidelines for systems integration', *International Journal of Electronic Commerce*, **7**(4), 9–35.

Lamb, R. and E. Davidson (2005), 'Understanding intranets in the context of end-user computing', DATA BASE, **36**(1), 64–85.

Lamb, R. and R. Kling (2003), 'Reconceptualizing users as social actors in information systems research', *MIS Quarterly*, **27**(2), 197–235.

Latour, B. (2004), 'Dialogue between a student and a professor about ANT', in C. Avgerou, C. Ciborra and F. Land (eds), *The Social Study of Information Technology – Actors, Context and Innovation*, Oxford: Oxford University Press.

Lerer, L. and M. Piper (2003), *Digital Strategies in the Pharmaceutical Industry*, New York: Palgrave Macmillan.

Nolan, R.L. (1973), 'Managing the computer resource: a stage hypothesis', *Communications of the ACM*, **16**, 399–405.

Scheepers, R. (1999), 'Key role players in the initiation and implementation of intranet technology', in O. Ngwenyama, L.D. Introna, M.D. Myers and J.I. DeGross (eds), *New Information Technologies in Organizational Processes: Field Studies and Theoretical Reflections on the Future of Work*, Proceedings of the IFIP TC8 WG8.2 International Working Conference, St Louis, MO, USA, 21–22 August 1999, Boston: Kluwer Academic Publishers, pp. 175–95.

Star, S.L. and K. Ruhleder (1996), 'Steps toward an ecology of infrastructure: Design and access for large information spaces', *Information Science Research*, **7**(1) March, 111–34.

Touraine, A. (2000), 'A method for studying social actors', *Journal of World-Systems Research*, **6**(3), 900–918.

Index